HEWLETT-PACKARD'S GUIDE TO COLOR PRINTING TECHNIQUES

How To Get The Most From Your
Black And Color HP DeskJet Printer

Gordon Padwick

RANDOM HOUSE
ELECTRONIC PUBLISHING
New York

To Kathy

Hewlett-Packard's Guide to Color Printing Techniques

How to Get the Most From Your Black and Color HP DeskJet Printer

Published in the United States by Random House, Inc., New York, and simultaneously in Canada by Random House of Canada, Limited.

Manufactured in the United States of America.

0 9 8 7 6 5 4 3 2 1

ISBN 0-679-75323-0

New York   Toronto   London   Sydney   Auckland

Contents

Part III

Acknowledgments

I offer my grateful thanks to all the people and organizations who have contributed to this book.

The book was initially proposed by Annika Bohl and Don Barnett, learning product managers at Hewlett-Packard's San Diego and Vancouver divisions. Many people in those facilities have contributed enormously by providing printers for me to work with me and answering what must have seemed like an unending stream of questions. They carefully reviewed various drafts of the book, caught many of my errors, and offered numerous suggestions. I particularly want to thank Ron Bondshu in San Diego and Rebecca Stille in Vancouver, B.C. for their help.

While other people have contributed to the accuracy of this book, the author is responsible for any errors that remain. Matters of opinion expressed in the book are entirely those of the author and are not necessarily shared by Hewlett-Packard or its employees.

Printers can, of course, only do what software directs. Consequently, there are many references to specific software applications throughout this book. My thanks go to the many companies who provided software and willingly answered my questions when I ran into problems. These companies include Adobe Systems (Photoshop), Aldus (PageMaker), Avery (LabelPro), Broderbund (3D Home Architect), Corel (CorelDRAW), Delrina (FormFlow), Digital Light & Color (Picture Window), Microsoft (Microsoft Office), and Software Publishing (Harvard Graphics). All the screen captures reproduced in this book were created with the help of Collage Complete, which was kindly supplied by Inner Media.

I'm grateful to my wife, Kathy, who has uncomplainingly put up with seeing the back of my head for many hours at a time during the months I have been working on this book. Her support and encouragement have made it possible for me to complete the project almost according to schedule.

Introduction

This book is about using your Macintosh or Windows-based computer to print color documents.

As technology advances, more and more demands are being made on personal computer users. One of the most recent skills that computer users are expected to have is to be able to make effective use of color. This came about because color printers, once a luxury affordable only to the aristocracy of the computer community, are now available at a price that is reasonable to consider for small offices and even home computer use. Today, you can buy a color printer for less than one-third of what a black-and-white laser printer cost only a couple of years ago.

The type of color printer we're talking about here is not just one that can print headlines in red, it's a printer that can print full-color, near-photo-quality pictures of people, products, scenery, buildings, or anything else. Of course, you also can use it to print ordinary black text as well as colorful charts and graphs.

While your color printer is a relatively tame beast, you do need to know how to gain its cooperation. That's the subject of this book. How you can use your printer to most effectively communicate with people—isn't that what it's all about?

Who Should Read This Book?

You should read this book if you have just purchased or are contemplating buying a color printer and are wondering how you would use it, or if you have access to a color printer and need some help in getting the best results from it.

If you work in an office, even a home office, and want to create color printed material or color presentations that have impact, this book is full of ideas and techniques you can use. Here, you will find out how to create reports in which color draws attention to important points and colorful charts make your data easy to grasp. You will also see how you can use your color printer to create overhead projection transparencies as well as audience handouts that contain miniature reproductions of your slides.

If you are a student, or a parent of a student, you'll learn how to use your color printer to enhance school and college reports, thereby improving grades.

At home, you can enjoy using your color printer to create personalized greeting cards, or to make plans for a new home or for remodeling your present home. If you're into photography, you can experiment with photographic retouching techniques to turn your not-quite-right photographs into masterpieces (at least in your own eyes).

As you read this book you'll find information about working with specific software. Most of the detailed examples are based on software that is the most popular of its type and, in many cases, available in almost identical versions for the Macintosh and Windows environments. If you have the software mentioned, that's great; if not, you can use most of the techniques described with similar software. What we're trying to do here is to show you what's possible.

In This Book

This book consists of three parts and some appendices.

Part I contains general information about using inkjet printers. Chapter 1, a brief introduction to inkjet printers, contains advice about what to consider when choosing a printer and outlines some of the benefits of owning a printer that you can use for printing ordinary black text as well as full-color graphics. Chapter 2 turns to the specific inkjet printers that are the subject of this book—the Hewlett-Packard DeskJet 560C, DeskWriter 560C, DeskJet 1200C, and DeskJet 1200C/PS printers. Here you will find detailed information about these printers.

Chapter 3 describes how to install printer hardware and software in the Macintosh and Windows environments. You will find detailed information about choosing paper to get the best results from your inkjet printer, as well as general information about printing from Macintosh and Windows applications.

Chapter 4 is about fonts and characters. It contains information about fonts that are built into the printers as well as fonts you can download from your hard disk.

In Chapter 5 you will read about the important subject of creating printed documents that effectively communicate your ideas. This chapter covers such topics as designing the overall page layout and choosing fonts. In addition, there is valuable advice about choosing colors for various types of documents.

Part II focuses on specific printing projects. Chapter 6 provides information about ordinary types of printing in an office, printing letters and memos, envelopes, labels, and forms.

The ability to print in color really makes a difference in business graphics. Chapter 7 describes how you can use your inkjet printer to create many kinds of graphs and charts that make your data easy to understand.

Desktop publishing, the subject of Chapter 8, means creating documents that combine text and illustrations, such as newsletters and flyers. In this chapter, you will learn the fundamentals of page layout as well as how to work with text and graphics. This subject continues in Chapter 9, which takes you step by step through the process of creating and printing a newsletter, and in Chapter 10, which deals with using graphics to enhance your desktop publishing projects.

You can use your DeskJet or DeskWriter printer to make high-quality transparencies for overhead presentations, as described in Chapter 11. This chapter contains general advice about preparing all types of presentations, as well as detailed information about printing full-color transparencies.

Turn to Chapter 12 for many suggestions about using an inkjet printer for personal projects. Here you will find useful hints about creating personalized greeting cards, using your printer for school and college reports, and planning your home. This chapter also shows how to enhance photographs and print near-photo-quality images on your inkjet printer.

Part III contains two chapters of advanced information. Chapter 13 deals with calibrating your system so that the colors you print closely match the colors on your screen. Chapter 14 provides some background on the commands that control your printer and shows you how to use these commands when you are working with DOS applications that cannot take advantage of the Macintosh or Windows printer drivers.

The book ends with four appendices and a glossary. Appendix A contains some hints and tips that you might find helpful when you run into problems. Appendix B lists sources of information about using inkjet printers and working with computer graphics. If you work with several applications, you will come across many different file formats, many of which are listed in Appendix C. Appendix D lists the companies and organizations whose products are referred to in this book. The glossary defines many of the specialized terms used in this book and in other publications about computer printing.

And So, To Work

Whatever your previous experience with printing in general and color printing in particular, I hope this book provides the information you need to create high-quality printed material that you are proud of. Also, I hope it contains many ideas that will trigger your thinking so that you can have fun while being productive with your inkjet printer.

Turn your printer on and see what you can do!

Gordon Padwick

Part I

Part I contains an introduction to computer printing, with particular emphasis on using Hewlett-Packard inkjet printers in the Macintosh and Windows environments.

Chapter 1 provides a general overview of inkjet printers. In Chapter 2, you learn about installing inkjet printers and how they work.

Chapter 3 provides information about installing HP's DeskJet and DeskWriter printers, and also about the basics of printing documents.

Chapter 4 focuses on printing character-based information. There, you learn the basics of the various fonts you can use in your printed documents.

The final chapter of this part, Chapter 5, deals with the concepts of document design, including how to use color effectively.

1

Introducing Inkjet Printers

For many years, computer experts have been talking and writing about the paperless office. They forecast that computers would eliminate the need for most paper documents. Instead of keeping paper in file cabinets, we would keep our records on computer disks and tape.

Except in a few isolated instances, this hasn't happened and doesn't seem likely to happen any time soon. Instead, the opposite has occurred. With computers connected to printers on our desks, and with high-speed copiers in our offices, we are creating more printed pages than ever before. At home, too, many of us have a computer with a printer churning out printed pages.

Printing is becoming increasingly important to many of us, and we are becoming more demanding of good print quality. There was a time, only a few years ago, when most of us were pleased to have a nine-pin dot matrix printer, although we were not always happy with the quality of what it produced. How times have changed. Now, we expect all our documents to look as though they have been professionally typeset and printed. And we'd like color, too.

The good news is that printing technology has progressed so rapidly that affordable printers are available that can meet these expectations.

This book is about getting professional-quality printing from printers that are affordable for use in our homes and offices, as well as for use with individual and networked computers in larger offices. The book focuses specifically on four Hewlett-Packard inkjet printers:

- The DeskJet 560C
- The DeskWriter 560C
- The DeskJet 1200C
- The DeskJet 1200C/PS

Note: Throughout this book, references to the 560C printer apply to the DeskJet 560C and the DeskWriter 560C. Also, references to the DeskJet 1200C apply to the DeskJet 1200C and to the DeskJet 1200C/PS.

All four printers can print high-quality black text. The DeskJet 560C is intended for use with IBM-compatible personal computers, whereas the Desk-Writer 560C is for the Macintosh environment. The DeskJet 1200C can be used with IBM-compatible personal computers, with workstations in various UNIX environments, and as a network printer. The DeskJet 1200C/PS provides Post-Script Level II and can be used with PCs, Macintosh computers, workstations in various UNIX environments, and as a network printer.

Introducing Printing Technologies

Printing is the process of creating visible images on paper or on other print media. Pen and ink is one printing technology we are all familiar with and use every day. Typewriters are another example of a printing technology. In this book, we deal with more sophisticated printing technologies that allow us to print black and color text and graphics from our computers.

When personal computers were first introduced, dot matrix printers were the predominant printers. Although their print quality left much to be desired and the noise they produced was hard to bear, dot matrix printers had one attractive feature: they were affordable. People who needed good print quality used more expensive daisy-wheel printers which were also very noisy.

Over the years, dot matrix printers have evolved to the stage where they can produce good quality text in black and color, but only very marginal quality graphics. These printers have one significant advantage for office applications over most other types of printers. Because they use impact to put ink from a ribbon onto paper, they can print on multilayer forms, something that inkjet printers cannot do.

Daisy-wheel printers have completely disappeared from the scene. They have been replaced by less-expensive and more versatile inkjet and laser printers.

The term *dot matrix printer* generally refers to a printer in which an array of pins strikes an inked ribbon, pressing the ribbon against paper so that dots of ink are deposited. In reality, though, laser printers and inkjet printers are also dot matrix printers; they create an image from a matrix of dots by non-impact methods. In only a few years, these printers have become very popular.

A Short History of Non-Impact Printers

IBM introduced the first laser printer in 1975, based on the xerographic technology that had become dominant for office copiers. This printer, however, was very expensive and intended for high-end, mainframe applications, and was of little interest to individual computer users. Three years later Xerox and Siemens offered similar printers, which were actually self-contained printing presses.

It wasn't until 1984 that Hewlett-Packard and Canon cooperated to make LaserJet laser printers available to personal computer users. Canon built the *printing engine*, the internal mechanism that converts electrical signals to dots on paper, and HP integrated the engine with electronics and software to make a printer that could be connected to a computer. Apple followed the next year (1985), also cooperating with Canon, to offer the LaserWriter laser printer for use with its Macintosh computers.

Since then, a few other companies have begun offering printing engines, and many companies integrate these engines into printers that are compatible with personal computers and workstations. As a result of all this activity, laser printers have become very attractively priced and widely used with home and office personal computers.

At the time this chapter is being written, laser printers have one very significant disadvantage. For most practical purposes, laser printers can only put one color (usually black) onto paper. If you need, or want, to put two or more colors onto a page, affordable laser printers can't do the job for you.

Having said that, let's go back a little and say that at least one company does offer a color laser printer. Also, it's reported that several other companies have color laser printers in the works. No doubt, several of these will be available by the time this book is in your hands, or soon after.

Color laser printers are very expensive and are likely to remain so for quite a while. They are not only expensive to purchase, they are also expensive to use. No doubt, there are high-end, multiuser applications that can justify the cost, but where does that leave the rest of us?

During the last few years, several printing technologies have emerged, of which one of the most successful is generally known as *inkjet*. This technology, used in the printers that are the subject of this book, has several advantages. It can be used to build printers that rival laser printers as far as printing quality and speed are concerned, but are less expensive. Furthermore, inkjet printers can offer color—not just colored text, but beautiful full-color graphics. While no one is going to claim that a color photograph reproduced by an inkjet printer would be mistaken for a photographic print, it does come close.

Inkjet printers that were initially available required special paper in order to print satisfactory images. By focusing on the development of special-purpose inks, Hewlett-Packard has developed inkjet printers that can print high-quality images on ordinary paper. Printers of this type are known as plain-paper printers. Few people will consider anything but a plain-paper printer for home and office use.

Having stated that HP's inkjet printers are plain-paper printers, it's necessary to temper this statement: to get the absolute best quality out of one of these printers, you should use specially manufactured paper which is available from HP dealers and some office supply stores. However, for normal work, you'll be very happy with your work printed on ordinary good-quality paper and or even on inexpensive copier paper.

> *Note:* Chapter 3 contains more information about choosing paper.

From now on, this book deals only with inkjet printers in general and specifically with HP's implementation of this technology in the DeskJet and DeskWriter printers.

Getting Professional Print Quality

Most of the computer printers used today print text and graphics as closely spaced dots on paper. When there are 300 or more dots per inch, individual dots are invisible at normal viewing distances to all but the most discriminating eyes, so text and graphics appear to be solid images. A dot density of 300 dots per inch is generally accepted as the lower limit of what is often called professional print quality.

Having a sufficient number of dots per inch isn't all that's necessary for good quality printing. These dots must be the optimum size, shape, and density. In the case of color printers, this consistency is required for dots of four different colors.

Printing is much more than just putting closely spaced, consistent dots on paper. It is a matter of creating an image on paper that gets people's attention and readily conveys information to them. When you have a printer capable of professional quality, you need to pay attention to choosing *fonts*, as well as using *graphics* and *color*.

> *Note:* Words that have a specific meaning in the context of printing are shown in italics when they first occur. Many of these words are explained in the Glossary at the back of this book.

Using Appropriate Fonts and Graphics

Your printer should be able to use fonts appropriate for your purposes, and to print them in various sizes. It should also be easy to print graphics such as business charts, and to print reasonable reproductions of photographs. Although the printers covered in this book can print photographs, these images are not of the same quality you see in magazines, where a resolution of up to 2400 dots per inch is used.

Printing in Color

We live in a colorful world and are accustomed to getting information and being entertained in color. Unfortunately, printing in color has been too expensive, too time-consuming, and too demanding of special skills to be used for the printing we do in our homes and offices.

When early humans began to communicate by means of rock painting, they used color. Why would they do otherwise when they saw color and they were only limited by the availability of the colors they could obtain from natural resources? Early books and manuscripts were created by hand and, in many cases, beautifully illuminated in color.

It was only when people started using the printing press that they became limited to one color on a page. Although methods of using two or more colors in printed material have evolved, until quite recently these all incurred expensive preparatory steps, the so-called prepress processes. Consequently, color has only been practical for publications that are printed in large quantity.

Now, affordable printers are available that can print just as easily, and almost as inexpensively, in color as in black. You are no longer limited to thinking about printing only in black ink on white paper or, if you had been really creative, in black ink on colored paper. Now, you can use color to create professional-quality printed material that grabs readers' attention and has an impact on their thinking.

Using Media That Suit the Task

Media are the materials, usually paper, on which images are printed. Paper has many characteristics, including size, thickness, texture, color, opacity, absorbency, and so on. In the context of home and office printing, where you need to print many different kinds of material, you need a printer that can handle quite a range of paper. You should think carefully before choosing a printer for which you must always buy special paper.

Some of the types of paper you can expect a home and office printer to accept include:

- Inexpensive copier paper for draft work, notes, and internal memos
- Bond paper
- Preprinted letterhead for correspondence
- Envelopes
- Labels
- Transparency material for presentations
- Heavier paper (card stock) for special purposes

You'll find more information about choosing media and, in particular, about what types of media to avoid, in Chapter 3 of this book.

> *Note:* Throughout the rest of this book, we'll use the word *paper* to mean whatever you print on, unless we're referring to a specific kind of medium.

The point here is that not only has printing technology made inexpensive, low-volume color printing possible, it has given you the advantage of printing on the paper you have at hand or choosing the paper that's most appropriate for your purpose. There are, of course, some limitations, such as size; don't expect to buy an inexpensive printer that can print on anything larger than ordinary legal-size paper.

Affordable Printing

When people think about buying a car, they compare initial costs and operating costs. The initial costs are fairly easy to find out, but the operating costs are more difficult to estimate—there are many factors to consider.

It's the same for a printer. You can look in advertisements or make a few telephone calls to find out how much it will cost you to buy one. The operating costs are much more difficult to estimate.

The generally accepted estimate for printing black text on ordinary paper is a few cents per page. This estimate is based on the assumption that you are using inexpensive paper and that you are printing ordinary business letters and memos. As an example, HP suggests that you can print about 900 pages of text from a black print cartridge for the DeskJet 1200C printer. You can expect to pay about $30 for the cartridge, so this works out at about 3.3 cents per page for ink.

To that, you have to add the cost of the paper, probably about one cent per page on average.

Be aware, though, that many factors affect your printing costs. The most obvious thing you can do to reduce your printing costs is to minimize the number of times you print each page. Do this by using your software's Print Preview capability to see on your screen what your work will look like and make corrections before you print it. Also, use inexpensive paper and use your printer's draft mode to print fast, lower-resolution copies for preliminary checking. See Chapter 3 for more information about printing draft copies.

Printing text in color costs only a little more than printing text in black, simply because color print cartridges (which contain the ink) are slightly more expensive than black print cartridges. However, if you only use color to emphasize headings, there is no significant increase in cost.

The cost of printing graphics is another story. Obviously, an area of a page that is completely covered in black or color uses much more ink than the same area filled with text. The cost of printing graphics is proportional to the percentage of the page covered with ink. In the real world of home and office use, you are not often likely to have large areas of filled graphics, so the cost of adding graphics to your work is small compared to the value and effect of those graphics. However, don't be surprised at how quickly you need to replace print cartridges if you print a lot of color transparencies in which ink covers most of the print area.

The Matter of Speed

Printing speed is an important, though not a simple, issue. Most printer specifications include some information about speed expressed in pages per minute (ppm) for text and minutes per page (mpp) for graphics. For the types of printers covered in this book, you will find figures of from one to seven pages of text per minute mentioned. After you consider what happens when you print a document, you may decide that specified printing speeds are less important than they initially seem to be. In my own work, I've found that I send a document to be printed, wait a short while to regain access to my computer, and then get on with other work while the pages are actually printed. Within reasonable limits, it doesn't really make much difference whether the printer is rated at four, six, or eight pages per minute.

Suppose you have created a document on your computer and give the command to print it. Briefly, what usually happens in the case of a page printer such as the DeskJet 1200C is:

1. The computer translates your document into a format suitable for the printer you are using.

2. The computer writes the printable form of your document to space on your hard disk or, perhaps, to memory in a print buffer or spooler.

3. The printer receives the data from the print buffer and starts to assemble it into a printable image.

4. The printer puts the image onto paper.

5. If you have requested two or more copies of each page, the printer repeats step 4 as often as necessary.

6. If the document consists of more than one page, steps 3, 4, and 5 are repeated as many times as necessary.

The sequence is a little different for the DeskJet 560C and DeskWriter 560C printers because these are serial, rather than page, printers. Rather than assembling a complete page and then printing that page, these printers receive and print a page line by line. When two or more copies of a page are requested, the printer repeats steps 3 and 4, rather than just step 4, once for each additional page.

When printer manufacturers talk about printing speed, they are usually referring only to the fourth step in this sequence for the reason that this is the only step over which they have some degree of control. Even the time taken for this step varies according to what is being printed.

In reality, most people don't buy a computer printer with the principal intention of printing multiple copies of each page. Consequently, the speed specified by the manufacturer is of little help in forecasting the time a printer will take to print your work. You can, of course, use this specification to compare one aspect of a printer's performance with that of another printer.

Some printer specifications include an estimate of the time required to print a color graphic image. The fact that this estimate is usually specified in terms of minutes per page (mpp) correctly suggests that graphics printing, and particularly color graphics printing, is much slower than text printing. The time required to print a color document that contains graphics is highly dependent on the complexity of that document. You can only discover this time by printing a representative document from a specific computer and on a specific printer.

In many cases, the time that is important is not the interval between the moment you give the Print command on your computer to the time you have printed paper in your hands. Rather, what is important is the interval between the moment you give the Print command and the time you can start using your computer again. This is the time required to complete the first two steps in the process outlined above. As you see, this time has little to do with the printer; it is something determined mainly by your computer hardware and software.

For the present, don't be overly concerned about printer speed unless you anticipate printing many pages on a regular basis.

The Benefits of Quality Printing

A quality product is one that completely satisfies its purpose. So, in this context, quality printing does not mean the most expensive, most impressive, or most elaborate printing, but rather printing that achieves what you intend. Most of us have different perceptions of print quality, depending on whether we are talking about a personal letter or a brochure.

Throughout this book, you'll find many examples of what you can do with an affordable color printer. Here are a few that might stimulate your imagination.

Printing in Your Home Office

If you have a home office—a full-time or part-time business—you need many types of stationery: letterhead and envelopes, business cards, forms, invoices, and so on. To impress people and be successful, you must have professional-looking printed material.

If you have recently won the lottery, you could save yourself a great deal of time by having all your material designed by a professional graphics artist and produced by a commercial printer. A better alternative for many people is to produce the material themselves using the type of computer printer dealt with in this book. The quality *might* not look quite as good to the professional eye, but it's sure to impress most of the people you deal with.

In your home office, you also need to create professional-looking correspondence and such other material as proposals, presentations, and invoices. All these can be printed quite satisfactorily with the types of printers covered in this book.

Printing in the Business Office

Business offices, large and small, have many requirements for printed material. Ordinary laser printers and office copiers can adequately deal with the run-of-the-mill need for black printing. Commercial printing companies offer services that can satisfy needs for large-quantity printing and for color printing. But there are many in-between needs, times when offices need relatively small quantities of material printed in color, and they need it *now*.

Take one example. A business manager has the opportunity to make a presentation to some senior people at a prospective client company. The manager knows that one of the most effective ways to make a presentation is to use color overhead transparencies and to leave the audience with handouts so they can remember the important details of the presentation.

By using a color printer, such as those described in this book, the manager or an assistant can easily prepare the overhead transparencies and handouts without concern for the budget.

Whether you have a small home business or are part of a large business organization, a color printer can solve a common problem. You need some printed material, it has to be in color to project a professional image, but the quantity you need is too small to justify the cost of professional printing. Without a color printer connected to your computer, the choice is simple: you either do without color printing, or pay a very high price to have someone else do it.

With a color printer you have a very practical alternative. If you need only a small quantity of printed pages, print them directly on your color printer. For a larger quantity, print one original on your color printer, then have that reproduced on a color copier at your local copy center. Either way, you can produce a few copies of a color document economically.

Your color printer can provide invaluable help even when you're preparing something like a newsletter or brochure that will be commercially printed in color. You can use your color printer to see what the final piece will look like, to get approval from other people in your organization, and to convey exactly what you have in mind to your commercial printer.

Color Printing at Home

Let's be up front about this. None of us *needs* a color printer at home. So why raise the subject? We don't *need* a TV, a VCR, or a video camera, either. But we have them, enjoy using them, and usually are glad we have them.

What would you do with a color printer at home? How about printing your own greeting cards in color? Your friends would be delighted to have personalized cards from you on their birthdays and at year's end. Then there are your family's sports and social clubs, most of which would enjoy newsletters and flyers printed in sparkling color and with graphics.

Are you into photography? With an adequately equipped computer and a color printer, you have the makings of a home photography lab, without all the hassles of a darkroom and chemicals.

And your kids, too: wouldn't school reports and other projects be more exciting to prepare, and get better grades, with some added color and illustrations?

Do you occasionally want to make a color copy of something in a magazine? If you have a scanner, you can use the combination of scanner and printer as a color copier. The process is slow, but more convenient and less expensive than using your local copy center.

Perhaps you want to let a landscape architect or interior designer know what you have in mind for a remodeling project. Inexpensive software and your color printer make it easy to sketch your ideas in a way that clearly conveys your intentions to the person you will be paying to make them happen.

As you read this book, you'll find detailed suggestions about these and other worthwhile things you can do with an affordable printer that has color capability.

You Also Need . . .

Don't buy your young daughter or son a camera unless you intend to provide supplies of film on an ongoing basis and pay for the processing. What's this piece of parental advice to do with color printers? Read on.

A printer is an output device. It needs to be fed. Apart from the fairly reasonable cost of paper and print cartridges, it needs data. This data comes from a computer. Not any computer, but a computer that is capable of handling the type of data you want to print.

For most of us, the choice is between using an Apple Macintosh computer or an IBM-compatible PC. A couple of years ago, the Macintosh was most people's choice for graphics work. Now, though, the PC with graphics applications running under Windows is at least the equal of the Macintosh. You can use either with equal ease and obtain good-quality results, providing you have a sufficiently powerful model.

We're talking here about color and about graphics, both of which require large amounts of memory and powerful processing. Memory is of two types: the internal RAM your computer has for the data and images you work with at one time, and the hard disk memory available to store your complete projects and the applications software you use to create them. Processing power is what you need to handle all the complexities of color and graphics in a reasonable amount of time.

You can't just buy a sophisticated printer and add it to your five-year old computer and expect to achieve all the results described in this book. The computer has to be powerful enough to take advantage of the software you are using and of the printer capabilities. The only guidance I can give on this subject is to advise that you should decide what you would like to do, choose appropriate software, look at the software specifications to see what type of computer is needed, and base your decisions on what computer you have, what hardware upgrades you are prepared to make, or what new computer you are prepared to buy.

Sophisticated printing, particularly color graphics printing, requires powerful software. There is a wide range of suitable software available for the Macintosh and Windows environments; new and improved software becomes available every month. One of the significant developments over the last year or two is that almost identical software is available for the two types of computer systems. In fact, in many cases, you can start creating a document on a Macintosh and then continue working with the same document on a PC, or the other way around.

As you read this book, you'll find references to specific software. Remember, though, that the references are to the software available at the time the book was written. By the time you read it, your software choices will probably be different.

To come back to the beginning of this section, quality printing requires ongoing feeding. Upgraded software often requires upgraded hardware. Almost all upgraded software requires double the RAM (system memory) and 50 percent more disk space than its predecessor; more sophisticated printing requires additional hardware and software. Once you become concerned about quality printing, be prepared for continuing expenses. You'll usually think of money you spend in this way as well spent!

A Word of Caution

High-quality printed text is exciting. High-quality printed graphics are even more exciting. If you're getting involved in printing and graphics for your own enjoyment, the only limitation is the amount of time and money you're prepared to devote to it. However, if you're using text and graphics for business purposes, temper your enthusiasm! How much is the work (time and money) you are putting into the project likely to add to your business reward? Are you spending time and resources on doing your own printing that you could better spend on your real business? Balance your effort with its worth.

The capabilities of using many fonts and of printing in various colors is exciting. It's only human nature to tend to go somewhat overboard, particularly when you first have access to fonts and colors. However, fewer fonts are usually better than many, and less color is usually better than more.

Ansel Adams, one of the world's most renowned photographers, worked entirely in black and white. But this book is not about artistic achievements: it's about using the capabilities of printers as an effective means of communication.

In most of our work, we can use fonts and color as enhancements. We can use them to draw attention, to imply a mood, to make information easy to digest, and to create an identity. When you use color, use it for a specific purpose, not just to advertise that you can afford it or that you like certain colors. Remember, color is a means of communication, whether you intend it that way or not. Make sure color reinforces, rather than detracts from, what you want to communicate.

When you choose fonts, select them with the intention of getting and keeping your readers' attention. For large blocks of text, make sure the font you use is easy to read. For titles and headings, use fonts that attract readers' interest.

2
CHAPTER

Getting Acquainted with Your Printer

This book will help you get the best possible results from computer printers that can print text and graphics in black and in color. Although much in this book will be useful for you no matter what type of printer you have, the information here is specifically about Hewlett-Packard DeskJet and DeskWriter printers.

You can choose between two approaches to using your printer. The first approach is simple: just follow the basic directions for connecting it to your computer, install the required software, open a document in your favorite word processor or other application, and choose the Print command. Wait a few moments for the new printer to give you a sheet of paper with some printing on it. That's simple. Now you know all about using the printer, so you can go back to work.

If you're satisfied with that approach, you don't need this book. You probably don't need the printer either!

The second approach is to start by realizing that your printer is a very powerful tool. The more you understand about it, the better printing you will get, and the more useful the printer will be to you. What's more, when things don't go quite the way you expect, as will surely happen (usually when your work is most urgent), the better you understand your printer, the easier it will be for you to solve the problem.

You don't have to study this chapter in detail. However, if you're the sort of person who likes to know how things work, you'll probably enjoy spending a little time getting to know how things are under the hood. If you're not really interested in how the printer works, then just skim this chapter for now and dip into it sometime later.

The 560C and 1200C Printers

For the remainder of this chapter, we'll focus on the specific HP inkjet printers shown in Figure 2.1:

- DeskJet 560C and DeskWriter 560C printers
- DeskJet 1200C printers

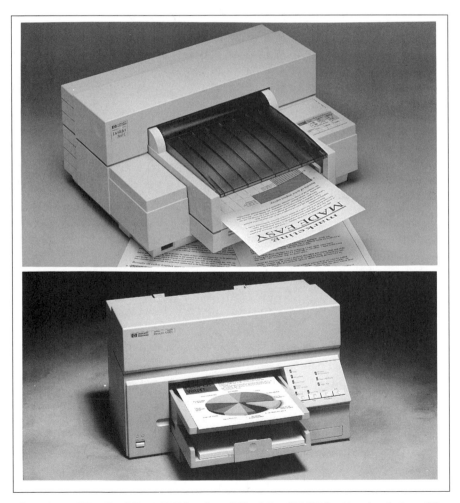

Figure 2.1 The DeskJet 560C (top) and DeskJet 1200C (bottom) printers. The DeskWriter 560C is almost identical in appearance to the DeskJet 560C.

The DeskJet 560C and DeskWriter 560C printers are mechanically and electrically very similar. The main difference between the two is that the DeskJet 560C is intended for use with IBM-compatible PCs, whereas the DeskWriter 560C is intended for use with Macintosh computers and with LocalTalk networks. Throughout this book, references to the 560C apply to both unless specifically stated otherwise.

1200C printers can be used with IBM-compatible computers, Macintosh computers, and UNIX-based workstations. They can also be used as network printers. The basic 1200C comes with a Centronics interface suitable for connection to IBM-compatible PCs. The 1200C/PS also has a LocalTalk interface suitable for connection to Macintosh computers. Optional interfaces are available for connection to various network configurations.

Perhaps the most obvious difference between 560C and 1200C printers is the price. The 1200C costs about three times as much as the 560C. Why would this be when, at first glance, both types of printers seem to be able to do much of the same?

Well, consider other products—cars, for example. Many car manufacturers offer a range of vehicles, with some priced four or more times higher than others. While all provide reliable, safe transportation, the more expensive ones offer additional features and capabilities. People who want the additions pay for the more expensive models.

It's the same with HP's printers. The 560C and 1200C can both print black and color text that's as good as (some people think better than) many laser printers. Both printers can also print graphics in black, shades of gray, and color.

There's the question of printing speed, also. In most situations, the 1200C is twice as fast as the 560C. However, as was mentioned in Chapter 1, there's a lot more to printing speed than just reading figures in a specification.

As you read the remainder of this book, this chapter particularly, you'll discover a number of other differences between the two printers and be able to decide which provides the value that best suits your needs. Basically, if you want a printer to connect to an individual computer, if you usually print only a few pages at a time, and mainly use business graphics, the 560C will prove an excellent choice. However, if you want to share a printer among computers, often print quite long documents, and like to use sophisticated graphics, you should consider the 1200C.

Putting Ink on Paper

The 560C and 1200C printers use a technique known as *on-demand thermal inkjet printing* to put ink on paper. Briefly, ink stored in disposable print cartridges is

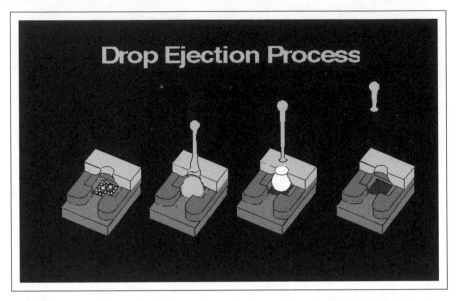

Figure 2.2 Schematic representation of on-demand thermal inkjet printing.

forced by heat through an array of tiny nozzles onto the paper. By incorporating the nozzles into the print cartridges, HP has minimized the problem of clogged nozzles that plagued earlier types of inkjet printers. With the 560C and 1200C, you get a new set of nozzles each time you replace a print cartridge.

The 560C uses two print cartridges, one for black ink and the other with separate reservoirs for cyan, magenta, and yellow ink. The 1200C uses four print cartridges, one each for black, cyan, magenta, and yellow ink.

With both printers, the black print cartridge is normally used to print black text and graphics. Colored images are created by using cyan, magenta, and yellow ink in various proportions.

Figure 2.2 shows how on-demand thermal inkjet printers work.

In each print cartridge, ink is constantly available behind an array of nozzles. There is a tiny resistor behind each nozzle. When a dot of ink is required from a specific nozzle, a pulse of electrical current flows through the resistor behind that nozzle, heating the ink in the immediate vicinity. The heat is sufficient to create a bubble that forces a drop of ink out of the nozzle and onto the paper. All this happens very quickly and very precisely.

Printer Features

In the next few pages, we'll draw your attention to some of the more important features of 560C and 1200C printers, noting the similarities and differences.

Physical Size

Both printers are quite small, occupying considerable less space on your desk than many laser printers.

Power Input

The 560C and 1200C printers are energy misers. They use very little power on standby and not a great deal more when they are printing.

The 560C comes with an external power module for 100 VAC (50/60 Hz), 120 VAC (60 Hz), 220 VAC (50 Hz), or 240 VAC (50 Hz) electricity outlets, depending on where you buy the printer. It has a power consumption of 8 W on standby and no more than 25 W when printing.

The 1200C has an internal power supply and can be plugged directly into power outlets supplying 100–240 VAC (50/60 Hz). The printer has a power consumption of 50 W on standby and no more than 250 W while printing.

When you compare this power consumption with that used by your office lighting, you will probably come to the conclusion that the cost of electricity used by a printer is not a significant consideration.

Input/Output Interface

There are significant differences between the I/O interfaces for the DeskJet 560C, the DeskWriter 560C, the DeskJet 1200C, and the DeskJet 1200C/PS. What we are talking about here is the electrical connection between a printer and the computer (or network) that provides the information to be printed.

The DeskJet 560C comes with a Centronics parallel interface (200 Kbps), shown in Figure 2.3, that you can use to connect to an IBM-compatible PC. This printer is intended for use with PCs; no interfaces for other computers are available.

The DeskWriter 560C printer comes with a single connector, shown in Figure 2.3, that you can use as an RS-422 serial (57.6 Kbps) interface to connect the printer directly to a Macintosh computer or as a LocalTalk (230.4 Kbps) interface to connect the printer to a LocalTalk network. No optional interfaces are available.

Like the DeskJet 560C printer, the DeskJet 1200C printer comes with a Centronics parallel interface (200 Kbps), as shown in Figure 2.4. Simply connect that to a parallel output port on your IBM-compatible PC and you're ready to print.

The DeskJet 1200C/PS printer is supplied with a LocalTalk interface in addition to the Centronics interface. You can purchase the LocalTalk interface separately and easily plug it into the vacant interface slot in a standard DeskJet

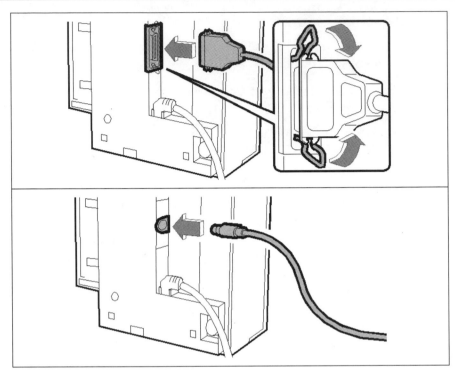

Figure 2.3 The Centronics interface connector underneath the DeskJet 560C (top) and the combined serial/LocalTalk connector underneath the DeskWriter 560C (bottom).

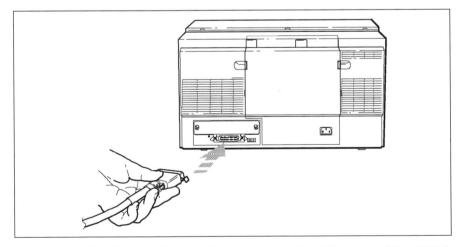

Figure 2.4 The Centronics interface connector is at the rear of the 1200C. The panel above the Centronics connector covers the space for an optional interface board.

1200C so that you can use this printer with a Macintosh computer. You can also purchase interfaces that allow you to connect a DeskJet 1200C to various types of UNIX-based computers and to most network cabling configurations.

I/O auto-sensing is a valuable extra feature of the 1200C, particularly when the printer is used on a network. The printer automatically senses the source of the data it is receiving so that it can process that data correctly. The 1200C can also sense whether incoming data is in PCL or HP-GL/2 format (or, in the case of a printer equipped with a PostScript module, PostScript format) and process the data accordingly.

Printer Drivers

You have been reading about I/O interfaces—the electrical connections between a computer or network and a printer. Now we turn to another aspect of how computers communicate with printers.

Everything you create on your computer is stored in memory and on disk in a particular coded format. Everything your printer does is in response to instructions in another coded format. In order for your printer to reproduce what you see on your screen, your computer's code has to be translated into your printer's code. That is what a *printer driver* does.

The Macintosh environment uses one format to store text and graphics data; the Windows environment uses a different format. Various DOS applications for PCs have their own individual formats.

The 560C and 1200C printers both understand HP's printer control language (PCL); however, the two printers do not respond in exactly the same way to all PCL commands.

Solving this language problem is a lot easier than solving the problem of communication between people who speak different languages. If you have a Macintosh computer and buy a DeskWriter 560C or DeskJet 1200C printer, just install the supplied printer driver on your computer—as a result, your computer and printer can communicate. Similarly, if you have a PC that runs Windows applications and buy a DeskJet 560C or 1200C printer, install the supplied printer driver and everything will be fine.

If you have a PC and want to work with DOS applications, you do not need a printer driver to print plain text. However, if you use a DOS application that works with other than plain text, you need to install a printer driver, which is usually available from the software supplier.

Print Cartridges

560C printers have two print cartridges, as shown in Figure 2.5. One cartridge contains black ink and the other contains separate reservoirs of cyan, magenta,

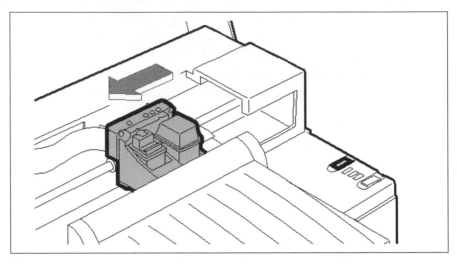

Figure 2.5 560C printers have two print cartridges. The black cartridge is on the left and the color cartridge is on the right.

and yellow ink. Black cartridges have 50 nozzles and color cartridges have 48 nozzles.

In contrast, 1200C printers have four print cartridges, as shown in Figure 2.6, one each for yellow, magenta, cyan, and black ink. Each cartridge contains 42 cubic centimeters of ink and has 104 nozzles.

Each 1200C print cartridge contains an ink-level indicator, a small window in the center of its label. The window is green when the cartridge is full. As ink is used, progressively more of the window becomes black. When the cartridge is empty, the window is completely black.

The differences between the print cartridges in the 560C and 1200C printers provide clues to the choices made by their designers, and may help you decide which printer better matches your needs.

One point to consider regarding the three-color print cartridge used in the 560C is the fact that you have to replace the cartridge when any one of the three color chambers is empty. In practice, most users use almost equal amounts of the three primary colors, so there is very little wastage. The reason for this is that printed colors are created by mixing the primary colors. Blue, for example, is created by equal amounts of cyan and magenta, green by equal amounts of cyan and yellow.

1200C printers, but not 560C printers, sense when one or more print cartridges are almost out of ink. When this happens, the printer completes the current page and then stops. The Check Print Cartridges indicator on the front panel lights to indicate why the printer has stopped.

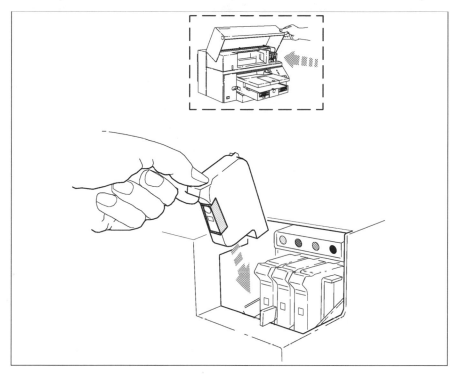

Figure 2.6 The 1200C has four print cartridges. From left to right, these are yellow, magenta, cyan, and black.

If necessary, run the self-test procedure to discover which print cartridge needs replacing. Replace that cartridge, and then continue printing.

Paper Trays

The 560C and 1200C printers have convenient paper trays that are easily accessible from the front, as shown in Figure 2.7. In each case, the input tray is at the bottom and the output tray is at the top.

The input trays of both printers can accept standard U.S. letter and legal size paper, as well as European A4 paper. The two printers have different methods of handling other sizes and types of paper.

The 560C input tray has space for up to 100 sheets of average weight paper or up to 20 envelopes. The 1200C input tray can hold up to about 180 sheets of ordinary paper.

HP recommends using paper in weights ranging from 16 to 36 lb for the 560C, and paper in the range from 16 to 24 lb in the 1200C's input tray—you can use heavier paper in the 1200C's manual feed slot. See Chapter 3 for information about how paper weights are specified.

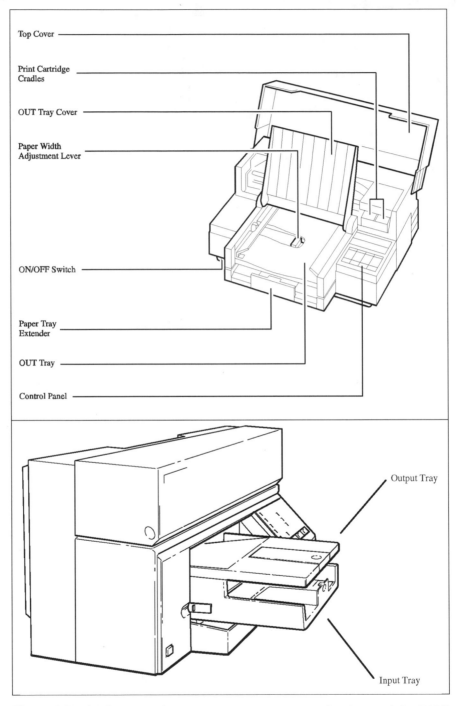

Figure 2.7 The input and output paper trays are at the front of the 560C printer (top) and the 1200C printer (bottom).

With the 560C, you can load executive size paper or envelopes in the input tray after you have moved a selector lever to the appropriate position. However, you cannot mix different sizes of paper. While this approach simplifies the printer design, contributing to a lower price, it does mean that each time you want to print an envelope, for example, you have to remove ordinary paper from the input tray, set the selector lever, and then load envelopes. After you have printed the envelope, you have to go through the same process to put ordinary paper back in the printer. You can minimize this small inconvenience by organizing your work so that you print envelopes in batches.

The 1200C has a manual feed slot at the back that you can use for printing envelopes and other special paper, without having to remove the normal paper in the input tray. When you feed in this way, the printer can handle ordinary business envelopes (#10) as well as DL and C5 sizes.

The 1200C's manual feed slot has another advantage when you are printing on thicker-than-normal paper or on folded paper such as an envelope. When you use the manual feed slot, the path the paper follows as it passes through the printer is less severely curved, resulting in less likelihood of printer jams.

You'll read more about selecting and using paper and other media in Chapter 3.

Using the Control Panel

The printers each have a control panel that has buttons and indicator lights, as shown in Figure 2.8. You will have little need to use the control panel except when things go wrong or, in the case of the 560C, when you need to install a new print cartridge. You'll find various references to the control panels at appropriate places throughout this book.

Inside Your Printer

Your computer sends signals to your printer by way of the I/O interface, and your printer responds by presenting you with text and graphics printed on paper. Let's see if we can understand how this happens.

Communicating Information

Text and graphics to be printed are generated by applications running on a computer, but not usually in a form the printer can understand. Software, known as a printer driver, translates the output from the application to a form a specific printer can understand.

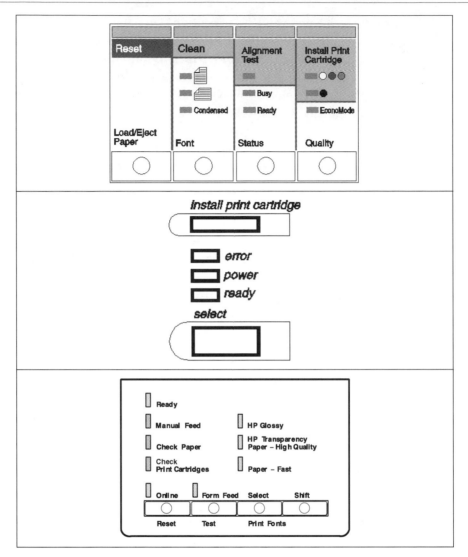

Figure 2.8 **Control panels for the DeskJet 560C printer (top), DeskWriter 560C printer (center), and DeskJet 1200C and DeskJet 1200C/PS printers (bottom).**

Printer drivers are available to communicate between the Macintosh and Windows environments and printers in PCL, the Hewlett-Packard printer control language. By using these drivers, output from Macintosh and Windows applications can be printed on any printer that understands PCL.

Some DOS graphics applications provide output in the HP-GL/2 language, a control language principally intended for plotters.

The DeskJet 560C, DeskWriter 560C, and DeskJet 1200C are all PCL printers, which means that they all expect to receive input in HPL. The DeskJet 1200C is bilingual—it can also receive input in the HP-GL/2 language and automatically switches between PCL and HP-GL/2.

The DeskJet 1200C/PS printer can receive input in PostScript as well as in PCL and HP-GL/2, and can automatically switch between the three languages.

The DeskWriter 560C takes a different approach to PostScript. As an option you can purchase a PostScript software package for installation on your Macintosh computer. This driver translates the PostScript output from certain applications to the PCL language your DeskWriter can understand.

The 560C printers and 1200C printers handle incoming information differently. The 560C printers receive text and graphics to be printed one section at a time and print each section as soon as it is received. The DeskJet 560C printer has a 64-Kbyte buffer memory that is used for this purpose; the DeskWriter 560C has a 48-Kbyte buffer.

> *Note:* You can add one or two 256-Kbyte memory modules to the DeskJet 560C, but these are used for downloaded fonts, not as a buffer memory for incoming data.

In contrast, the 1200C printer receives a complete page of text and graphics to be printed and then prints that page. This printer has a 2-Mbyte memory that you can expand to as much as 26 Mbyte (20 Mbyte in the case of the 1200C/PS). Most of this memory is used to store incoming data, but some of it is used for other purposes.

Processing Information

The incoming information is of two quite different types:

- Control data that does such things as setting margins, starting a new page, selecting fonts, and much more
- Data that represents characters to be printed in the case of text, or positions of dots or descriptions of shapes in the case of graphics

The process of converting the incoming data into dots that can be printed on a page is known as *rasterization*. This process is complex, very complex in the case of graphics, and requires the use of a microprocessor within the printer. The 560C printer uses a relatively simple microprocessor, the Zilog Z80 running at 8 MHz, for this purpose. The 1200C printer uses the advanced Intel i80960SA RISC processor running at 11 MHz.

With more memory and a more powerful processor, it's not surprising that the 1200C is faster than the 560C.

Using Fonts

The subject of fonts is another area where there are distinct differences between the 560C and the 1200C, and also between the non-PostScript and PostScript versions of these printers.

Font Facts

There are a few facts about fonts that need to be clarified. First, there are *bitmapped* fonts and *outline* fonts. Bitmapped fonts are the shapes of characters that are stored in the computer memory as the dots necessary to reproduce those characters on the screen and in the printer memory to print characters on paper. One characteristic of bitmapped fonts is that a complete set of characters has to be stored for each size you are going to use.

Outline fonts, on the other hand, are stored as mathematical descriptions of the shape of each character. When you display or print a character, the micro-processor in your computer or printer generates that character at the size needed. This eliminates the need to store each character separately in every size. Outline fonts are also known as *scalable fonts* because they can be scaled to many different sizes.

The fonts used to display text on the screen are different from those used to print text on paper. This is because monitor screens have a different number of dots per inch from printers. In the case of bitmapped fonts, you need a separate set of screen fonts and printer fonts for every size character you want to use. In the case of scalable fonts, your software must be able to generate suitable screen and printer fonts.

People sometimes encounter the problem that printed text looks different from that on the screen. In particular, line breaks and page breaks occur at different positions. This is usually because the screen fonts and printer fonts don't match. Slightly different character widths cause the differences between printed and on-screen appearance. For this reason, it's important to have matching screen and printer fonts.

When you're working on an IBM-compatible PC and using an application that runs directly under DOS, you can use the standard fonts defined in the PC's read-only memory (ROM) to display characters on your monitor. You can use fonts built in to the printer, fonts available in plug-in cartridges, or fonts downloaded from your computer to the printer to print your work.

In the case of Macintosh and Windows applications, you can use scalable fonts, such as TrueType, Intellifont, or ATM fonts that come with those applications or that you have purchased separately. These fonts can produce matching screen and printer fonts in a wide range of sizes.

Macintosh and PC applications using a PostScript driver can print with the standard PostScript fonts, or with additional downloaded PostScript fonts.

Supplied Fonts

DeskJet 560C and 1200C printers are supplied with scalable fonts. The 560C is supplied with 16 general-purpose internal fonts you can use with DOS applications, and also with 14 TrueType fonts on disk. You can install the TrueType fonts into your computer and use them with Windows applications, creating matching screen and printer fonts.

The 1200C printer comes with 45 scalable fonts (35 Intellifont and 10 True-Type) stored within the printer in ROM. You can also request the same fonts on disk from HP so that you can create matching screen fonts.

The DeskWriter 560C is supplied with 35 TrueType scalable fonts; the DeskJet 1200C/PS is supplied with 35 internal PostScript scalable fonts in addition to those supplied with the 1200C.

Font Cartridges

As already mentioned, the DeskJet 560C and 1200C printers have internal fonts that are stored internally in a ROM. You can add to this ROM by plugging font cartridges into the printers. The font cartridges you can use are those offered by HP (and by some independent suppliers) for its LaserJet printers. There is no provision to add font cartridges to a DeskWriter 560C because this printer works solely with TrueType and Adobe Type 1 fonts.

The ability to accept font cartridges is somewhat of an anachronism. Before scalable fonts became available for the PC, font cartridges provided a convenient, though not inexpensive, way to use various fonts and font sizes with laser printers. Now, though, scalable fonts provide a much more convenient, less expensive, and more versatile way to do this.

The only time you are likely to want to use a font cartridge with your DeskJet printer is if you have standardized on a font that is only available in a cartridge. Font cartridges are interchangeable between HP LaserJet printers and DeskJet 1200C printers, but not between LaserJet printers and DeskJet 560C printers.

Margin Limitations

Like most laser printers, inkjet printers cannot print to the exact edge of the paper.

According to the HP specifications:

- The 1200C printer can print to within 0.167 inch of the top, bottom, left, and right margins.
- The 560C printer can print to within 0.33 inch of the top margin, 0.67 inch of the bottom margin, and 0.25 inch of the left and right margins.

> *Note:* The margins for the 560C printer quoted above are true for Macintosh and Windows applications. The specific printer drivers used with DOS applications may result in different margin specifications.

If you're a 560C user, you should pay particular attention to the 0.67-inch bottom margin. This is because word-processor and other applications commonly use 0.5 inch as the default vertical position for footers. If you do not change this setting, none of your footers will be printed.

Unfortunately, not all applications allow you to change the footer position. Microsoft Excel version 4 had this problem. However, the newer Excel version 5 allows users to change the footer position.

Watch for this possible problem in the applications you use.

3

Installing and Using Your Printer

This chapter provides the basic information you need to install and use your DeskJet or DeskWriter printer. If you need more details, refer to the Setup Guide and User's Guide that were supplied with your printer.

Installing the Printer

The steps involved in installing 560C and 1200C printers are slightly different, so they are described separately in the next few paragraphs.

Installing a 560C DeskJet or 560C DeskWriter Printer

The following steps assume you are installing a new printer.

The cable necessary to connect the printer to a computer or network is not supplied with the printer, so you must purchase this cable separately. For a DeskJet printer, the cable required is a standard Centronics parallel printer cable with a Centronics connector at one end. The connector required at the other end of the cable is a 25-pin male D-connector, unless your computer requires a different connector.

For a DeskWriter printer, you need a LocalTalk connector box if you are going to attach the printer to a LocalTalk network, or a standard Macintosh serial cable if you are going to connect the printer directly to your computer.

33

After removing the printer and accessories from the packing case, do the following:

1. Set the printer on a firm, level surface.

2. Remove the tape that holds the paper output tray in place.

3. Open the paper output tray, remove the packing material inside it, and close the tray.

4. Open the top cover, remove the tape that secures the print cartridge cradles, and close the cover.

5. Make sure the on/off switch at the left end of the front of the printer's base is in the off position. If necessary, press the left end of the switch to set it to the off position.

6. Remove the paper output tray, then turn the printer on its side so that the bottom of the printer faces you.

7. Plug the power module connector firmly into the printer's power socket.

8. Place the power module on the floor, and plug the power cord into a grounded electrical outlet.

> *Caution:* The power module emits some magnetic interference. Make sure it is not in a position where you might place floppy disks on it or close to it. The module should be at least one inch away from your computer.

9. With the printer still on its side and turned off, plug the interface cable into the interface port.

   • For a DeskJet printer, push the Centronics connector firmly into the printer's interface port, then snap the spring clips into place to secure the connector. Plug the other end of the printer cable into a parallel printer port on the back of your computer, and tighten the screws to hold it in position.

   • For a DeskWriter printer connected to a LocalTalk network, plug the LocalTalk connector box into the printer's interface port and connect the connector box to the network with standard LocalTalk interface cable.

   • For a DeskWriter printer connected directly to a computer, plug one end of a standard Macintosh serial cable into the printer's interface port and connect the other end of the cable to either the printer port or the modem port on the back of the computer.

10. Return the printer to its upright position, making sure that it does not rest on the power cable or interface cable, and replace the paper output tray.

11. Set the on/off switch to the on position and verify that the lights on the front panel come on. If the lights do not come on, it is probable that you have not pushed the power connector all the way in or, perhaps, the electrical outlet you are using is not energized. Correct these problems before proceeding.

Before you can use your printer, you must load some paper into the input paper tray and install the print cartridges. To load paper:

1. Open the paper output tray cover. On the bottom of the paper output tray, you can see markings for three paper widths and two sizes of envelopes.

2. Move the green paper width adjust lever (which you can see through a slot in the bottom of the paper output tray) to suit the width of paper you intend to use.

3. Pull out the paper tray extender at the front of the paper input tray.

4. Remove a stack of paper about half an inch thick from its packaging. Fan the paper to make sure sheets are not stuck together, and tap the stack on a smooth surface to make sure the sheets of paper are evenly aligned.

5. Slide the stack of paper into the paper input tray with the print side (the side to receive printing) down. Make sure the right edge of the paper is touching the right side of the paper tray, and make sure you slide the paper in as far as it will go.

6. Push the paper tray extender in until it just touches the outer edge of the paper. Don't push it in enough to make the paper buckle.

7. Close the paper output tray cover.

To install print cartridges:

1. Open the printer's top cover and make sure the packing tape that secured the print cartridge cradles has been removed.

2. If necessary, set the on/off switch to the on position and check that some of the indicator lights come on. The printer must be turned on before you install print cartridges.

3. Press the Install Print Cartridge button on the control panel. This causes the print cartridge cradles to move to the left side of the printer.

4. Open the black print cartridge package and the container inside the package. Grasp the cartridge by the green top and remove it from the container.

5. Remove the two pieces of tape that cover the nozzles, being careful not to touch the nozzles or the copper contacts.

6. Drop the black print cartridge into the left cradle. Make sure the green arrow on the cartridge top points to the black dot on the top of the cradle.

7. Push the green arrow toward the black dot until the cartridge snaps into place.

8. Open the color print cartridge package and the container inside the package. Grasp the cartridge by the green top and remove it from the container.

9. Remove the two pieces of tape that cover the nozzles, being careful not to touch the nozzles or the copper contacts.

10. Drop the color print cartridge into the right cradle. Make sure the green arrow on the cartridge top points to the color dots on the top of the cradle.

11. Push the green arrow toward the color dots until the cartridge snaps into place.

12. Press the Install Print Cartridge button on the control panel to return the print cartridge cradles to the right side of the printer.

13. Close the top of the printer.

When initially installed, the two print cartridges may not be aligned optimally. The following alignment procedure lets you correct any misalignment:

1. Press the Alignment Test button on the control panel. This causes the printer to print a sample page with seven different horizontal alignment patterns.

2. Choose the best horizontal alignment, and press the control panel button indicated on the sample page. This causes the printer to print a sample page with seven different vertical alignment patterns.

3. Choose the best vertical alignment, and press the control panel button indicated on the sample page. This causes the printer to print a sample page showing the horizontal and vertical alignment. If the black and colored line segments are aligned, the procedure is complete. If they are not aligned, repeat these three steps.

Your printer should now be completely installed and ready to use. As a final step, run the printer self-test, using the following steps:

1. Make sure the printer is connected to a computer that is turned on or to a live network.

2. Turn off the printer.

3. Press and hold down the Load/Eject Paper button on the printer. Keeping the button pressed down, turn on the printer.

4. Keep the Load/Eject Paper button pressed until the top sheet of paper in the paper input tray begins to move into the printing position, then release the button.

The printer should print a color test pattern followed, in the case of the DeskJet 560C, by samples of the internal fonts. If your printer does not print, the most likely reasons are:

- You did not remove the tape that covers the nozzles of new print cartridges.
- You did not install the print cartridges correctly.
- The printer is not connected to a computer or network.
- The computer is not turned on or the network is not live.

After you satisfactorily complete the self-test, you are ready to install a printer driver and then print from the applications installed on your computer.

Installing a 1200C or 1200C/PS DeskJet

The following steps assume you are installing a new printer.

The cable necessary to connect the printer to a computer or network is not supplied with the printer, so you must purchase this cable separately. If you are going to connect your 1200C or 1200C/PS printer directly to an IBM-compatible PC, the cable required is a standard Centronics parallel printer cable with a Centronics connector at one end. The connector at the other end of the cable is a 25-pin male D-connector, unless your computer requires a different connector.

If you have a 1200C/PS printer and are going to connect it directly to a Macintosh computer, you need a standard Macintosh serial cable or LocalTalk connector box. To connect the printer to a LocalTalk network, you need a LocalTalk connector box.

To use your printer with any other type of computer or network, you need the appropriate JetDirect kit and cables.

After removing the printer and accessories from the packing case, do the following:

1. Set the printer on a firm, level surface.

> *Note:* During operation, the rapid horizontal movement of the print cartridges generates considerable sideways forces. If the table or desk on which you place the printer is not rigid, you will experience noticeable shaking. Although this will not harm the printer, you will probably not enjoy it.

2. Remove the tape that holds the paper trays in place.
3. Open the top cover, remove the tape that secures the print cartridge cradles, and close the cover.

4. Attach the control-panel overlay over the indicators and switches at the right end of the printer.

5. Make sure the on/off switch at the left end of the front of the printer's base is in the off (out) position.

6. Plug the power module connector firmly into the printer's power socket and plug the power cord into a grounded electrical outlet.

7. Plug the interface cable into the interface port.

   - For a printer to be connected directly to a PC, push the Centronics connector firmly into the printer's interface port, then snap the spring clips into place to secure the connector. Plug the other end of the printer cable into a parallel printer port on the back of your computer, and tighten the screws to hold it in position.

   - For a printer to be connected to a LocalTalk network, plug the LocalTalk connector box into the LocalTalk JetDirect card and connect the connector box to the network with standard LocalTalk interface cable.

   - For a printer to be connected directly to a Macintosh computer, plug one end of a standard Macintosh serial cable into the LocalTalk JetDirect card and connect the other end of the cable to either the printer port or the modem port on the back of the computer.

   - For a printer to be connected to a different type of computer or network, use the appropriate JetDirect card and cable.

8. Set the on/off switch to the on (in) position and verify that the lights on the front panel come on. If the lights do not come on, it is probable that you have not pushed the power connector all the way in or, perhaps, the electrical outlet you are using is not energized. Correct these problems before proceeding.

Before you can use your printer, you must load some paper into the input paper tray and install the print cartridges. To load paper:

1. Push the green media selector on the right side of the input paper tray all the way in if you are going to use U.S. letter or legal paper, or pull the level all the way out if you are going to use European A4 paper.

2. Set the #7 switch at the back of the printer (at the right side of the Centronics interface port) in the down position if you will be using U.S. letter or legal paper, or up if you will be using European A4 paper.

3. Pull out the paper tray extender at the front of the paper input tray.

4. Remove a stack of paper about half an inch thick from its packaging. Fan the paper to make sure sheets are not stuck together, and tap the stack on a smooth surface to make sure the sheets of paper are evenly aligned.

5. Slide the stack of paper into the paper input tray with the print side (the side to receive printing) down. Make sure the right edge of the paper is touching the right side of the paper tray, and make sure you slide the paper in as far as it will go.

6. Push the paper tray extender in until it just touches the outer edge of the paper. Don't push it in enough to make the paper buckle.

To install print cartridges:

1. Open the printer's top cover and make sure the packing tape that secured the print cartridge cradle has been removed.

2. Open the black print cartridge package and the container inside the package. Remove the print cartridge from the container, touching only the black areas of the cartridge.

3. Remove the green tab and the blue transparent tape from the print cartridge to expose the nozzles, being careful not to touch the nozzles or the copper contacts.

4. Drop the black print cartridge into the stall at the right end of the cradle. Push the cartridge forward firmly until it snaps into position.

5. Repeat steps 2, 3, and 4 to place the cyan, magenta, and yellow print cartridges into their stalls in that order from right to left. Each print cartridge is keyed to prevent it being placed in an incorrect stall.

6. Close the top of the printer.

Unlike the cartridges in 560C printers, the 1200C print cartridges are aligned automatically. This alignment procedure occurs each time the printer is turned on, when the top cover is opened, and when a new cartridge is installed.

Your printer should now be completely installed and ready to use. As a final step, run the printer selftest. The 1200C printer does not have to be connected to a computer or network to run the selftest. To run the selftest:

1. Turn the printer on and wait until the Ready and Online indicators on the control panel are on.

2. Press and hold down the Shift button on the control panel, press and release the Test button, then release the Shift button.

After a few seconds, the Ready indicator starts flashing to indicate that the printer is processing data. A few seconds later, a sheet of paper moves from the paper input tray into the printing position and the printer starts to print the self-test page.

The self-test page shows whether there are problems, such as clogged nozzles, with any of the four print cartridges, and provides detailed information about the printer setting and options. If your printer does not print some or all of the test pattern, the most likely reasons are:

- You did not remove the tape that covers the nozzles of new print cartridges.
- You did not install the print cartridges correctly.

If you see streaks in a color bar, this indicates that a print cartridge is low in ink or has clogged nozzles. The procedure for unclogging nozzles is described later in this chapter.

As a separate procedure, you can obtain a printed sample of the internal fonts in a 1200C printer. To do this:

1. Press the Online button on the front panel to turn off the Online indicator.
2. Press and hold down the Shift button while you press the Print Fonts button.
3. Release the Shift button.

After several seconds' delay, the printer prints pages showing the internal scalable and bitmapped fonts.

After you satisfactorily complete the selftest and obtained a list of the internal fonts, you are ready to print from the applications installed on your computer.

Clearing Clogged Print Cartridge Nozzles

If you use your printer regularly, it is unlikely that you will experience clogged nozzles. If nozzles do become clogged, you will see the effect as streaks in your printed material.

The easiest way to unclog nozzles is to print several pages, making sure you are using the color that is causing the problem. In the case of a DeskJet or DeskWriter 560C printer, if this does not solve the problem, first make sure there is some paper in the paper tray. Then, in the case of the DeskJet, press the Clean button on the printer's control panel. For a DeskWriter, open the printer's Setup dialog box and choose Clear Nozzle. This initiates a cleaning process that includes printing color bars.

In the case of the 1200C printer, you can usually clear a clogged print cartridge by running the self test once or twice. When you do this, you will usually see the clogging problem gradually disappear.

You can also use a manual method for clearing nozzles. To do this:

1. Run the self test to identify the print cartridge that has clogged nozzles.
2. Open the top cover of the printer.

3. Move the print cartridge selector lever (in front of the print cartridges) so that it is in front of the problem cartridge.

4. Press the green plunger (at the right of the black print cartridge) down once, then release the plunger.

5. Close the top cover of the printer and run the self test again.

This procedure usually solves the problem. Occasionally you may have to repeat the procedure several times.

Another way you can sometimes clear clogged nozzles is to wipe them with a clean, lint-free tissue moistened with distilled water.

Printing from Applications

The 560C and 1200C printers can print text and graphics that you create by working with applications on your computer. For this to happen, your applications have to send instructions to the printer in a language the printer can understand. Applications use add-on software called printer drivers to convert the data the applications themselves work with to data a printer can understand.

Working with Windows Applications

Most people who use IBM-compatible PCs do most of their work in applications that run in the Microsoft Windows environment. One of the benefits of using Windows is that all applications share the same printer drivers and HP provides these drivers with DeskJet printers.

> *Note:* The 560C and 1200C printers require different drivers. If you use both printers, you must install separate drivers for each.

If you are using a 560C printer or a standard 1200C printer without a PostScript module, you need to install the driver that comes with the printer. This driver uses HP's PCL language to communicate with the printer. All you have to do is to install the supplied driver and then you can print text and graphics from any document you create in a Windows application.

To install the PCL printer driver for Windows:

1. Start Windows version 3.1 or later on your computer and display the Program Manager window.

2. Open the File menu and choose Run to display the Run dialog box.

3. Insert the printer driver disk, or the first disk if there is more than one, into one of your floppy disk drives.

4. To install drivers for the 560C printer, type A:\HPSETUP or B:\HPSETUP (depending on which floppy disk drive you are using), and then click OK.
   To install drivers for the 1200C printer, type A:\INSTALL or B:\IN-STALL (depending on which floppy disk drive you are using), and then click OK.

5. Follow the on-screen instructions to complete the installation process.

As part of the installation process, you are asked whether you want to make the new driver the default. If you do so, all your Windows applications will automatically print using the DeskJet printer. If you do not make the new driver the default, your Windows applications will use whatever printer you previously chose, but will give you the option of selecting the DeskJet printer.

After you install the 560C driver, you need to install the TrueType fonts on the driver disk onto your hard disk. To do this:

1. Double-click Main in the Windows Program Manager window to open the Main window.

2. Double-click Control Panel to open the Control Panel window.

3. Double-click Fonts to open the Fonts dialog box.

4. Click Add Fonts to open the Add Fonts dialog box.

5. Open the Drives drop-down list box and select the disk drive that contains the driver disk. After a few seconds delay, the List of Fonts list box shows the beginning of the fonts on the installation disk. You can use the vertical scroll bar to scroll down the list of fonts.

6. Click Select All if you want to install all the fonts. Otherwise select those fonts you want to install.

7. Click OK to install the selected fonts.

8. Click Close to close the dialog box.

Using PostScript

The standard PCL drivers that come with 560C and 1200C printers provide access to all of those printers' capabilities and will serve your needs well for most home and office purposes. However, circumstances may arise in which you need PostScript capability.

To satisfy a need for PostScript, you can purchase a 1200C/PS printer instead of a 1200C, or you can add a PostScript module to your existing 1200C printer. In either case, the printer can accept PostScript input as well as PCL and HP-GL/2.

Why might you need PostScript? Here are just two of several possible reasons.

Some applications offer capabilities that you can only use if you have a printer that can accept PostScript. For example, in CorelDRAW (a popular PC graphics application) you can generate textures that are based on PostScript filling algorithms. Although you can see these textures on your screen, you can print them only if your printer accepts PostScript.

Another reason you might need PostScript is a matter of compatibility. You may be preparing a brochure or newsletter that will be professionally printed. After you have prepared your material on your PC and have printed proof copies, the next stage is to give your computer files to a service bureau that will prepare them for commercial printing. The chances are that the service bureau will require PostScript files. If you have previously used a PCL printer to proof your work, there will be small but significant (sometimes major) differences between what you printed on your PCL printer and what comes off your commercial printer's press. You can minimize these sorts of difficulties by working in PostScript.

To install the PostScript driver on your PC, use almost the same procedure as for installing the PCL driver, described previously, but using the PostScript driver disk. To start installation, in the Windows Program Manager dialog box, type A:\SETUP or B:\SETUP.

Working with OS/2 Applications

When you install OS/2 onto a computer, you can choose an OS/2 and a Windows DeskJet printer driver in order to print OS/2 and Windows applications.

If you did not initially install DeskJet printer drivers, you can return to the OS/2 setup procedure to add these drivers, as described in your OS/2 documentation.

Working with DOS Applications

A DOS application is one that runs directly under DOS and does not require Windows. Each DOS application requires its own printer drivers if it is to take advantage of a DeskJet printer's capabilities.

When you purchase a major DOS application such as the DOS versions of Microsoft Word or WordPerfect, you receive one or more disks that contain printer drivers for many different printers. If these disks do not contain drivers for your specific DeskJet printer, you may find that your applications supplier can provide the driver you need, often without charge. You can also look for printer drivers that are available for downloading from computer bulletin boards.

If you are unable to locate a printer driver that exactly matches your application to your DeskJet printer, another alternative is to use a similar printer driver. Such a driver will allow you to print, but may not provide access to all of the printer's capabilities. For example, you can use a printer driver intended for the HP DeskJet 500C or 550C printers to print on a DeskJet 560C. The 500C driver supports black and some color printing, but does not provide the same envelope printing capabilities as the 560C driver. You can also access some of your DeskJet printer's capabilities with an HP LaserJet printer driver.

There is one more way to print on a DeskJet printer without using a printer driver: that is to embed printer codes within the text to be printed. That method, though, is beyond the scope of this book.

Working with Macintosh Applications

As with Windows, the Macintosh environment uses one printer driver for all applications. To install the driver and fonts provided with your DeskWriter printer:

1. Insert the driver disk into a floppy disk drive.
2. Double-click the Installer icon to install the printer drivers and background printing files.
3. When you are asked to do so, provide a name for your printer.
4. Use the Chooser to choose your printer.
5. Insert the fonts disk into a floppy disk drive.
6. Double-click the Install icon to install the HP fonts into your system folder.

After doing this, you can use the supplied fonts and print from your Macintosh documents.

Using PostScript with a Macintosh

If you are working with a high-end graphics application that is intended for use with PostScript, you can usually choose between ignoring the PostScript-specific capabilities or installing a PostScript software package on your computer. This software accepts the PostScript output from your application, rasterizes the image, and sends that image to the printer in PCL form. The package also allows you to use the standard set of PostScript fonts.

You install the PostScript software in the same way that you install the standard driver, as described above.

Selecting Paper and Other Print Media

DeskJet and DeskWriter printers are technology marvels. Not just one technology, but several!

We don't often stop to wonder about the mechanical, electrical, electronics, software, and manufacturing engineering achievements that make it possible for a printer to deposit tiny dots of ink so precisely on paper as the print cartridges move from side to side and paper moves through the printer. Nor do we often consider the achievements of the materials and chemistry scientists who have developed the inks that work so well on a wide variety of paper and other media. But there, sitting on your desk, is a compelling example of what scientific and engineering talent can achieve.

Inkjet printers have been available for several years, but the early versions required special, and expensive, print media. There are, perhaps, three reasons why HP's DeskJet and DeskWriter printers have become so popular:

- They provide print quality that is as good as, if not better than, many laser printers.
- They are available at a very reasonable price.
- They can print on a wide variety of paper and other media.

Let's pay attention, now, to the last point.

Choosing Appropriate Paper

If you're like most people, when you first get a DeskJet or DeskWriter printer, you steal some paper from the nearest copier, put it into the paper input tray, and do some printing. You're probably very happy with the results. Yes, these printers do an excellent job of printing on the least expensive copier paper you can find at your local discount office supply store.

Please don't stop there. If you do, you're not being fair to the printer or to yourself. Your printer can do much better.

Inexpensive copier paper is fine for printing drafts and, perhaps, internal memos. When you want quality printing, though, you should pay more attention to the paper you use.

Printing with an inkjet printer is somewhat similar to the commercial four-color offset printing process. In each case, tiny drops of ink are deposited onto paper. Some of the requirements are the same. For example, the paper should absorb just enough of the ink so that the dots stay in place, but not too much so that the ink spreads. With these common requirements, it's not surprising that good-quality offset paper usually works well with inkjet printers.

The requirements for copier paper are different. In a copier or laser printer, dry toner is deposited on paper and then fused into the paper by heat. Copier paper is not optimized for a wet ink process.

HP offers two special papers that work exceptionally well with DeskJet and DeskWriter printers. These are the HP LX JetSeries Special paper and the HP LX JetSeries Glossy paper. A small sample of both is supplied with your printer. Try these papers. You'll be very impressed with the results, particularly with the vivid colors produced. However, these papers are expensive, so you will want to use them only for final work.

There are many other sources of paper that you'll find advertised in computer magazines. Take the time to look at samples, such as those from PaperDirect, and see how well they satisfy your needs. Sometimes you'll be very pleased, other times you'll be disappointed.

How Paper Thickness Is Specified

Printer manufacturers usually specify the thickness of suitable paper in terms of weight, or what is more properly called the *basis weight*. If you look at the label on a package of ordinary copier paper, you'll probably see 20 lb, or perhaps #20 or Substance 20. This means that the weight of the paper is 20 pounds.

> *Note:* Paper thickness is sometimes measured in points. In this case a point is one thousandth of an inch.

Obviously, one sheet of paper doesn't weigh 20 pounds, nor does one package that normally contains 500 sheets (a ream). So what does the 20 pounds refer to?

In the case of copier paper (*bond*) the weight is that of 500 sheets that are 17 by 22 inches in size, four times the size of the paper we normally use. The most common paper of this type has a weight of 20 pounds; a slightly thinner paper has a weight of 18 pounds; and a somewhat thicker paper, the letterhead often used for correspondence, has a weight of 24 pounds.

From here, things get more complicated. Only bond is specified in terms of the weight of 17 by 22 inch sheets. Another widely used type of paper is known as *book*. This type of paper is specified in terms of the weight of 500 sheets 25 by 38 inches in size, about two and a half times as big as the standard bond size. What this means is that the 20-pound bond is about equal in weight to the 50-pound book.

There are seven common types of paper, each specified by the weight of 500 sheets of a certain size. You guessed it! The size is different for each type. So you can't judge the thickness by the number on the package.

We of the computer age find ourselves inevitably involved in the ancient art of papermaking. The terminology is not going to change, so learn to adapt to how paper is specified.

Fortunately, most of the paper you see in a paper supply store is of only two types. If its weight is specified in the range 50–80, it's not bond, so divide the number by 2.5 and you'll have the weight in the terms you're used to thinking about and those that HP uses in the specifications for its printers. For example, if you see a paper labeled 65, it's about the same thickness as a 26-pound bond.

Using the Correct Side of the Paper

Have you ever noticed that paper has two sides? Let's rephrase that question. Have you ever noticed that paper has two *different* sides? Take a piece of HP JetSeries paper in your hands. You can easily detect that the two sides have a different feel. One side is intended to be printed on, the other is not. Look at the label on a package of good quality paper. You'll probably see an arrow with a note such as *Print This Side Only*. Sheets of HP JetSeries paper have a small watermark in one corner on the reverse side.

Take care to print on the printing side of quality paper for best results. Note that you put paper into the input paper tray of DeskJet and DeskWriter printers with the print side down. This is the reverse of what you do with most laser printers. If you are using the 1200C's manual feed tray, insert the paper with the printing surface facing the front of the printer.

Inexpensive copier paper usually doesn't have a preferred printing side, so you don't have to be concerned about this point when you are using this paper for drafts.

Avoiding Paper Problems

You can avoid most paper problems by using the right kind of paper, not mixing types of paper in the paper input tray, and storing paper properly. You should avoid using paper that:

- Has a deep texture (some light textured papers work very well)
- Is prepunched or has cutouts of any sort
- Has perforations
- Is wrinkled or has bent edges
- Has already been printed by a laser printer or xerographic copier

The first four points should be fairly obvious when you think about them. Perhaps the last point requires some explanation. The point is that laser printers and xerographic copiers print by depositing a dry toner onto the surface of the paper and then using heat to make the toner adhere to the paper. On a printed page, the toner lies on top of the paper. If you use this printed page in your DeskJet or DeskWriter printer, some of the toner may get scraped off and deposited onto the internal surfaces of the printer. After a while, this can affect the operation of the printer.

If you are having trouble feeding heavier paper into the 1200C from the paper input tray, try using the manual feed slot. When you do this, the paper follows a path that does not have sharp curves, so it feeds more easily.

You can use colored paper, but HP recommends that you do not use paper to which a colored coating has been added after the paper has been manufactured, This, or course, includes preprinted papers. A more liberal, perhaps more reasonable approach, is to suggest cautious use of preprinted paper. For the 1200C, the inks used for preprinting should be heat-resistant so that they do not melt or vaporize, and they should be nonflammable. For any printer, preprinted inks must not contain any substance that could adversely affect the printer's rollers.

Always store your paper properly. Leave paper in its original sealed packages until you are ready to use it. Keep it in a cool, low-humidity area. Stack it flat on a level surface.

Printing Overhead Transparencies

The inks in the print cartridges are transparent, so you can use them to print overhead transparencies. HP recommends that you use only LX JetSeries Transparency film for this purpose. There are at least two good reasons for this recommendation:

- The film has a surface to which ink can satisfactorily adhere.
- The film has an opaque strip on one edge that allows the printer to detect the presence of a sheet.

See Chapter 11 of this book for more information about preparing overhead transparencies.

Printing Envelopes

The 560C and 1200C printers can both be used to print envelopes. Both printers can print ordinary U.S. #10 and European DL envelopes. The 1200C can also print European C5 envelopes. If you need to use other envelopes, you can print labels and attach them to the envelopes.

In general, you should use quality envelopes that have sharply creased folds and are made of paper not heavier than 24 pound. Avoid envelopes that:

- Are poorly manufactured
- Are damaged, curled, or wrinkled
- Have shiny, textured, or embossed surfaces
- Have clasps
- Have already been printed (unless you are sure the ink is heat-resistant)
- Do not stack neatly when placed in a pile

The 560C and 1200C handle envelopes differently. With the 560C, you must remove whatever paper is in the paper input tray, adjust the paper width adjustment lever, and place a stack of up to 20 envelopes face down in the paper input tray. You can then print envelopes automatically, one after the other.

The 1200C uses the separate manual feed slot for envelopes. This allows you to print envelopes without removing the paper in the paper input tray, but restricts you to printing one envelope at a time. You place an envelope in the manual feed slot with its top surface facing the front of the printer.

See Chapter 6 for more information about printing envelopes.

Labels Can Be a Sticky Problem

Pun intended! Labels are intended to stick to things. Unfortunately, labels can stick to things you don't want them to stick to. There lies the problem.

It's very convenient to print labels because you can stick those labels to envelopes, packages, and containers of any size and almost any material. The problem is that labels can stick to rollers within your printer and, if that happens, you can be faced with expensive repairs.

HP has specific guidelines about printing labels. The 560C User's Guide tells you not to print on adhesive labels; the 1200C User's Guide recommends certain kinds of labels and tells you how to use them.

The reason for the difference is that the 1200C has a manual feed slot, whereas the 560C does not. When sheets of labels pass through the 1200C from the manual feed slot, they only have to follow a 90-degree bend. In contrast, if you were to try to feed labels from the paper tray of either printer, they have to follow a fairly sharp 180-degree bend, which can cause labels to become detached from the sheet and to stick inside the printer.

To print labels on a 1200C, be sure you follow HP's guidelines in the 1200C User's Guide. These are:

- Use only recently manufactured labels, because old ones can become brittle.
- Use paper labels only, not clear plastic labels.
- Do not use any sheets of labels on which any labels are missing.
- Do not print within 0.5 inch from the top edge of the sheet.

- Use the manual feed slot to load individual sheets of labels.
- Do not use label sheets in which there are spaces between labels.
- Use only HP LaserJet or DeskJet approved label stock.
- Be sure to set the media size selector to suit the width of the label sheets.

You can buy HP-brand labels from your HP dealer. You can also purchase a much broader range of labels manufactured by Avery and marked for use with laser or inkjet printers from computer-supply stores. These labels include sizes suitable for floppy disks.

Printing Your Work

When you are ready to print a document, you can just select your application's Print command, wait a little while, and see the results on paper. You may be happy with what you get, or you may be disappointed. You would be unhappy, for example, if you create a color document but the printed version is just black.

To understand why the printed results may not be what you want, you need to be familiar with the controls you have over your printer, some of which may be provided by the application you're using, but most of which are provided by the printer driver.

The way in which you control the printer varies to some extent according to the application you're using and depends on the printer driver. We can't illustrate all possibilities in this book, so we'll use just one example. Suppose you have prepared a document in Microsoft Word for Windows version 6.0 and you're ready to print it on a 1200C printer.

To start, open the File menu and choose Print to display the Print dialog box shown in Figure 3.1.

To print the entire document using the current Word for Windows printing options and the current 1200C printer driver options, just click the OK button. However, you should normally examine these options before you start to print and, if necessary, change them.

Choosing an Application's Printing Options

To look at the Word for Windows printing options, click Options in the Print dialog box to display the Options dialog box shown in Figure 3.2.

It's not our purpose here to look at all these options in detail. One option, however, is particularly important. Notice in Figure 3.2 that the Reverse Print Order check box is selected. This makes Word for Windows print pages in the reverse order starting from the last page.

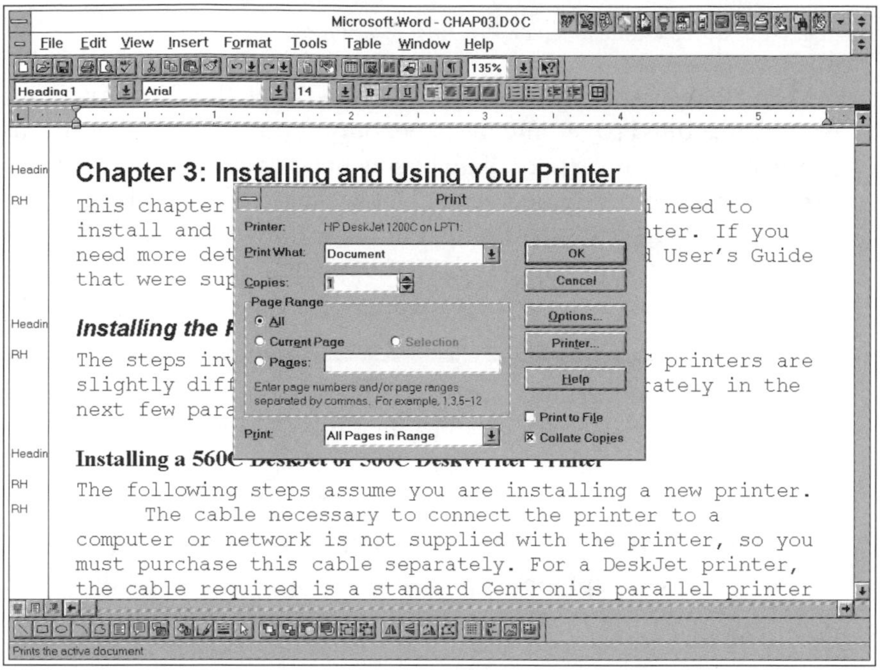

Figure 3.1 The Word for Windows Print dialog box.

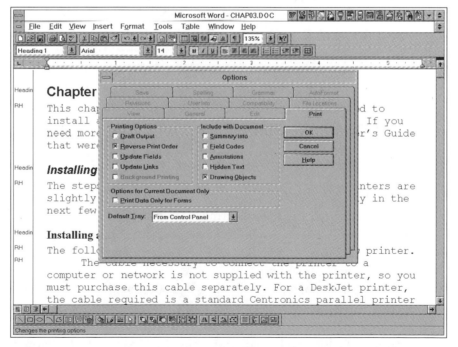

Figure 3.2 The Word for Windows Options dialog box with the Print tab selected.

You have probably already discovered that the 560C and 1200C printers deliver printed pages into the paper output tray face up. This means that pages are stacked in reverse order, which is not a significant problem in the case of two- or three-page documents. However, if you have long documents, it is irritating to have to reverse their order after they are printed. By selecting the Reverse Print Order option in your application, you eliminate the need to do this.

> *Note:* Reverse Print Order, or a similar option, is available in major word processors and desktop publishing applications. It is not available in all applications.

After you have chosen the print options you want, click OK in the Options dialog box to accept those options and return to the Print dialog box.

Choosing a Printer Driver

The top line of the Word for Windows Print dialog box shows the name of the currently selected printer. Most Windows applications do the same. In fact, this line shows the name of the current printer driver and the computer port to which the printer is connected. In Figure 3.1 the current printer driver is HP DeskJet 1200C and the printer is connected to the LPT1 port.

If you need to change to another printer driver, click the Printer button in the dialog box to display the Print Setup dialog box, shown in Figure 3.3. This dialog box lists all the printer drivers currently available for Windows applications on your computer, with the currently selected printer driver highlighted.

If you want to choose a different printer driver, click its name.

Choosing Printer Driver Options

Having accepted the default printer driver in the Print Setup dialog box, or selected a different one, click Options to display a Setup dialog box such as those shown in Figures 3.4 and 3.5. It is here where you take detailed control over your printer.

The Setup dialog box for the DeskJet 560C printer has five sections. The top section is where you select a color mode. By default, the printer driver chooses ColorSmart, HP's built-in color optimizer. You can also choose Black Text, Color Graphics, Color Photo, and Grayscale. See Chapter 13 for more information about using these color options.

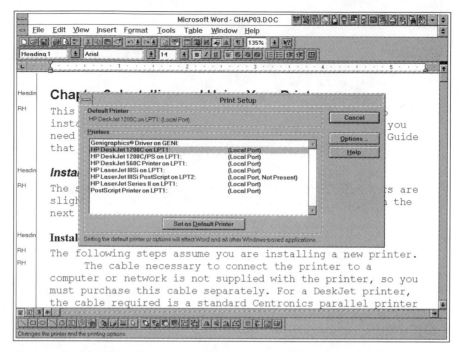

Figure 3.3 The Print Setup dialog box with the available Windows printer drivers listed.

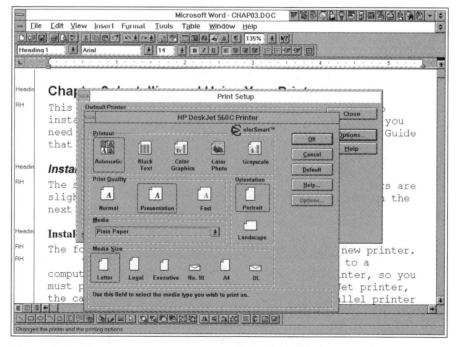

Figure 3.4 The Setup dialog box provided by the DeskJet 560C printer driver.

53

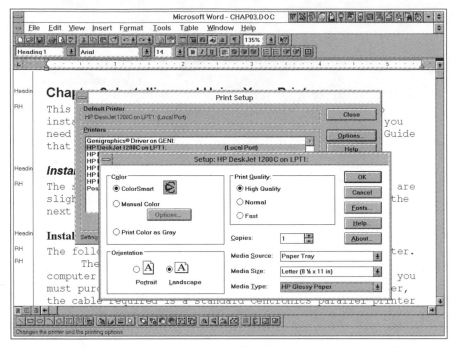

Figure 3.5 The Setup dialog box provided by the DeskJet 1200C printer driver.

Note: ColorSmart is available in PCL drivers for the 560C and 1200C printers. ColorSmart is not yet available in PostScript drivers.

The second section of the DeskJet 560C dialog box allows you to choose between Normal, Presentation, and Fast printing. Normal, the default option, is suitable for most purposes. Presentation uses more ink to produce a richer image but results in slower printing. Fast, which uses the least amount of ink and consequently results in faster printing, is a good choice for draft printing.

The Media section of the dialog box offers the choice of Plain Paper, Transparency, Transparency (Extra Dry Time), HP Glossy Paper, HP Glossy Paper (Extra Dry Time), and HP Special Paper. The default Plain Paper is suitable for most ordinary papers. You can enhance the quality of output onto other surfaces by making the appropriate choice.

The Media Size and Orientation sections of the dialog box allow you to choose the size of paper and whether printing is to be horizontal or vertical.

The buttons at the right side of the Setup dialog box are conventional.

This Setup dialog box for the DeskJet 1200C printer has four sections. The top-left section gives you control over color. By default, the 1200C printer driver chooses ColorSmart, HP's built-in color optimizer. You can also choose Manual Color if you want to control colors yourself. See Chapter 13 for more information about using these color options.

The top-right section of the dialog box allows you to choose between High Quality, Normal, and Fast printing. High Quality uses more ink to produce a richer image but results in slower printing. Fast, which uses the least amount of ink and consequently results in faster printing, is a good choice for draft printing. Normal gives in-between results.

The bottom-left section of the dialog box is where you choose the orientation of your document on a page. The orientation you choose here should normally match the orientation you chose in the application.

The bottom-right section of the dialog box contains some choices that are also available in the application's Print dialog box. In most cases, the settings in the application's Print dialog box override the settings in the driver's Setup dialog box. In some cases, though, you may get unexpected results if there are conflicting settings in the two dialog boxes, or if you set the number of copies in the driver's Setup dialog box to anything other than 1.

One situation in which you *would* set the number of copies in the driver's Setup dialog box is when you want to print more than one copy of a document created in an application that does not allow you to specify the number of copies. For example, the version of Collage Complete used to capture the screens illustrated in this book allows you to print a copy of screens, but has no provision for printing more than one copy. You can overcome this limitation by setting the number of copies you want in the driver's Setup dialog box.

The last item at the bottom-right of the dialog box is Media Type, from which you can choose Plain Paper, HP Special Paper, HP Glossy Paper, or HP Transparency. Your choice here affects the time allowed for ink to dry during printing. If you are not satisfied with the printing you are getting, some experimentation with these settings might provide worthwhile improvements.

The buttons at the right side of the Setup dialog box are conventional, with the exception of the Fonts button. Click this button to open the Fonts dialog box that you use to install fonts from HP's MasterType library of IntelliFont fonts.

The DeskJet 560C and 1200C setup dialog boxes allow you to choose fast draft printing, though in different ways. In the case of the 560C, choose Black Text for Printout and Fast for Print Quality. For the 1200C, for Color, choose Print Color as Gray and, for Print Quality, choose Fast. You should also choose these options if you want to print a document that will be copied on a black-and-white copier or will be faxed.

After you have chosen the options you want in the Setup dialog box, choose OK to return to the Print Setup dialog box, then choose Close to return to the Print dialog box.

Printing the Document

The Print dialog box shown in Figure 3.1 is typical for Windows and Macintosh applications, although there are minor differences between applications. You will almost certainly be able to choose how many copies you want to print and which pages of a multipage document to print.

After you have made the appropriate choices of application and printer driver options, click the OK button to start sending your document to the printer. If the Print Manager is enabled, Windows sends your document to a temporary file on your hard disk and then from that file to the printer. If the Print Manager is not enabled, Windows sends the file directly to the printer.

If the Print Manager is enabled, you don't have to wait until a document is printed before you can continue working on your computer. This is because applications can send the document to a temporary file much faster than to the printer. The disadvantage of using the Print Manager is that it requires enough free space on your hard disk to accommodate the temporary file, which, in the case of a document containing graphics, can be very large.

> *Note:* To enable or disable the Windows Print Manager, open the Main window from the Program Manager window, open the Control Panel, then select Printers. In the Printers dialog box, check the Use Print Manager check box to enable the Print Manager, or uncheck the check box to disable the Print Manager.

As soon as the printer starts receiving the document, the Ready indicator on the printer control panel begins to flash and continues to flash until the document is completely printed.

There is more information about controlling printers in Chapter 6 and elsewhere in this book.

To end this chapter, here's some advice. Make it a habit to check printer options before you print every document. By doing this, you can choose those options that provide the print quality you need and you can avoid using an unnecessary amount of ink when all you need is a quick draft version of a document.

Using Fonts

When you read the title of this chapter, you had a good idea of what you expected to find, right? Unfortunately, the word *font* has different meanings for different people. To a traditional printer (the person), a *font* is a *complete assortment of printing types of one size and style*. To the computer user, *font* has a much broader meaning.

What does the traditional definition mean? In most cases, *a complete assortment of printing types* means all the letters of the alphabet in uppercase and lowercase forms, together with the numerals 0 through 9 and the commonly used punctuation characters. As a group, these are referred to as the *character set* in the font. *Size* refers to the space occupied by the characters. *Style* refers to a family shape and possible variations of that shape. Within each family shape there are such variations as italic (slanted) and bold (thick).

Understanding Fonts

In traditional printing, each character set in one size and one style is a font. In today's computer world, the word *font* refers to the general shape of a set of characters. A font can contain characters of many sizes and several variations of the basic family shape.

While working with fonts on your computer, you will find references to fonts by names such as Arial. This is the name of a complete set of characters that you can use in many different sizes and variations.

57

Font Classes

There are two major classes of fonts you will come across:

- Those that contain the full set of uppercase and lowercase characters, numbers, and punctuation marks
- Those that contain special technical symbols, such as mathematical, musical, and mapping symbols

We're primarily concerned with the first because those are the ones we use the most. Within this group, there are serif fonts and sans serif fonts for general use and also decorative and other special-purpose fonts.

Serif fonts have small decorative additions (serifs) at the ends of the character strokes, as in the Times New Roman example in Figure 4.1. *Sans serif* fonts do not have these decorations, as shown in the AvantGarde example in the figure.

Serif fonts are generally used in large bodies of text (*body copy*) in books and magazines. It is widely believed that the serifs help a reader to perceive words as a whole, rather than as individual letters, and so aid reading.

Sans serif fonts are often used for headlines and titles, so-called *display type*. The bolder appearance of sans serif type makes it stand out. Because headlines and titles are short, the linking effect of serifs is not needed.

Decorative and other special-purpose fonts are used in greeting cards, advertisements, packaging, and similar printed material.

Times New Roman (18-point)
abcdefghijklmnopqrstuvwxyz
ABCDEFGHIJKLMNOPQRSTUVWXYZ
0123456789

AvantGarde (18-point)
abcdefghijklmnopqrstuvwxyz
ABCDEFGHIJKLMNOPQRSTUVWXYZ
0123456789

Figure 4.1 Examples of a serif font (top) and a sans serif font (bottom).

Font Names

Each font has a name. The name represents the general appearance and shape of a complete set of characters. By law, font names can be copyrighted but the appearance and shape of the characters cannot. This explains why fonts that look the same often have different names. When you look at descriptions of fonts, you will often find a name you don't recognize, followed by a phrase such as *similar to. . . .* You are being told that the company that wants to sell you the font has imitated the shape of a well-known font (something that is perfectly legal), but cannot copy the well-known font's name.

When we computer users were first released from the boredom of one-font-fits-all, we were often offered two fonts, Dutch and Swiss, from Bitstream. Dutch looked like Times Roman, and Swiss looked like Helvetica. Indeed, the two computer-usable fonts were all but identical to the traditional fonts. The only significant difference was their names.

Font Sizes

In the typewriter and early PC worlds, font sizes were defined in terms of pitch—the number of character per inch in a line; every character, whether a narrow *i* or a wide *w*, was allocated the same space. The choice was easy: you could choose between 10 (pica) and 12 (elite) characters per inch. Whichever you chose, your work was normally spaced at six lines per inch. Really sophisticated software allowed you to cram your lines together or spread them out.

In the typesetting business and, now, in the computer world, font sizes are measured in terms of height. Thanks to history, fonts are not measured in such convenient units as inches or centimeters—they are measured in points, a point being approximately $\frac{1}{72}$ of an inch.

Some references will tell you that you can determine the size of type by measuring the distance from the top of an ascender (the stroke that extends upwards in a *d* or an *h*) to the bottom of a descender (the stroke that extends downwards in a *g* or a *y*), but this is not exactly true. In common with many printing-related terms, height is defined in terms of the original technology.

Setting type for a page used to involve handling individual metal characters, each of which consisted of a roughly rectangular body with the mirror-image shape of the character to be printed protruding from one edge. Characters with ascenders almost reached the top of the body and characters with descenders almost reached the bottom. The distance from the bottom to the top of the body was referred to as the type size.

Goudy Old Style (18-point)
abcdefghijklmnopqrstuvwxyz
ABCDEFGHIJKLMNOPQRSTUVWXYZ
0123456789

Bookman Old Style (18-point)
abcdefghijklmnopqrstuvwxyz
ABCDEFGHIJKLMNOPQRSTUVWXYZ
0123456789

Figure 4.2 Two examples of the printed alphabet, both set in 18-point type. The characters at the top are set in a font (Goudy Old Style) that has a smaller x-height than those at the bottom (Bookman Old Style).

Most of what we read is set in lowercase. The visual impression we get of type size depends on the size of lowercase letters—not the distance from the top of an ascender to the bottom of a descender, but the height of most lowercase letters. The technical term for this is the *x-height*, the height of a lowercase *x*.

There is no standard that relates the x-height of letters to the font size, nor should there be. Some fonts have a relatively small x-height, while others have a relatively large x-height, as shown in Figure 4.2. This figure clearly shows that the size of type specified in points is not necessarily a good indication of the actual size on the printed page. Quite often, as shown in this example, characters in a font that has a large x-height are wider than characters in a font having a smaller x-height. Keep this point in mind when you read about choosing font sizes later in this book.

Font Styles

Fonts come in various styles. For example, the Zurich font supplied with CorelDRAW comes in 22 styles, as shown in Figure 4.3. This is an extreme example, but most widely used fonts are available in several styles.

In most cases, the basic font (the one you normally use for body copy) is known as *roman*. A lighter style is known as *light*; heavier styles are called by such names as *bold* and *black*. A narrower style is called *condensed*, and a wider

Zurich Roman
Zurich Italic
Zurich Light
Zurich Light Condensed
Zurich Light Italic
Zurich Light Extra Condensed
Zurich Light Condensed Italic
Zurich Bold
Zurich Bold Italic
Zurich Bold Condensed
Zurich Bold Condensed Italic
Zurich Bold Extended
Zurich Bold Extra Condensed
Zurich Black
Zurich Black Italic
Zurich Black Extended
Zurich Condensed
Zurich Condensed Italic
Zurich Extended
Zurich Extra Black
Zurich Extra Condensed
Zurich Ultra Black Extended

Figure 4.3 The Zurich font supplied with CorelDRAW comes in 22 styles.

style *extended*. A tilted style is *italic*. Combinations of these styles have such names as *bold condensed italic*.

In many Macintosh and Windows applications you can choose a font by its name—Zurich, for example—and then choose a style, as shown in Figure 4.4.

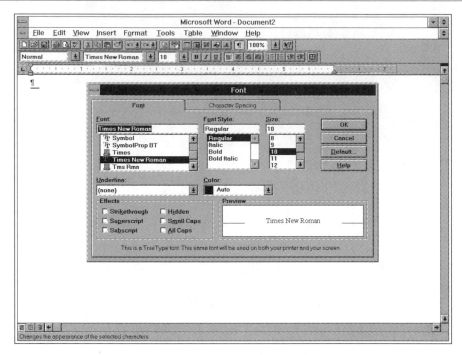

Figure 4.4 The Word for Windows Font dialog box in which you can choose a font, font style, font size, and other font attributes.

Contrary to what you may have previously assumed, the bold style of a font is not just the roman style with the strokes made slightly thicker, nor is the italic version the roman version tilted. Most fonts are supplied with completely different designs for the various styles. You can often see this most easily by comparing the lowercase *a* and *f* in the roman and italic styles, as shown in Figure 4.5. You can easily see that the *a* and *f* have completely different shapes in the roman and italic styles.

Figure 4.5 Notice the significant differences between the roman and italic styles of the Garamond font shown here.

a f Garamond Book (roman)

a f Garamond Book (italic)

Figure 4.6 The derived italic style that Windows creates by slanting the roman style.

Now, let's see what happens if you only install the roman version of a font into your computer. Windows still lets you choose an italic style. In this case, Windows creates an italic style for you by slanting the roman style. The result, as you see in Figure 4.6, is a derived italic style, not the real thing.

Note: Although the example shown here specifically illustrates how Windows handles TrueType fonts, it is typical of other scalable fonts.

What's the point of going into all this in a book about printing? You want to get professional-looking results, don't you? To do so, you have to dig below the surface as far as fonts are concerned. The proper use of font styles is one area in which people tend to go astray.

Choosing Fonts

We print a wide variety of documents that consist mainly of text. Text appears in one font or another, so choosing appropriate fonts is something we all have to do. An appropriate choice of fonts helps to give our documents a professional appearance; the wrong choice makes our work look amateurish.

Whole books have been written about the proper use of fonts, but there is only a limited amount of space available for this important topic here. So, only a few basic points are covered.

Perhaps the most important idea to grasp is that the fonts you use should contribute to your document. They should reinforce the meaning of your document. They should draw attention to the document, not to themselves.

Understanding Character Sets

Each font contains a set of characters, known as a character set. So far in this chapter, we have thought of the characters in a set as the uppercase and lowercase characters in the alphabet, numerals, and commonly used punctuation marks. In fact, a character set can consist of up to 255 separate characters, many more than we customarily use.

Computers represent each character in a set as a number. For various reasons, computers handle data in 8-bit groups (bytes). There are 256 possible combinations of 8 bits, ranging from 00000000 to 11111111, hence the possibility for 256 characters in a set.

Much of the way things work in computers is derived from earlier technologies. The way characters are represented by numbers comes from teleprinters, machines you could use to send a typed message from one place to another over telephone lines, before the days of the now-ubiquitous fax machines. Teleprinters used a 7-bit code to transmit data, a code that could represent 128 different characters. The first 32 of these were used for control information and the remaining 96 for characters. There are 52 uppercase and lowercase characters in the English language, 10 digits, 10 commonly used symbols, and about 20 punctuation characters; so 128 numbers were just adequate. The set of 128 control and printing characters became a standard known as the American Standard Code for Information Interchange, usually abbreviated to ASCII (pronounced ask-ee).

When computers arrived with 8 bits used as a basic element of information, another 128 possible numbers became available. Originally, there was no standard for these extra characters. IBM used them in PCs for various geometric shapes and some mathematical symbols. You could use the geometric shapes to draw lines and rectangular boxes on your screen. The Macintosh computer used the extra numbers to represent many of the accented characters used in European languages other than English.

The Macintosh and Windows environments have brought a more useful standard for character representation to the computer world. Macintosh and Windows applications don't need characters to draw lines and boxes, so the geometric shapes have been replaced by accented characters and symbols. Figure 4.7 shows the complete Windows character set. The Macintosh environment offers a similar, though different, character set.

You are not limited to working with fonts that contain the alphabetical character set. When you install Windows, you also install a Symbol font that contains many mathematical and other symbols, and a Wingdings font that contains decorative symbols.

032		064	@	096	`	128		160		192	À	224	à
033	!	065	A	097	a	129		161	¡	193	Á	225	á
034	"	066	B	098	b	130	,	162	¢	194	Â	226	â
035	#	067	C	099	c	131	*f*	163	£	195	Ã	227	ã
036	$	068	D	100	d	132	„	164	¤	196	Ä	228	ä
037	%	069	E	101	e	133	…	165	¥	197	Å	229	å
038	&	070	F	102	f	134	†	166	¦	198	Æ	230	æ
039	'	071	G	103	g	135	‡	167	§	199	Ç	231	ç
040	(	072	H	104	h	136	^	168	¨	200	È	232	è
041	)	073	I	105	i	137	‰	169	©	201	É	233	é
042	*	074	J	106	j	138	Š	170	ª	202	Ê	234	ê
043	+	075	K	107	k	139	‹	171	«	203	Ë	235	ë
044	,	076	L	108	l	140	Œ	172	¬	204	Ì	236	ì
045	-	077	M	109	m	141		173	–	205	Í	237	í
046	.	078	N	110	n	142		174	®	206	Î	238	î
047	/	079	O	111	o	143		175	‾	207	Ï	239	ï
048	0	080	P	112	p	144		176	°	208	Ð	240	ð
049	1	081	Q	113	q	145	'	177	±	209	Ñ	241	ñ
050	2	082	R	114	r	146	'	178	²	210	Ò	242	ò
051	3	083	S	115	s	147	"	179	³	211	Ó	243	ó
052	4	084	T	116	t	148	"	180	´	212	Ô	244	ô
053	5	085	U	117	u	149	•	181	µ	213	Õ	245	õ
054	6	086	V	118	v	150	–	182	¶	214	Ö	246	ö
055	7	087	W	119	w	151	—	183	·	215	×	247	÷
056	8	088	X	120	x	152	~	184	¸	216	Ø	248	ø
057	9	089	Y	121	y	153	™	185	¹	217	Ù	249	ù
058	:	090	Z	122	z	154	š	186	º	218	Ú	250	ú
059	;	091	[	123	{	155	›	187	»	219	Û	251	û
060	<	092	\	124			156	œ	188	¼	220	Ü	252	ü
061	=	093	]	125	}	157		189	½	221	Ý	253	ý
062	>	094	^	126	~	158		190	¾	222	Þ	254	þ
063	?	095	_	127	▓	159	Ÿ	191	¿	223	ß	255	ÿ

Figure 4.7 The Windows 3.1 standard character set.

Accessing Characters

From what you have read so far, you know that a font contains a maximum of 256 characters. In fact, not all these possible characters are used, but there are over 200 characters available in most fonts. You don't have 200 keys on your keyboard, so it's not immediately obvious how you can use them.

There's no problem with the usual alphabetic characters, digits, and symbols. Just press the appropriate key on the keyboard.

For the remaining characters, you can do things the hard way or, with support from your application, do things the easy way. The hard way on a Macintosh computer is to hold down the Option key while you press a key. Instead of getting the character shown on the key's label, you get the character that is coded 128 higher. You can also open the Finder menu and choose Key Caps to see a display of the keyboard. Press the Option key to see the alternative characters.

On a PC, you access the higher characters slightly differently depending on whether you are using a DOS application or a Windows application. In DOS, press and hold down the Alt key, type the three-digit number (using the numeric keypad) that represents the character, and then release the Alt key. You can also access any of the characters in the lower 128 the same way. In Windows, press and hold down the Alt key, type 0 (zero) followed by the three-digit number (shown in Figure 4.7) that represents the character, then release the Alt key.

Some applications make it easier for you to access the upper 128 characters. For example, in Windows, you can open the Character Map window, shown in Figure 4.8, from the Accessories group. This shows you all the characters available in the selected font. To select characters from this window:

1. Point onto the character you want to use, then press and hold down the mouse button. While you are pressing the mouse button, the selected character becomes enlarged (particularly useful if you have a small screen with low resolution).

2. Release the mouse button. The character you selected is indicated by a dark outline.

3. Click Select to copy the character into the Characters to Copy box at the top of the screen.

4. Repeat steps 1 through 3 to copy additional characters into the box.

5. Click Copy to copy all the characters in the Characters to Copy box to the Clipboard.

6. Click Close to close the Character Map window.

7. In your application, open the Edit menu and choose Paste to copy the character or characters into that application.

This method should work with all Windows applications that support the Clipboard.

Some applications make life even easier. For example, in Word for Windows, you can open the Insert menu and choose Symbol to open the Symbol dialog box, which is similar to the Character Map. In this dialog box, click the symbol you want to use, then click Insert to insert that symbol directly into your document. Click Close to close the Symbol dialog box.

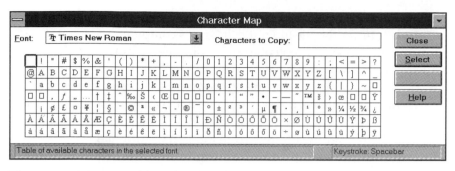

Figure 4.8 The Windows Character Map window.

It's not possible here to illustrate how other Windows applications and Macintosh applications deal with special characters. Many have similar capabilities to Word for Windows. You should look for these and learn to use them.

Using Hot Keys to Access Special Characters

Hot keys (also known as shortcut keys) are key combinations that provide fast access to many things you might want to do within an application that would otherwise involve several keystrokes. On Macintosh computers, you access hot keys by holding down the Option or Command key while you press another key. On the PC, you press one of the function keys or hold down the Ctrl or Alt key while you press another key.

In PageMaker, for example, you can insert the registered trademark symbol ® into a document:

- On a Macintosh computer, hold down the Option key while you type R.
- On a PC, hold down the Ctrl key while you type G.

Other applications provide similar facilities. Unfortunately, there is no standard shared by applications, so you have to consult your applications User's Guide, or open on-line Help, to find the hot keys you can use. No one said that life should be that easy!

Sharing Documents between Computers

The availability of so many fonts and character sets gives us the power to create very impressive documents. A side effect can be equally impressive headaches!

You might have taken a great deal of time and trouble to create an important document. The document uses carefully chosen fonts, and includes color graphics. Unfortunately, your printer can only print in black, so you need to use a colleague's color printer to see what the printed version looks like. No problem, just transfer the file to your colleague's computer and print it.

Unfortunately, your colleague's computer doesn't have the fonts you've used. That's why the headaches start.

When you open a document, the application can use the correct fonts if those fonts are available. If those fonts are not available, most applications substitute the specified fonts with similar ones. The characters in the substituted fonts may look only slightly different from those in the original fonts, which may or may not be important. Quite likely, though, some of the characters in the substituted fonts have slightly different widths from those in the original. This can cause line breaks at different positions which, in turn, can affect page breaks.

It's possible that the substituted fonts may contain different characters in the upper 128 of the character set, so the document opened on the second computer may contain characters that are different from those you intend.

Clearly, then, it's important that computers that share documents have the same fonts available. There are two ways to ensure this. The obvious is to purchase and install the same fonts on all the computers involved. TrueType fonts provide another solution to this problem.

The design for TrueType fonts includes the ability to embed those fonts within a document; however, the font designer has the option to allow this to be done or not. If the TrueType fonts you are using permit, you can save a document and, in the same file, save the fonts as well.

In Word for Windows, for example, you can open the Tools menu and choose Options. Then, in the Options dialog box, choose the Save tab. If you check Embed TrueType Fonts, any document you subsequently save will include the TrueType fonts used in the document, providing the fonts allow this to happen. You can open the saved file on another computer, see the document on screen with the original fonts, and print it with the original fonts.

Communicating in Print

The title of this chapter is intended to give a strong clue about its theme—encouraging you to think about printing as a method of communicating. All the decisions you make about preparing material for printing should be based on how they affect communication. The final printed pages should be judged on how well they communicate.

Life used to be much simpler than it is now. If we wanted to prepare something for printing, we could choose between using the only tool we had, a typewriter, or handing the whole project to a professional designer. Now we have computers on our desks, all kinds of applications software to use, many fonts available, easy-to-use graphics, and the capability to use color. The only problem is, all this power challenges us to make the right choices.

This chapter contains many suggestions that will help you make good choices, and avoid making bad ones, from all the capabilities of your hardware and software.

Printed pages contain text and graphics, both of which can appear in one color (usually black) or in two or more colors. This chapter provides basic information about text and color, leaving graphics to later chapters.

Working with Text

All aspects of page design serve three principal purposes:

- To attract the reader's attention
- To keep the reader's attention
- To communicate

First you want to attract attention so that readers will begin to read the page. After they begin to read the page, you want them to continue and you want them to absorb the material the page contains. These three elements have different priorities for various types of documents.

Attracting the Reader's Attention

Consider attracting the reader's attention first. Every day, all of us see a great deal of printed material, but actually read and digest only a small proportion of it. Some we read because we have to. The people who design income tax forms don't have to pay much attention to attracting our attention! In most cases, though, we choose what we are going to read because of the initial impact a printed page, poster, or whatever, has on us.

Do you ever stand in front of a magazine rack, thumbing through magazines to see if any *look* as if they are worth buying? Your judgment will be highly influenced by how pages attract your eye, rather than by the content of paragraphs.

If your work is going to influence people, it must be read. If people are going to read it, they must first be attracted to it. Your number-one priority in most cases should be to make sure your printed pages grab readers' attention.

Making Pages Easy to Read

After you have been successful in getting a person's attention, the next issue is to hold that attention. You can do this by making your pages easy to read. Being easy to read is partly a matter of writing style (which is outside the scope of this book) and partly a matter of page design.

Page design includes such matters as choice of fonts and font sizes, character and line spacing, and column width. These and other factors affect how easily a reader's eye can flow from word to word and from line to line without fatigue. People are much more likely to read something that is packaged attractively than the same material that is thrown together without concern for the reader's comfort.

If your text is too small or too closely spaced, reading it requires too much concentration. On the other hand, if text is too large or too loosely spaced, people see individual characters rather than words. This, also, makes reading hard work. Width of columns is another factor that can encourage or discourage reading. When columns are too narrow, it becomes difficult to grasp sentences; if columns are too wide, the eye doesn't easily move from the end of one line to the beginning of the next.

Choosing Fonts and Font Sizes

A typical printed page uses text for different purposes. Some of these are:

- Headings and titles
- Body copy (the text in paragraphs)
- Captions (the text that identifies illustrations)
- Quotations
- Page numbers

You should choose a font, font size, and font style for each of these and use those choices consistently throughout the publication. Because there are usually a limited number of different elements on a page, you should use a limited number of fonts and use each one to help readers identify those separate elements.

Above all, resist the temptation to demonstrate how many fonts you have. This is a crime often indulged in by people who create advertisements and flyers. The result is chaos and confusion.

Fonts for Body Copy

For body copy, choose one of the commonly used serif fonts. Times Roman, or one of its imitations, is often recommended, but it is overused, probably because several of the first font packages available for Macintosh computers and PCs contained it. Among the many widely available fonts that are good substitutes for Times Roman are Bookman Old Style, Century Schoolbook, and Garamond. Samples of these four fonts are shown in Figure 5.1.

Normally, use these fonts in sizes ranging from 10 to 12 points for body copy. In many cases, a good choice is 11 or 11.5 points.

Don't be misled by the range of font sizes your application appears to offer. Most applications let you choose font sizes over much wider ranges than you might think. For example, PageMaker offers you a choice of certain font sizes, as shown in Figure 5.2. However, the application actually lets you specify type

> This is Times New Roman, 11.5 points
> This is Bookman Old Style, 11.5 points
> This is Century Schoolbook, 11.5 points
> This is Garamond, 11.5 points

Figure 5.1 Four fonts, shown here at 11.5 points, to consider using for body copy.

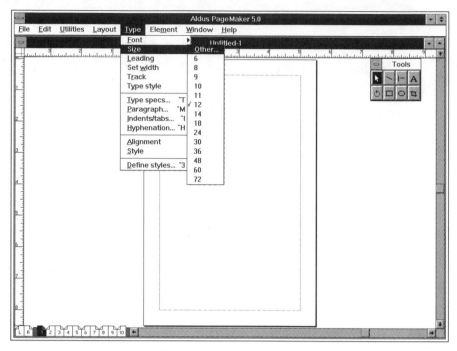

Figure 5.2 PageMaker offers a limited choice of font sizes, but there are many more you can specify.

in size from 4 to 650 points in one-tenth point increments. Word for Windows, on the other hand, lets you specify fonts in the range from 1 to 1638 points in half-point increments.

Don't use decorative fonts for body copy. These fonts are fine for personal invitations or, perhaps, if you are putting together a book of romantic poetry. For almost all purposes, stay with the traditional serif fonts.

Fonts for Captions and Quotations

It is common practice to use the same font for captions and quotations as for body copy. You might consider using the font at a size about two points smaller than the body copy to help the reader clearly distinguish what is ordinary body copy and what is not.

If the font you have selected has an easy-to-read italic style, you might consider using that style for captions and quotations. Make sure, though, that you use the real italic style, not the imitation italic style created by your application (see Chapter 4 for information about this).

This is Arial, 14 points
This is Arial Narrow, 14 points
This is Futura, 14 points

Figure 5.3 Samples of fonts, shown here at 14 points, that can be used for titles and headings.

Fonts for Titles and Headings

The rules about choosing fonts for titles and headings are different from those for body copy. Titles and headings contain only a few words and you want them to stand out. For these page elements use sans serif fonts that complement the fonts you are using for body copy.

Many of the font packages that were initially introduced for PCs contained the serif Times Roman (or an equivalent with a different name such as Dutch) for use as body copy, and the sans serif Helvetica (or an equivalent with a name such as Swiss) for use as display type in titles and headings.

For your documents, you can consider using such fonts as Arial, Arial Narrow, or Futura (in one of its many variations), as shown in Figure 5.3. Arial is quite similar to Helvetica but has a somewhat larger x-height.

For main chapter or section headings, use a font size that is significantly larger than the body copy, perhaps as large as 24 or even 36 points.

The font size you use for section headings depends on how much you want sections to stand apart. You've probably noticed that novels rarely break up chapters with section headings. This is because the author wants the chapter to flow smoothly. On the other hand, in technical books, chapters are often divided into quite short sections. This is done so that readers can digest the information in short segments.

If you have section headings, they should usually be at least two points larger than the body copy so that readers can easily distinguish them. Make section headings even larger if you want to make separate sections stand out well.

Nonfiction books, such as this one, usually have two or three levels of headings. If this is the case, choose different size fonts for each level so that readers don't get confused. In most cases, avoid numbering sections unless you are creating a reference book or something similar that can benefit from a very formal appearance.

Spacing Lines and Paragraphs

The proper choice of line spacing can make a document easy to read; inappropriate line spacing makes a document difficult to read. If lines of a paragraph are too close together, the descenders of characters on one line almost touch ascenders of characters on the line below, giving a cramped, unattractive effect. On the other hand, if there is too much space between lines, the lines don't seem to belong together.

Line spacing is measured in points, the same units used to measure the size of type, and is known as *leading* (pronounced ledding). Typically, leading for body copy is about 20 percent larger than the size of type, spacing that is automatically provided by many applications. For example, leading for body copy set in 11-point type should be about 13.2 points.

> *Note:* In traditional typography, extra space between lines was created by inserting strips of lead between slugs of type, hence the term leading. In that era, leading referred to the extra space between lines of type. Now, leading usually refers to the entire space occupied by a line of type, the height of the characters plus any extra space between lines.

For larger display type, the same proportion of leading is too much. In many cases, display type is *set solid*, that is, with no extra space between lines.

There are two ways to separate one paragraph from the next. You can either indent the first line of each paragraph, or leave extra space between paragraphs. Don't do both.

If you choose to use extra space between paragraphs, the so-called block format, the space should normally be less than the height of lines in paragraphs. The easiest way to set consistent paragraph spacing is to use the paragraph formatting capability of your word-processing or desktop publishing software to add space before or after paragraphs.

Setting the Column Width

The width of columns is related to the font size. For easy reading, a good rule-of-thumb is to make the column width equal to the space occupied by one-and-a-half to two alphabets of lowercase characters in the font and font size you are using for body copy.

For example, if you choose 11-point Century Schoolbook for your body, type a line with one-and-a-half alphabets and another line with two complete alphabets, print them, and measure their widths. The ideal column width is somewhere between the widths of the shorter and longer lines. Figure 5.4 shows an example.

If you must use narrower columns, you should usually reduce the leading. For wider columns, increase the leading.

abcdefghijklmnopqrstuvwxyzabcdefghijklm
abcdefghijklmnopqrstuvwxyzabcdefghijklmnopqrstuvwxyz

Figure 5.4 The ideal column width for body copy set in 11-point Century Schoolbook is between 3 and 4 inches.

Aligning and Justifying Text

Lines of text can be:

- Left aligned so that the left ends of lines are vertically aligned and the right ends of lines are ragged
- Right aligned so that the right ends of lines are vertically aligned and the left ends of lines are ragged
- Center aligned so that the centers of lines are vertically aligned and the left and right ends of lines are ragged
- Justified so that the left and right ends of lines are vertically aligned

There is no such thing as left, right, or center justification!

In the case of all three types of alignment, the spacing between characters in a word and the spacing between words is dictated by the design of the font. Justification is achieved by evenly changing the space between individual characters and between words so that both edges of paragraphs are aligned.

> *Note:* Older applications attempted to justify paragraphs by adding standard-sized spaces between some words, resulting in very ugly text. Some current applications only change the spacing between words (not between characters), but do so evenly. Desktop publishing applications, such as PageMaker, produce the most satisfactory justification by evenly changing the spacing between words and between characters.

For most purposes, you will choose between left-alignment and justification for body copy. Left aligned paragraphs are usually easier to read, mainly because the different lengths of lines helps the eye to move from one line to the next. Justification, though, is often thought to look more *professional*, so many people prefer it. My preference is to use left-aligned paragraphs.

A Matter of Style

Having made choices of fonts, font sizes, line spacing, column widths, and so on, that dictate the look of a page, it is important to be consistent within a document and also within a family of documents.

Word processors and desktop publishing applications make it very easy to maintain consistency in the look of our documents by offering styles, style-sheets, and templates. You can define a style for body copy, another style for captions, and other styles for headings of various levels. After you have defined these styles, you just apply them to the appropriate parts of the document to achieve consistent formatting.

Unfortunately, it takes some time to learn how to use styles, so many people ignore them. The truth is that every minute you spend learning about styles is likely to save you hours in the future as you work with documents. You should take the time to learn about styles unless, of course, you don't care very much about the appearance of your documents.

Miscellaneous Hints and Tips

When you prepare documents for printing, you are getting into the discipline of typography, which is distinctly different from typing. Many of the rules you should follow are different from those that apply to typing business correspondence on a typewriter.

Here are some hints and tips you should follow to give your documents a professional appearance:

- Use a single space, not a double space, after a period, question mark, or exclamation point at the end of sentences.
- Use hyphens to hyphenate words. Use an *en-dash* (not a hyphen) to indicate a range or as a minus sign. Use an *em-dash* (not a double hyphen) to indicate a pause, as shown in Figure 5.5. There should be no space on each side of an en-dash or em-dash.
- Use boldface or italic type for emphasis, not underlining.
- Be generous with empty space. Don't cram too much on a page.
- In most cases, avoid abbreviations in body copy. There are certain exceptions in which the abbreviation is better understood than the words it represents.
- Generally, use bullets to mark items in a list. Use numbers only when the order is significant.

One more point! By all means use spell and grammar checkers to check your work, but don't rely too heavily on them. When you have finished a document and are ready to have it printed in quantity or sent to the people for whom it is intended, find someone who has not seen it before to give it one last check. The golden rule in proofreading is that there is always one more error to find!

Use a hyphen to hyphenate words

> Cost-effective

Use an en-dash for a range

> 2–3 hours

Use an em-dash for a pause

> A pause—such as this.

Figure 5.5 Use a hyphen to hyphenate words, an en-dash to indicate a range, and an em-dash for a pause.

Using Color

Color can make your documents interesting, attractive, and attention-grabbing. Color can make your documents look more professional and authoritative, but only if it is used wisely and well. Be aware that color used carelessly or tastelessly can have the opposite effect: it can make your documents look amateurish or even childish. Use color, but use it thoughtfully.

Color can add another dimension to the documents we print. Color can be used to:

- Add emphasis
- Establish a mood
- Display an identity
- Make information easier to understand

You can use some or all of these purposes to your advantage in all the documents you create. Here are some examples.

Using Color for Emphasis

In a report or similar document, you can use color for headings to help readers easily find the topics they are looking for. You might use different colors for various level headings.

Another way to use color is to use a light color as a background for information you want to emphasize. Suppose you are writing a pamphlet about how to ride a bicycle and you want to draw strong attention to the importance of wearing a helmet. One way to do this would be to create a separate paragraph with a light red background behind it. The red should be just bright enough to attract attention, but not so bright that the paragraph itself is difficult to read. The red background used in this way is known as a *screen*.

Using Color for Mood

Colors have an emotional impact. Red, for example signifies danger or heat; blue signifies cold or calm; yellow conveys caution; white indicates purity and cleanliness. You should choose colors that are compatible with the purpose of your document. Be aware, though, that people with different cultural backgrounds don't always associate colors in the same way. In China, for example, brides traditionally wear red because that color is associated with good luck.

Using Color for Identity

Within a specific context, certain colors are associated with specific companies or organizations. In the world of photography, a certain shade of yellow means Kodak and a certain shade of green means Fuji.

Use colors to reinforce identity. Be careful that the colors you use don't imply an association that's not appropriate.

Using Color to Provide Information

Colors can make your publications easier to understand. You can't tell from a black-and-white photograph whether a car is red, blue, green, or gray. With a color photograph, you can see the car's color and the shade of that color. Numerical data is easy to understand if it is presented in charts with color identifying the categories of data.

Choosing Colors Wisely

Color is like many of the pleasures of life—some color is good, too much is bad. When you're using color, keep it simple. If in doubt, use less color, not more.

If you're using color for contrast, don't use more than seven distinct colors. Any more colors than this usually conveys an impression of chaos.

The golden rule is *Keep it simple*.

Printing in Color

When you are preparing documents for printing, you should be aware of the capabilities and limitations of the printer you will be using. Fortunately, the HP 560C and 1200C printers we are dealing with here are generous in capabilities and, for most purposes, don't have very significant limitations.

As far as color is concerned, the printers can reproduce approximately 16.8 million colors—two to three times more than the human eye can distinguish. The printers do this by placing tiny dots of cyan, magenta, yellow, and black ink on paper in much the same way commercial printing presses do.

Fundamentally, the printers are capable of reproducing eight colors:

- Cyan—cyan ink
- Magenta—magenta ink
- Yellow—yellow ink
- Black—black ink
- Green—cyan and yellow inks
- Blue—cyan and magenta inks
- Red—magenta and yellow inks
- White—no ink

The visual effect of other colors is achieved by grouping dots into cells, with one cell representing each pixel of the image, and choosing appropriate colors for each of the dots within a cell. The human brain mixes the colors of the individual dots to give the perception of a single color. This process of creating the perception of many colors is known as *dithering*.

From this, you might assume that your printer can print every possible color. As you will see later when you read about color matching, this isn't quite true. However, for most practical purposes, the problem is relatively minor.

If these printers have a limitation, it's in terms of resolution, that is, the number of dots per inch they can place on the paper. Both printers have a resolution of 600 by 300 dots per inch for black ink and 300 by 300 dots per inch for colored ink. While that resolution can provide excellent quality, it's not up to the quality provided by the 1270 or 2540 dot-per-inch resolution achieved on imagesetters used in commercial printing. But don't let this bother you too much. The print quality produced by the 560C and 1200C printers is very impressive.

Creating Color

At one time, people thought that color was an innate property of objects: a ripe tomato *is* red; a cucumber *is* green. Now we know that this isn't true.

Here is why we describe a ripe tomato as being red. The sun emits electromagnetic energy over a wide range of frequencies. The human visual system, but by no means that of all animals, responds to a small part of the range of the sun's energy with a sensation of colors in the spectrum from violet through red. We call the range of energy to which our eyes respond *light* and the sensation we perceive when the entire range falls on our eyes *white*.

The surface of a tomato or cucumber absorbs some of the sun's energy and reflects some of it. A tomato absorbs most of the violet, blue, green, and yellow energy, but reflects most of the red energy. When we look at a tomato, we see only the reflected red energy, so we say the tomato is red. A cucumber absorbs violet, blue, yellow, and red, reflecting only the green, so we say the cucumber is green.

This oversimplified explanation makes it easy to understand one of the pervasive problems with color—the problem of why colors don't always look the same. If you shine green light on a tomato it appears to be almost black. The reason is that if the light falling on the tomato contains no red, the tomato reflects no light at all.

In our daily lives we see objects under different lighting conditions, sunlight, tungsten light, fluorescent light, for example. Most objects appear to have a different color under each of these types of lighting.

When we look at an illuminated object, the color we see is the result of subtracting colors from the light that's falling on the objective because the object absorbs certain colors. That's why colors produced in this way are known as subtractive colors. Colors on a printed page are subtractive. The colors we perceive are the colors that are reflected, rather than absorbed by, the ink on the paper.

The color you see when you look at your computer monitor is different. The inside of your screen is coated with tiny dots known as *phosphors*. When electrons fired at these dots from the back of the CRT tube hit the phosphors, they emit energy that our eyes can detect as colors. At each point (pixel) on the screen there is a dot that emits red light, another that emits green light, and a third dot that emits blue light.

When all three dots in a pixel are equally stimulated by electrons, they emit equal amounts of red, green, and blue light that our visual system mixes together to give us the sensation of white light. If the three dots in a pixel are stimulated by different intensities of electrons, they emit different amounts of red, green, and blue light. Our eyes mix these colors to provide the sensation of light over a wide range of colors.

The colors we see when looking at a computer monitor are, as you have just seen, created by adding (mixing) individual colors. That's why the process is known as additive and the three colors used are referred to as the additive primary colors.

Reproducing Color

"Why are the colors that I print different from the colors on my monitor?" If you haven't already asked that question, you soon will.

One answer to this question is that there are colors you can see on your monitor that no printer can reproduce. This is because you are using two distinctly different processes—the additive process to see colors on your monitor, and the subtractive process to see colors on the printed page.

A monitor can produce a wide range of colors, technically known as the monitor's color gamut. A color printer can reproduce a wide range of colors, known as the printer's color gamut. In addition, the human visual system can perceive a wide range of colors, known as the human color gamut. Most of the colors in the three gamuts are the same; however, some are not. This is the fundamental problem we face in attempting to match colors.

After understanding that there are limitations to how well on-screen colors can match printed colors, we can see what can be done to optimize the situation. This involves using a color calibration procedure, such as those described in Chapter 13 of this book.

Specifying Color

When we want to communicate precise information about color, we need a better method than using words like red, blue, pink, and purple because words are vague and don't mean exactly the same to everyone. Over the years, many ways of specifying color have come into use, often called color models. The color models described here are often used in a computer environment.

The RGB Color Model

The RGB color model describes colors in terms of proportions of red, green, and blue, and is appropriate for defining colors as they appear on the screen of a monitor. Many applications that support color allow you to define colors in this way, as shown by the example in Figure 5.6.

The left-center of this dialog box contains three spin boxes, one for red, one for green, and one for blue. You can choose values in the range 0–255 in each of these spin boxes to create one of over 16 million colors. The computer uses eight data bits for each of the three colors. There are 256 possible combinations of eight bits, hence the range 0–255.

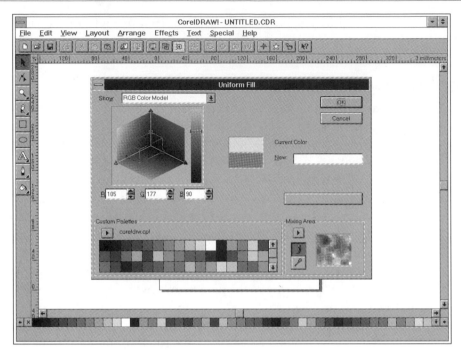

Figure 5.6 The CorelDRAW dialog box in which you can define colors using the RGB color model.

As in most applications, you can also create a color by dragging in a color box. When you do this, the values in the spin boxes change accordingly.

The dialog box shown here (and in the next three illustrations) is typical of how applications allow you to choose colors. Although other applications have different dialog boxes, you use them in a similar manner.

The CMYK Color Model

The CMYK model describes colors in terms of percentages of cyan, magenta, yellow, and black inks, and is appropriate for defining colors in terms of how they appear when printed. Many applications that support color allow you to define colors in this way, as shown by the example in Figure 5.7.

The left-center of this dialog box contains four spin boxes, one for cyan, one for magenta, one for yellow, and one for black. Each spin box can contain numbers in the range 0–100, corresponding to the percentage of that color ink. You can use these numbers to define colors to be printed commercially on a four-color press.

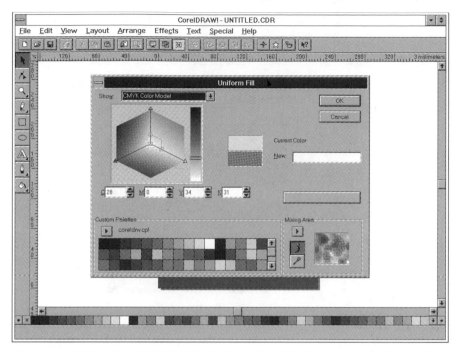

Figure 5.7 The CorelDRAW dialog box in which you can define colors using the CMYK color model.

The HSB Color Model

The HSB color model defines colors in terms of the sensations perceived by the human visual system. *Hue* represents the position of the color in the spectrum. *Saturation* represents how much the color is diluted with white. *Brightness* represents how much the color is darkened with black. Many applications that support color allow you to define colors in this way, as shown by the example in Figure 5.8.

The left-center of this dialog box contains three spin boxes, one for hue, one for saturation, and one for brightness. You can choose a color by setting the three values in the range 0–255.

Using Spot Colors

Commercial printers use two methods to print color. One method is to use a four-color press and to print specific percentages of cyan, magenta, yellow, and black ink. This method has the advantage of being able to print many different colors, necessary when printing color photographs. The disadvantage of this

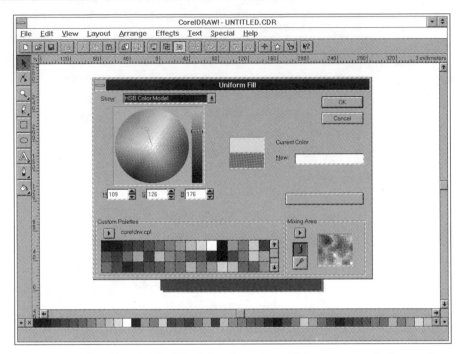

Figure 5.8 The CorelDRAW dialog box in which you can define colors using the HSB color model.

method is that it is not always possible to match a specific color, such as the color an organization uses in its logo.

The other method commercial printers use to print color is by using spot color inks, which are available in many exact colors. This method is used to print a few closely controlled colors.

Several proprietary ranges of spot color inks are available, of which PANTONE is the oldest and best known. PANTONE spot colors are specified by numbers. Many applications that support color allow you to define colors by PANTONE numbers, as shown by the example in Figure 5.9.

Most, but not all, PANTONE colors can be simulated by mixing cyan, magenta, yellow, and black inks. Although print cartridges containing PANTONE inks are not available, you can simulate these colors with your 560C or 1200C printer. The Windows driver for the 1200C printer includes the capability to print PANTONE-approved colors.

Designing with Color

Color can reinforce your message, or it can distract from it. You would probably be confused if you approached a construction site while driving and saw

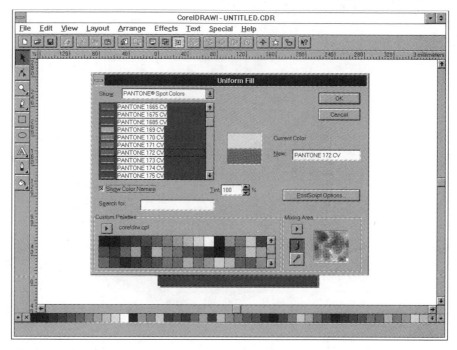

Figure 5.9 The CorelDRAW dialog box in which you can define colors using PANTONE numbers.

someone holding up a green sign with the word *Stop* on it. On the highway, green conveys the message to go, completely the opposite of the word *stop*.

This may be an extreme example, but it illustrates the point. Take care that colors don't fight the message. If you print a map of the Hawaiian islands, you probably wouldn't color the islands blue and the ocean around them brown. Your map would look like lakes on a continent. In the context of a map, blue usually means water and brown means land. As far as possible, try to follow cultural conventions so that readers can easily grasp your meaning.

Be consistent in your use of color. If you are creating a slide presentation, choose a background color, a color for headings, a color for bulleted text, and so on, and stick with those colors for the complete presentation. There might be an exception to this in the case of one or two isolated slides that you really want your audience to notice. By using a different color for these slides you are telling the audience that there is something different here.

The colors you use should be aesthetically pleasing and harmonious. Many of us don't have a natural instinct for color harmony, nor do we have the benefit of art school training. Fortunately, there are rules we can follow that will help to make our work pleasing. The color wheel, shown in Figure 5.10, is a good place to start.

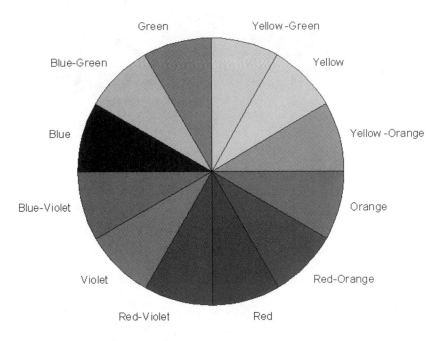

Figure 5.10 The color wheel.

The colors in the color wheel consist of the following proportions of the additive primary colors:

Color Name	Red	Green	Blue
Yellow-green	128	255	0
Yellow	255	255	0
Yellow-orange	255	191	0
Orange	255	128	0
Red-orange	255	64	0
Red	255	0	0
Red-violet	255	0	128
Violet	255	0	255
Blue-violet	128	0	255
Blue	0	0	255
Blue-green	0	128	128
Green	0	255	0

You can use these proportions to print a color wheel from any application that lets you specify RGB colors.

Using Warm and Cool Colors

The color wheel divides colors into those we intuitively describe as warm and those we describe as cool. The warm colors at the long-wavelength end of the spectrum—yellow-green, yellow, yellow-orange, orange, red-orange, and red—are on the right, and the cool colors at the short-wavelength end of the spectrum—green, blue-green, blue, blue-violet, violet, and red-violet—are on the left.

Warm colors are bright and stimulating—they tend to grab attention. Cool colors are quieter and are suitable for use as backgrounds. Warm colors are usually best used in relatively small areas when fully saturated, but can be used in larger areas when in pastel (low-saturation) shades.

For charts and diagrams, particularly in slides, you should consider using cool colors for backgrounds and warm colors for data.

Using Complementary Colors

Complementary colors, those that are opposite each other on the color wheel, provide strong contrast. In fully saturated shades, complementary colors compete for attention, so you should use a large area of one with a smaller area of another. In an organization chart, for example, you might choose violet from the color wheel as a background and yellow for the blocks on the chart.

Be careful about one aspect of complementary colors. One of the common forms of color-blindness is a limited ability to distinguish between red and green. Although these are contrasting colors, a significant number of people who see your work may not be able to distinguish between them.

Using Split Complementary Colors

For each color on the color wheel there is a complementary color at the opposite position on the color wheel. Also for each color, there are two split complementary colors. The split complementary colors are the colors on each side of the complementary color. For example, the color complementary to red is green; the split complementary colors for red are the colors on each side of green, yellow-green and blue-green.

Split complementary colors provide a somewhat more subtle contrast than complementary colors. Another benefit of split complementary colors is that they provide two colors to contrast with a main color.

Learning About Colors from the Experts

Choosing colors may be a subject you'd rather not have to deal with. If so, one way out is to learn from the experts.

Look critically at professionally printed material to see what you can learn about using color. News magazines contain many examples of how color can be used to enhance data in charts. Computer magazines, also, often contain charts comparing features of computer hardware and software.

The manuals that come with your computer hardware (including HP printers) and software is another place you can find good examples of how color can be used effectively. Some use color for titles and screens to set sidebars apart. Others, such as HP User's Guides, use color more extensively to draw attention to specific parts of illustrations. Some, such as the User Guide that comes with Adobe Photoshop, use color very liberally to illustrate application capabilities.

Some applications offer you a variety of color combinations from which you can choose. Microsoft PowerPoint, an application in which you can develop presentations, provides many possible color combinations for you to look at and possibly use. You can, of course, use the suggestions in PowerPoint, even if you are working in a completely different application.

Fortunately, ideas about using color in printed material cannot be copyrighted. Feel free to learn from the experts.

Part II

Part II contains information about preparing documents for printing on inkjet printers. It contains general information about printing as well as many suggestions about working with text and graphics.

Chapter 6 deals with the most common home and office tasks, including letters, envelopes, labels, and various types of cards.

The focus of Chapter 7 is business graphics, the types of illustrations you use in reports and school projects. In addition to the common charts that present numerical data, the chapter also contains information about organization and flow charts, and maps.

Once you get beyond ordinary letters and reports, you are in the world of desktop publishing, which is the subject of Chapter 8. This chapter introduces you to the concepts of desktop publishing and shows you how to print impressive publications with your inkjet printer.

Chapter 9 focuses on text. This chapter shows you how to prepare a newsletter, using the power of your inkjet printer to get and keep readers' attention.

In Chapter 10, you learn how to prepare graphics for printing. Here, you find many of the secrets about working effectively with graphics you can create within a desktop publishing application, as well as with general-purpose and specialized graphics applications.

Chapter 11 turns to the subject of preparing presentations. It covers not only what you present on the screen from overhead transparencies and 35 mm slides, but also audience handouts and speaker's notes.

Inkjet printers aren't all business. Chapter 12 contains many suggestions about using your printer for personal projects.

6
CHAPTER

Printing in Your Home and Office

This chapter covers printing the ordinary types of character-based documents you regularly work with at home and in your office, such as letters and memos, envelopes, labels, business cards, postcards, and forms. While you read about printing these documents, you will learn about some of the controls you have over your printer.

Inkjet printers do an excellent job of printing most types of office documents. Being able to enhance documents with color printing is a distinct benefit color inkjet printers have over most other types of printers.

In this book we primarily use Microsoft Word as an example of a typical word processor because, at the time of writing, Word is the most popular Macintosh and Windows word processor, and the two versions are almost identical. If you use a different word processor, you'll be able to do most of what is described here, though by using different commands.

> *Note:* Throughout this book, Word refers to Word for Windows or Word for Macintosh, but not to the DOS versions of Word.

Preparing to Print

The essential, one-time task in getting ready to print is to connect your printer to your computer or network, install the printer driver software and, if necessary, install the fonts you will be using. See Chapter 3 of this book for information about these tasks and consult the documentation that came with your printer.

Don't forget to look for files on your printer driver installation disk that may contain information more current than that in your printed documentation. This information is usually in files named README.TXT. You may also find useful information about printing in your application's User's Guide and, possibly, in README files on your application's distribution disks.

Preparing to Create a Document

There are a few things you should do before starting to create any document. The purpose of these is to ensure you don't get any unpleasant surprises when you get to the printing stage. Although the Macintosh and Windows environments do a good job of showing you on screen what your document will look like when it is printed, they sometimes need some help from you.

Choosing the Default Printer

Your application needs to know what printer you will be using to print the final version of your document. This is so that the application can format the document appropriately and, possibly, warn you if you try to do some things your printer can't handle. For example, some printers can only print in portrait orientation. If you specify such a printer, a well-behaved application will not let you choose landscape orientation or will warn you about the incompatibility if you do choose landscape.

You should specify the *target printer* that will print the final version of your document—not necessarily the printer connected to your computer. You may want to print a draft version of the document on the printer connected to your computer, but the final version on a different printer. In this case, specify the target printer so that the application can optimize your document for that. When time comes to print the draft document, many applications let you temporarily override the printer choice. When you do this, the draft printed document may differ somewhat from what you see on your screen and from the final document printed on the target printer.

To specify the target printer in Word, you choose from a list of installed printer drivers. Open the File menu and choose Print to display the Print Dialog box shown in Figure 6.1. The top of this dialog box shows the name of the current target printer driver. This is normally the driver for the printer connected to

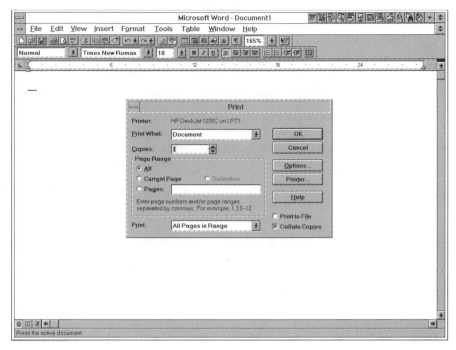

Figure 6.1 The Word for Windows Print dialog box, showing the target printer driver.

your computer. Refer to Chapter 3 for additional information about printer drivers.

If you want to change the target printer driver, choose Printer to display the Print Setup dialog box that lists print drivers installed on your Macintosh or in Windows, as shown in Figure 6.2. Some applications have a Print Setup command in the File menu that you can use to display the Print Setup dialog box.

In this dialog box, click the name of the printer driver you want to use, then click the Set as Default Printer button to select that printer as the target. From this point, you could click the Options button to check, and possibly change, the printer driver options. Alternatively, click the Close button to return to the Print dialog box that shows the name of the new target printer. Click Close in the Print dialog box to return to the document window.

From this point on, your application creates a document suitable for printing on the target printer you have specified.

Matching Screen and Printer Fonts

Chapters 3 and 4 of this book contain information about screen and printer fonts, so mentioning them here is in the way of a reminder. If you find that text

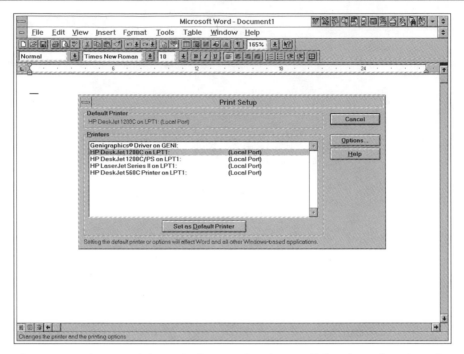

Figure 6.2 **The Word for Windows Print Setup dialog box showing the printer drivers installed in Windows.**

in your printed pages has different line breaks and different page breaks from what you see on your screen, it's likely that your screen and printer fonts don't exactly match.

One easy way to make sure you have matching screen and printer fonts is to use TrueType, Intellifont, PostScript, or other fonts that generate individual screen and printer characters. If you are using your printer's built-in fonts, make sure that matching screen fonts are available for your computer. Also, if you are going to download bitmapped fonts from your computer to the printer, make sure that matching screen fonts are available on disk.

Choosing the Paper Size and Orientation

Most applications let you choose a paper size, usually from the range of paper sizes specified for the target printer you have specified. In addition, many applications let you choose a custom size for which you specify a height and width. The choice of paper size is not quite as straightforward as it may seem at first glance.

Obviously, the paper size you choose in your application has no effect on the actual size of paper in your printer's paper input tray. Normally, you do specify

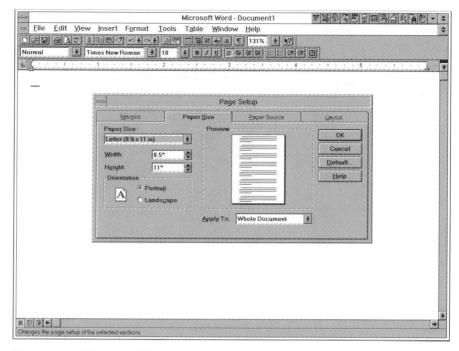

Figure 6.3 The Word for Windows Page Setup dialog box in which you specify a paper size.

the actual size of the paper on which you are going to print your document. You can, however, specify a size smaller than the paper on which you are going to print. You would do this, for example, if you intend to trim the paper after the document is printed. Some graphics and desktop publishing applications can print crop marks to show where the paper is to be trimmed.

In many applications, you choose paper size by opening the File menu and choosing Page Setup to display the Page Setup dialog box. In Word, you choose the dialog box's Paper Size tab, shown in Figure 6.3, to choose a paper size.

The choice of portrait (upright) or landscape (sideways) orientation is available for most printers, including the 560C and 1200C. The orientation you choose from within an application normally overrides the orientation setting in the printer setup dialog box.

Setting the Margins

Word processing and other applications let you set the top, bottom, left, and right margins for printed pages. These applications also let you set the positions of headers—text printed at the top of every page—and footers—text printed at the bottom of every page. Margins as well as header and footer positions are

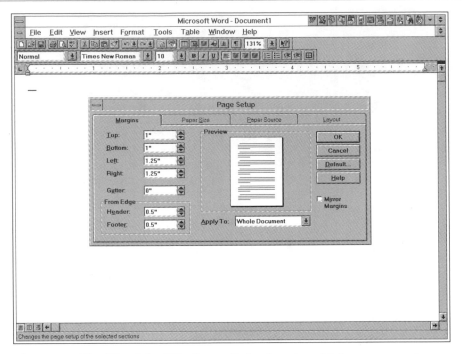

Figure 6.4 The Word for Windows dialog box in which you can set margins as well as header and footer positions.

usually specified in terms of the distance from the edge of the paper. In most cases, you can set default values that apply to every document, and subsequently change the default settings to other values for individual documents.

If you have specified a custom paper size that is smaller than the sheets of paper in the printer's paper input tray, the margins are distances from the edges of the custom size, not distances from the edges of the paper on which the document is printed.

As mentioned earlier, most home and office printers do not print quite to the edge of standard-sized pages. What's more significant is that different printers have different minimum margin settings. You must choose settings that are acceptable to your printer. If you don't, some of your text will not be printed.

You should pay particular attention to this point if you are using a 560C printer. Notice that the minimum top margin for this printer is 0.33 inch and the minimum bottom margin is 0.67 inch, whereas the minimum top and bottom margins for the 1200C are 0.167 inch. Many laser printers can print to within 0.25 inch of the edge.

Most applications provide a dialog box similar to the one shown in Figure 6.4 that you can use to set the margins. In the Word dialog box shown here, you can

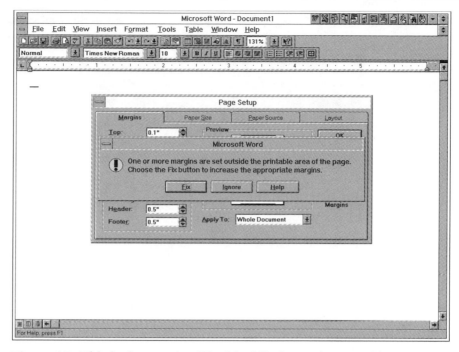

Figure 6.5 This is the warning Word for Windows gives you if you choose margins your printer can't handle.

set the margin values (also the header and footer positions) and then click OK to apply those settings to your current document. Alternatively, you can click the Default button to save these settings for all subsequent documents as well as the current document.

Word, but not all applications, makes it difficult for you to define margins that are smaller than the minimum value for your printer. If you try to do so, Word warns you when you click OK to apply margins to your document, as shown in Figure 6.5. Unfortunately, you don't get this warning if you set header and footer positions too close to the top or bottom edges of the paper.

If you sometimes print on one type of printer and sometimes on another, you can easily run into the problem that some text printed on one is missing when you print on the other. You might, for example, have a DeskJet 1200C in your office and a DeskJet 560C at home. Characters close to the edge, particularly the bottom edge, that are on the document printed by the 1200C might be missing from the pages printed on the 560C. This type of problem can also occur if you have access to several different types of printers on a network.

Take care, then, that the margins you choose for your document match the capabilities of the printer you intend to use.

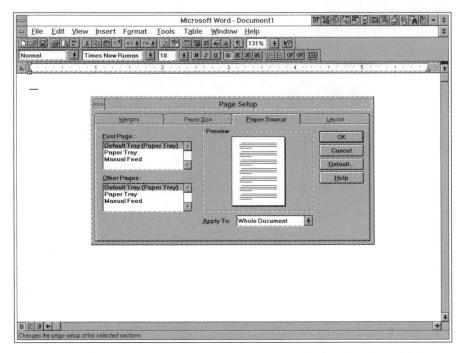

Figure 6.6 The Word for Windows Page Setup dialog box in which you can choose one paper source for the first page and another paper source for other pages.

Choosing Other Page Setup Parameters

Most applications also let you set such parameters as the paper source and the layout.

The paper source is the paper input tray or manual feed slot that contains the paper on which your document will be printed. Some printers have several paper input trays. Others, such as the 1200C, have one paper input tray and one manual feed slot. The 560C has just one paper input tray.

In many applications, you use the Page Setup dialog box to specify the paper source. In the case of Word, this dialog box is slightly different for various printers. If the default printer is a 1200C, the dialog box, shown in Figure 6.6, lets you choose a source for the first page and a separate source for other pages. By default, Paper Tray is chosen for the first page and for other pages. You can change either or both paper sources to Manual Feed.

If the default printer is the 560C, you can only choose the In Tray because no other paper source is available in this printer.

The effect of choosing a paper source for the 1200C printer is not exactly what you might think. If you choose Paper Tray and then print a document, the printer will print on paper from the paper input tray if there is no paper in the manual feed slot. However, if a sheet of paper is loaded in the manual feed slot, the printer will print on that, even if you have selected Paper Tray as the source.

If you choose Manual Feed and then print a document, the printer will print on the paper in the manual feed slot if there is a sheet of paper there. However, if there is no paper in the manual feed slot, the printer's Ready indicator flashes and the Manual Feed indicator lights, but nothing is printed. As soon as you load a sheet of paper in the manual feed slot, printing starts.

In Word, Layout refers to the control of headers and footers. Layout options allow you to do such things as:

- Omit headers and footers on the first page of a document.
- Print different headers and footers on odd and even pages.

Creating and Printing a Document

It's not the purpose of this book to provide detailed information about using specific applications, so what follows here is of the nature of hints and tips that you can use with many Macintosh and Windows applications.

Let's assume you are creating a one-page business letter. Perhaps the most important single piece of advice is to create a template and make use of your application's styles capability. Together, templates and styles simplify the task of creating consistently formatted documents, without having to bother with formatting details for individual documents.

After you have typed your document, you're ready to print, but resist the temptation at this stage. You can save yourself time and money, as well as preserve your good reputation, by going through some preliminary steps. The purpose of these steps is to minimize the number of draft copies you print, thus saving time and money, and to avoid mailing or distributing documents that contain errors. If you follow these suggestions, you will save the many draft copies that would otherwise end up in the trash can.

You should check a document from two points of view—for accuracy and for appearance.

Checking Your Document for Accuracy

Most word processors contain tools for checking the spelling and grammar in documents. You should make a habit of using both tools, but not relying too much on them.

The spell checking tool checks all the words in your document and warns you if any are not in the application's dictionary. If the tool alerts you about a particular word, it doesn't necessarily mean that word is incorrect, just that it isn't in the dictionary. Most spell checking tools let you create custom dictionaries containing words you frequently use that are not in the standard dictionary. By taking a little time to create one or more custom dictionaries, you can save yourself time and frustration whenever you check spelling.

Don't assume your document has no spelling errors just because the spell checking tool doesn't find any. There are many words in the English language that are easily confused. If you type *to* instead of *too*, *is* instead of *if* or *as*, *on* instead of *no*, *advise* instead of *advice*, or *alternate* instead of *alternative*, the spell checking tool won't object.

Your next line of defense is the grammar checking tool that will alert you to possible grammar and style errors. Your grammar checking tool may let you choose which types of errors it should look for and which it should ignore. The Word grammar checking tool lets you choose any combination of 19 grammar problems and 25 style problems for checking.

It's worth taking the time to tune the grammar checking tool to your specific needs, and each time you create a document to look at the suggestions it makes. Some you will not agree with, but others you will. At least, this way, you won't send out documents with such obvious goofs as singular verbs with plural nouns.

Most of us, even professional writers, are not good at proofreading our own work. We tend to see what should be there, not what really is. There is no substitute for having a colleague take a look at your work. It's particularly easy to do this if you can share files on a network. A good arrangement can be to pair up with someone so that you check each other's work. That way the playing ground is even—each of you gets to be critic and each gets to ignore the comments he or she disagrees with.

> *Note:* The Revisions and Annotations features in Word make it very easy for one person to add suggestions or comments to another person's work, and for the second person to accept or reject them.

If you work alone and can't have someone else check your work, try the next-day method. Do all you can to finalize a document one day, then let it rest overnight. Take another look at it the next day. You'll almost always find that the fresh look helps you see errors you didn't notice before so that you can significantly improve your work.

Checking Your Document for Appearance

There's one last check to make before you are ready to commit the document to paper. Look at an on-screen view of the document as it will appear when printed. To do this in Word, open the File menu and choose Print Preview.

The purpose of this is not so much to check words and sentences, but to see how the document looks on a page. You may find, for example, that a letter occupies only slightly more than one page and that all there is on the second page is the space for the sender's signature and name. In this case, you need to make some adjustments, perhaps altering some of the text or its format so that the whole letter fits on one page, or perhaps inserting a hard page break so that the last paragraph moves to the second page with the signature. An easy way to save a line or two is to hyphenate a long word at the beginning of one or two lines so that some syllables move to the preceding lines. However, don't overdo hyphenation.

Other layout faults to look for at this stage are widows and orphans—not the human kind. A *widow* is the last line of a paragraph when it is by itself at the top of a page. The word *widow* is also used to mean the last word (or few short words) of a paragraph that are on a separate line. An *orphan* is the first line of a paragraph that occurs as the last line on a page. If you see widows or orphans in your document, you should make adjustments to the text to eliminate them.

> *Note:* Word and other applications provide options that give some automatic control over widows and orphans.

Only when the document looks correct in the print preview are you really ready to print.

Printing Draft Copies

For one or more reasons, you probably need to print most documents twice, the first time as a draft and the second time as the final version. However, if you follow the suggestions above, you should only need to print one draft copy.

For some reason, documents on paper look different from documents on the screen. No matter how careful you are, you will often see things in the printed copy you didn't see on the screen. That's one reason why many people need a draft printed copy. A second reason is that there may be someone in your organization who insists on approving a printed draft copy.

The reality is, therefore, that you are likely to need to print a draft copy of your work. When you do this, you should select your printer's draft mode to save money and time. In draft mode:

- Printing uses less ink.
- Printing is faster than in other modes.

For draft printing, it is usually acceptable to use ordinary, inexpensive copier paper. This paper is much less expensive than the special types of paper recommended for high-quality documents.

To select draft mode to print a typical Macintosh or Windows document on the 560C or 1200C printer, open the File menu and choose Print to open the Print dialog box, shown previously in this chapter. This dialog box confirms that the correct printer driver is selected. In the Print dialog box, click Printer to open the Print Setup dialog box and, in that dialog box, click Options to display the Setup dialog box.

The Setup dialog box is displayed by the printer driver you have selected, not by your application. It is somewhat different for each printer driver. The procedure for different printers is described separately in the following paragraphs.

Using Draft Mode with the DeskJet 560C Printer

If you are using a DeskJet 560C printer, the Setup dialog box is similar to that shown in Figure 6.7.

For draft printing, click Black Text in the Printout section near the top of the dialog box, and click Fast in the Print Quality section near the middle of the dialog box. Orientation should be the same as the orientation you specified in the application's Page Setup dialog box. Choose Plain Paper from the Media drop-down list box. Make sure the Media Size selection corresponds to the paper in your printer. Click OK to return to the Print Setup dialog box, and click Close to return to the Print dialog box.

Press the Quality button on the printer control panel to select EconoMode. To send your document to the printer, click OK in the Print dialog box.

> *Note:* EconoMode is only available when the Fast mode is selected.

Using Draft Mode with the DeskWriter 560C Printer

If you are using a DeskWriter 560C printer, the Setup dialog box is similar to that shown in Figure 6.8.

To select EconoMode, open the Quality drop-down list box in the dialog box and choose Economode.

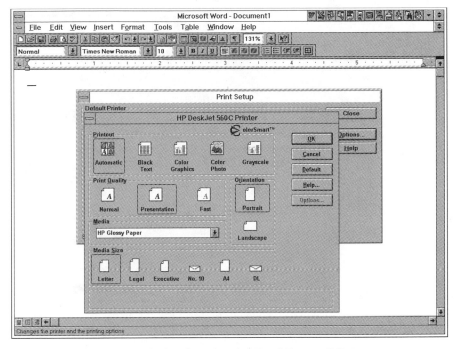

Figure 6.7 The Setup dialog box for the DeskJet 560C Printer.

Using Draft Mode with the DeskJet 1200C Printer

If you are using a 1200C printer, the Setup dialog box is similar to that shown in Figure 6.9.

For draft printing, you should normally choose Print Color as Gray in the Color box at the top-left and Fast in the Print Quality box at the top right. Orientation should be the same as the orientation you specified in the applica-

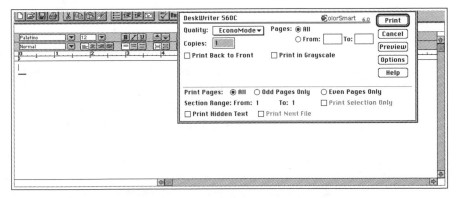

Figure 6.8 The Setup dialog box for the DeskWriter 560C Printer.

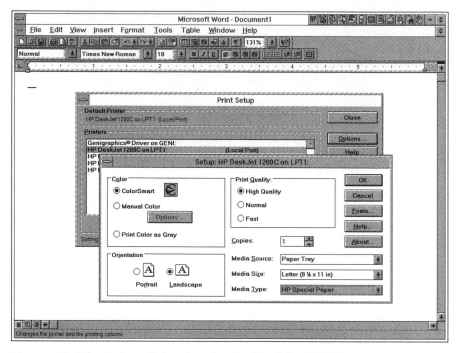

Figure 6.9 The Setup dialog box for the DeskJet 1200C printer.

tion's Page Setup dialog box. Choose Plain Paper from the Media Type drop-down list box. Choose OK to return to the Print Setup dialog box and choose OK to return to the Print dialog box.

To send your document to the printer, click OK in the Print dialog box.

Using Draft Mode with the DeskJet 1200C/PS Printer

If you are using a 1200C/PS printer, the Setup dialog box is similar to that shown in Figure 6.10.

To select draft printing, click Features to display the Features dialog box shown in Figure 6.11. In this dialog box, choose Yes from the Print Color as Gray drop-down list box and choose Fast from the Print Quality drop-down list box. Click OK to return to the Setup dialog box, click OK to return to the Print Setup dialog box, and click Close to return to the Print dialog box.

To send your document to the printer, click OK in the Print dialog box.

Printing Final Copies

For final copies, you normally want to get the highest possible quality from your printer. To do so, you should use paper such as:

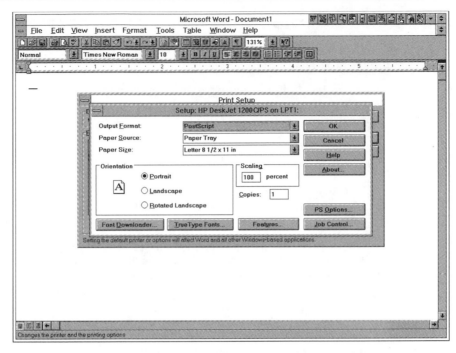

Figure 6.10 The Setup dialog box for the DeskJet 1200C/PS printer.

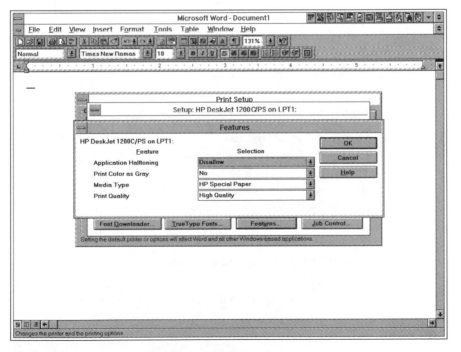

Figure 6.11 The 1200C/PS Features dialog box.

- HP LX JetSeries Paper
- Good-quality bond or offset paper
- Your company letterhead

For best results, do not use inexpensive copier paper!

The procedure for selecting high-quality printing mode is somewhat different for the various printers.

Using Quality Mode with the DeskJet 560C Printer

Figure 6.7 shows the Setup dialog box for the DeskJet 560C printer.

For quality printing, click Automatic in the Printout section near the top of the dialog box, and click Presentation in the Print Quality section near the middle of the dialog box. Choose the type of paper you are using from the Media drop-down list box. Make sure the Media Size selection corresponds to the paper in your printer. Click OK to return to the Print Setup dialog box, and click Close to return to the Print dialog box.

To send your document to the printer, click OK in the Print dialog box.

Using Quality Mode with the DeskWriter 560C Printer

Figure 6.8 shows the Setup dialog box for the DeskWriter 560C printer.

For quality printing, open the drop-down Quality list box and choose Best. Open the Options dialog box and choose the type of paper you are using. Make sure the correct size paper is selected, then click OK to return to the Setup dialog box. Click Print to send your document to the printer.

Using Quality Mode with the DeskJet 1200C Printer

Figure 6.9 shows the Setup dialog box for the DeskJet 1200C printer.

For quality printing, you should normally choose ColorSmart in the Color box at the top-left and High Quality in the Print Quality box at the top right. Orientation should be the same as the orientation you specified in the application's Page Setup dialog box. Choose HP Special Paper from the Media Type drop-down list box. Choose OK to return to the Print Setup dialog box and choose OK to return to the Print dialog box.

To send your document to the printer, click OK in the Print dialog box.

Using Quality Mode with the DeskJet 1200C/PS Printer

Figure 6.10 shows the Setup dialog box for the DeskJet 1200C/PS printer. To select quality printing, click Features to display the Features dialog box shown in Figure 6.11.

In this dialog box, choose No from the Print Color as Gray drop-down list box and choose High Quality from the Print Quality drop-down list box. Click OK to return to the Setup dialog box, click OK to return to the Print Setup dialog box, and click Close to return to the Print dialog box.

To send your document to the printer, click OK in the Print dialog box.

Printing Multipage Documents and Multiple Copies

The assumption so far has been that you want to print one copy of a single-page document. Here are some suggestions that can help when you need to print multipage documents and when you need more than one copy of a document.

The 560C and 1200C printers both deliver pages to the output tray face up. If the pages of a multipage document are printed in order starting from the first page, the result is that the last page is on top of the pile. To put the pages in correct order, you have to reverse the order in which they are stacked, a tedious task for long documents.

To avoid this problem, many word processors and desktop publishing applications can send pages to the printer in the reverse order. In Word, for example, you can open the Tools menu, choose Options, choose the Print tab, and then check the Reverse Print Order check box. In PageMaker, click Reverse Order in the Print Document dialog box.

There are two ways in which you can print several copies of a multipage document: collated or not collated. If you choose to print the copies collated, your application sends every page of the first copy, one at a time, to the printer, then every page of the second copy, and so on. The advantage of this is that each copy of the document comes out of the printer assembled in correct page order. The disadvantage is that the printer has to rasterize each page several times, once for each copy of the document. For this reason, printing collated documents can be quite slow, particularly if the pages contain graphics.

When you print on a DeskJet 1200C, you can print multiple pages faster by choosing not to collate the document. In this case, the application sends each page to the printer just once, the printer rasterizes the page, then prints however many copies you request. This process is much faster than printing collated documents, but has the obvious disadvantage that you have to collate the copies manually.

> *Note:* The 560C printers do not store an entire page internally. For this reason, every page has to be sent from the computer to the printer each time it is printed.

In Word, click the Collate Copies check box in the Print dialog box to print collated copies. Leave this check box unchecked to print in uncollated order. Set the number of copies you want to print in the Copies box.

In PageMaker, you check the Collate check box in the Print Document dialog box to print collated documents. If this box is not selected, documents are printed in uncollated order. Set the number of copies you want to print in the Copies text box.

You have probably noticed that you can define the number of copies to be printed in the DeskJet 1200C printer driver's Setup dialog box. Normally, you should leave the number here set to 1, and use your application's Print dialog box to define the number of copies. Only if your application does not allow you to set the number of copies should you do so in the printer driver's Setup dialog box.

If you set the number of copies to be printed in an application's Print dialog box and in the printer driver's Setup dialog box to other than 1, the result is not consistent among applications. In some cases, one setting overrides the other; in others, the number of copies you get is the result of multiplying the two numbers.

Printing Special Documents

Most of the printing we do is on ordinary letter-size or A4 paper. There is no more to say at this time about that.

Are you one of the many people who use a word processor, but keep a typewriter on their desks for printing envelopes and labels? If so, it's time to retire the typewriter (and recover the desk real estate it occupies) and start using your printer for envelopes and labels.

Printing Envelopes

Many word processors can print envelopes with almost no effort on your part. This way, you avoid having to type the addressee's address twice, once on the letter and once on the envelope, or you avoid the cost of window envelopes.

Word can take the addressee's address from the top of your letter and automatically reformat it to print an envelope. If your envelopes are preprinted with your return address, there's nothing more to do. If not, you can type your return address just once and have the word processor keep it for use on all envelopes.

Suppose you have typed a letter in Word, and want to print an envelope. With the letter open as a document, open the Tools menu and choose Envelopes and

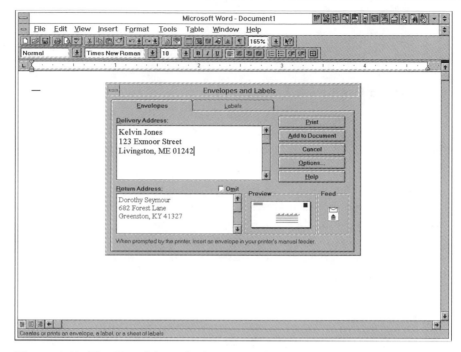

Figure 6.12 The Word for Windows Envelopes and Labels dialog box.

Labels to display the Envelopes and Labels dialog box. If necessary, click the Envelopes tab to show the addressee's and return addresses all ready to print, as shown in Figure 6.12.

If either address is incorrect, you can edit it in the dialog box. If you wish, you can click Options and choose to have Word automatically add the delivery point bar code to the address, to speed the delivery of your mail. You can also choose fonts for the delivery and return address. Now you are almost ready to print, but first you must have an envelope in your printer.

Using envelopes in the 560C and 1200C printers is a little different, so the two printers are dealt with separately below. Whichever printer you use, you should follow the advice in Chapter 3 about suitable envelopes.

Printing Envelopes on a 560C Printer

To print envelopes on the 560C, remove all the paper from the paper tray, set the paper width selector position for the specific size of envelopes you are using, and insert up to 20 envelopes in the tray. The envelopes should be face down with the stamp corner leading. If you are using Word for Windows, the drawing in the Feed box at the bottom-right of the Envelopes and Labels dialog box reminds you of the envelope orientation. You can then start printing.

Because you have to replace your normal printing paper in the paper tray with envelopes, it's efficient to print envelopes in batches, rather than one at a time. You can do this in Word, using the Mail Merge capability.

Printing Envelopes on a 1200C Printer

You must feed envelopes from the manual feed slot in the DeskJet 1200C printer one at a time. To feed an envelope, first move the media size selector to the position for the specific size of envelopes you will be using, then insert an envelope into the slot with the printing surface facing the front of the printer and the stamp corner leading. If you insert the envelope correctly, the printer grabs it and draws it down to the printing position. Sometimes, the printer doesn't immediately grab the envelope; in that case, jiggle the envelope up and down gently in the slot until the printer grabs it. When the envelope is in the correct position, the Manual Feed indicator on the front panel lights. Then you can start printing.

Printing Labels

Hewlett-Packard is cautious about printing on labels. This is because labels are adhesive and it's possible for them to stick to rollers or other components within a printer. If this happens, you face quite expensive repairs. I understand the problem. Before the days of laser printers, I had a label stick inside a dot matrix printer and subsequently spent an hour or two dismantling the printer, removing the label, and getting things running again.

HP does not recommend printing labels on the 560C printer, but does tell you how to print labels on the 1200C. If you choose to print labels, use only those recommended by HP or those manufactured specifically for use in laser and inkjet printers. Avery is the best known source of such labels, but they are available from other sources.

You can use your word processor to create labels to print. In Word, for example, open the Tools menu and choose Envelopes and Labels to open the Envelopes and Labels dialog box. If necessary, choose the Labels tab to display the Labels section shown in Figure 6.13.

In this dialog box, you can check the Use Return Address to use your return address, the same one you use for envelopes, as the address to print on the label. Alternatively, you can click an insertion point in the Address box and then type the address or whatever else is to be printed on the label.

The print section of the dialog box is where you specify whether you want to print a full page of the same labels, or just one label on a sheet of labels. Note that HP advises that you should not use sheets of labels on which any labels

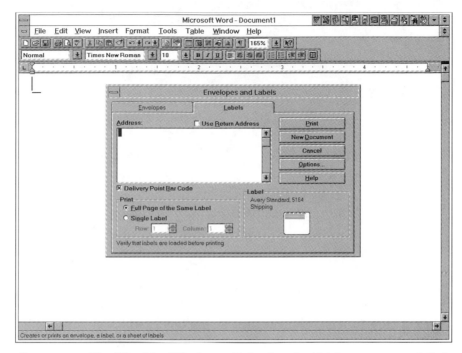

Figure 6.13 The Word for Windows dialog box in which you create a label.

have been removed. I have ignored that advice and have not had any problems. Ignore it or not as you wish, but don't blame HP or me if it does get you into problems.

To choose the type of label you are going to print on, click options to display the Label Options dialog box, shown in Figure 6.14. In this dialog box, you can choose the size of label you are going to use. Word lets you choose labels in terms of the Avery product number, using the numbers available in the United States or those used in Europe.

If you want to use a label of a size other than that specified in the Label Options dialog box, you can click Details to show the Custom Label Information dialog box, shown in Figure 6.15. Here you can specify custom label dimensions. After you have specified the label dimensions, click OK to return to the Labels dialog box.

After you have chosen the labels you are going to use, click OK to return to the Labels dialog box.

To print labels on the DeskJet 1200C printer, insert sheets of labels one at a time into the manual feed slot. In most cases, you will get best results if you choose ColorSmart in the Color section of the printer Setup dialog box, and Normal in the Print Quality section.

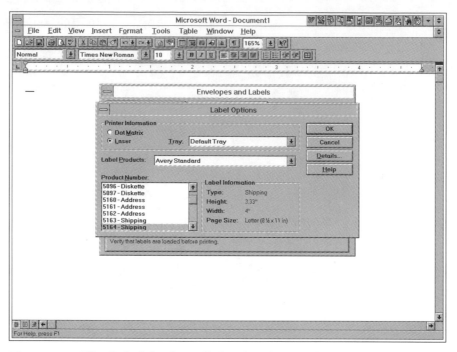

Figure 6.14 The Label Options dialog box in which you choose the type of label.

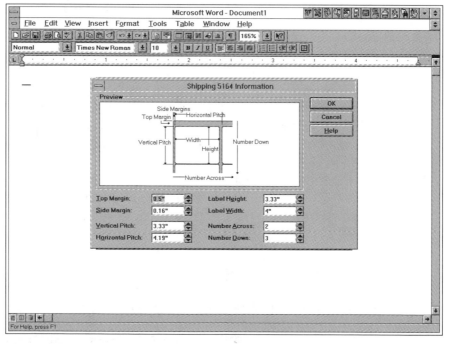

Figure 6.15 The Custom Label Information dialog box in which you specify custom label dimensions.

Printing a Series of Labels

The preceding information about printing labels primarily focused on individual labels and sheets of the same label. You can also use Word to print sheets of different labels by using the Mail Merge capability. Detailed information about this is beyond the scope of this book, but is covered in the application's User's Guide and other books.

Printing Labels with Graphics

Word's label-printing capability allows you to print text labels in black or color, but does not easily allow you to include graphics. If you need to create labels with graphics, one option is to use Avery's LabelPro application that is available in Windows and DOS versions, or the same company's MacLabelPro application for Macintosh computers.

When you open LabelPro and start a new label design, the application presents you with a choice of labels, such as that in the Product list in Figure 6.16.

After you have chosen a label, the program displays an outline of that label. You can use this outline to place graphics and text wherever you want on the

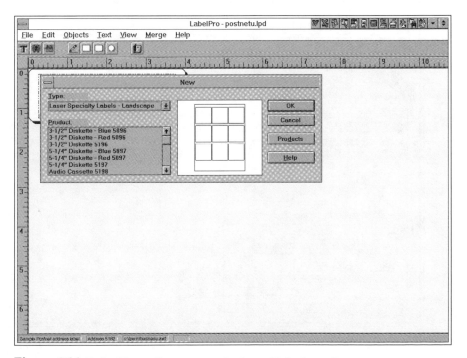

Figure 6.16 LabelPro offers you a choice of label products.

label. After you have completed a label's design, you can merge the design with a list of data, such as names and addresses, to print any number of individual labels.

Printing Business Cards

Standard business cards and postcards are too small to print on ordinary inkjet and laser printers. However, there is one easy way around this problem.

You can purchase sheets of business cards from Avery (Product No. 5371). You use these sheets in just the same way as Avery's sheets of labels. Instead of being attached to a backing sheet, the business cards are made as sheets of thin cards with micro-perforations between the individual cards. After you have printed the cards, just tear them apart.

The resulting cards are barely distinguishable from professionally printed cards. They are, perhaps, a little thinner than some cards. The micro-perforations leave almost no evidence of their existence after the cards are torn apart.

You can, of course, use graphics applications to create more elaborate business cards than you can do with a word-processing application.

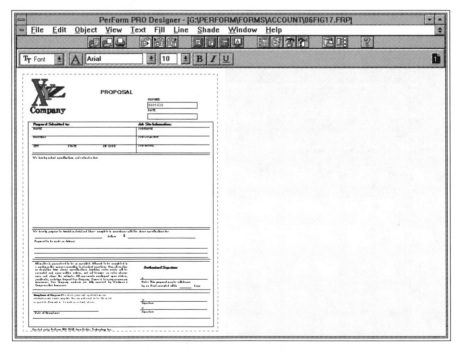

Figure 6.17   A form prepared in FormFlow and printed on a DeskJet 1200C printer.

In addition to business cards, Avery offers a range of other card products in sheet form that you can use in your inkjet printer. These include postcards, name tags, and index cards.

Printing Forms

Forms are another type of document for which your inkjet printer is ideally suited. The ability of DeskJet and DeskWriter printers to print in a variety of fonts and font sizes, to print graphics, and to print in color lets you easily create forms that are better designed and easier to use than those you often find in stationery supply stores.

You can create forms the hard way using a word processor or graphics application, but there is an easier way. Use an application such as FormFlow that is specifically intended for creating and managing forms. With FormFlow, you can choose among the many form examples that are supplied, using these forms as they are or with modifications, or you can create forms from scratch.

The proposal form shown in Figure 6.17 is a slightly modified version of a form supplied with FormFlow. If your office submits proposals to clients, you will present a successful, businesslike image by submitting a form that is well designed and uses color to draw attention to certain areas.

7
CHAPTER

Working with Business Graphics

The term *business graphics* usually refers to the types of graphics that are commonly used in business reports and presentations, primarily graphs and charts. This chapter deals with these types of graphics, and also introduces working with clip art.

Although our focus is on graphics used in business, much of this chapter applies equally to graphics used to enhance school and college reports.

HP inkjet printers are an excellent choice for printing business graphics, whether you need original vivid colors for reports, transparencies for presentations, or black-and-white originals for reproduction. The illustrations in this chapter are excellent examples of DeskJet and DeskWriter printer capabilities.

The Purpose of Graphics

The purpose of graphics is to communicate, not to decorate. This number-one principle should be at the front of your mind whenever you work with business graphics. Graphs and charts communicate numbers and relationships; maps communicate positions.

There are two components to graphics: shape and color. Both should work together to communicate. If we think in terms of corporate logos, for example, most high-technology companies—AT&T, Hewlett-Packard, IBM, Kodak, for example—have simple, bold, bright-colored logos. At first, the familiar Apple Computer logo might seem to be an example of something different. I suspect, though, that in choosing the company name and logo, the founders intended to indicate that they were different from the usual high-technology company. The apple with a bite out of it certainly does that.

Graphics should convey ideas simply and in a way people can readily understand. A map is a good example of the use of graphics to convey complicated ideas in a simple manner. The graphs and charts we use to present numerical data are other examples of graphics being used to simplify communication of information.

Creating Graphics from Spreadsheet Applications

In business, word processing is the most widely used Macintosh and PC class of application, closely followed by spreadsheets. Spreadsheet applications, such as 1-2-3, Excel, and Quattro Pro, are primarily used to maintain records of numerical data and to perform calculations on that data. They are, however, excellent tools for creating graphs and charts.

Each of these spreadsheet applications can produce many types of graphs and charts. You can use other applications, such as CorelCHART and Harvard Graphics, to create an even wider variety of graphs and charts, far too many to describe in detail here.

The simple rules for charts are to choose the simplest ones that convey your meaning clearly, and to make sure that the different elements of the chart are clearly distinguishable, preferably by use of color. If you are not able to use color, then choose distinctive shading patterns. If you intend to make copies on a black-and-white copier, create the original with shading patterns, rather than with colors. If you try to copy colored originals on a black-and-white copier, the copies will have elements in various shades of gray that are very difficult to distinguish.

Tip: To optimize printing of shades of gray, choose the Print Color as Gray in the printer Setup dialog box.

Creating a Pie Chart

Suppose you have to create a report that provides detailed information about sales of various products and services throughout a year. One way to do this (not the recommended way) is to present all the figures in one table, such as that in Figure 7.1, and leave it to your readers to pick out the information they need. This guarantees that all but the most dedicated readers will ignore your report.

	Q1	Q2	Q3	Q4	Total Year
East					
Hardware	93	134	119	156	502
Software	47	75	74	96	292
Supplies	29	54	53	52	188
Service	23	42	27	45	137
Total	192	305	273	349	1119
North					
Hardware	132	176	143	182	633
Software	58	87	76	98	319
Supplies	28	56	62	63	209
Service	28	51	54	68	201
Total	246	370	335	411	1362
South					
Hardware	197	134	146	156	633
Software	28	54	56	63	201
Supplies	11	25	29	39	104
Service	10	27	32	43	112
Total	246	240	263	301	1050
West					
Hardware	155	162	153	162	632
Software	117	115	106	102	440
Supplies	73	76	54	58	261
Service	39	52	63	69	223
Total	384	405	376	391	1556
Grand Total	1068	1320	1247	1452	5087

Figure 7.1   **An example of a spreadsheet table containing a lot of information.**

The second way is to use the figures in the table to generate a series of charts that graphically show the information you want readers to grasp. This way, a person who just scans your report gets the gist of the information. If you think some readers might need detailed information, supplement the chart with the detailed table.

If one of your purposes is to compare total sales for the four quarters of the year, you can use the totals at the bottom of the table to create a pie chart. With Excel, for example, you can use the ChartWizard to create the chart almost automatically. Just select the data in the table that is to appear in the chart, click the ChartWizard button in the Standard toolbar, and make choices in the ChartWizard dialog boxes. The result is a pie chart in which the sales of the four

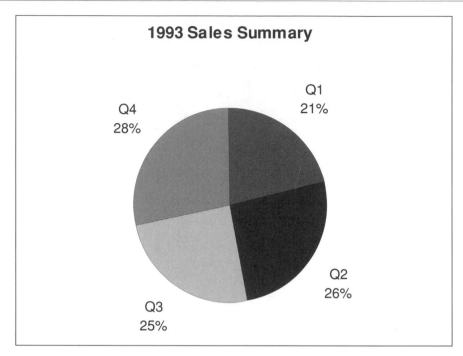

Figure 7.2 A pie chart created automatically by Excel.

regions are shown in color, with the percentages marked, as in Figure 7.2. The colors shown in this chart are those chosen automatically by Excel. You can choose other colors if you wish.

After you have created a report in Word, you can easily copy the chart to the Clipboard and then paste it into the report. However, if the report will be printed in black rather than color, you might find that there is not sufficient contrast between the shades of gray that represent colors. If this is the case, you should replace the colors Excel uses to identify the slices of the pie into shading patterns, such as those in Figure 7.3.

You can make your chart more attractive by converting it to a three-dimensional form, as shown in Figure 7.4. Many people find three-dimensional charts more appealing than those in only two dimensions. Another advantage is that a three-dimensional chart often fits more easily on a page because it occupies less vertical space.

By default, Excel creates three-dimensional pie charts with an elevation angle of 15 degrees, that is, a chart appears as if you are looking at it from an angle of 15 degrees to the surface. In Excel, as well as other applications, you can change this angle. You can also rotate the pie so that whatever slice you wish is at the front.

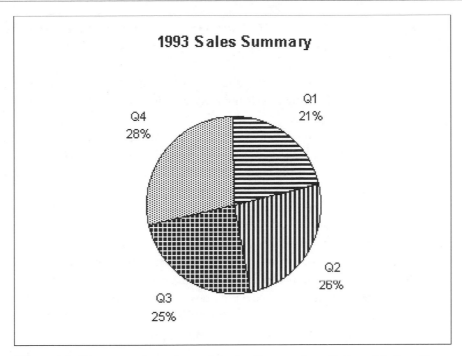

Figure 7.3 The same time chart with shading used to distinguish the slices.

Using Pie Charts to Compare Sets of Data

A pie chart is an excellent way to show the proportion of parts in a whole such as, in this case, the contribution of each product to total sales. This type of chart, though, does have some limitations. You wouldn't want to use a pie chart if there are more than about six or eight slices, because the chart gets too crowded.

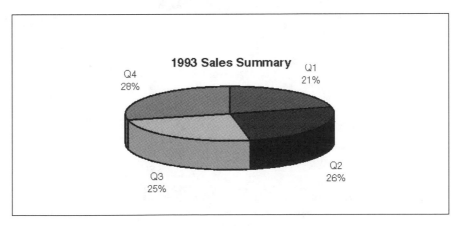

Figure 7.4 A three-dimensional pie chart created in Excel.

Tip: If you need to use a pie chart and have too many slices, you can combine several of the smaller slices into a single slice named Other.

Another limitation of a pie chart is its inability to show more than one set of values. What if you wanted to show the contribution of parts to total sales in four separate regions?

Harvard Graphics has a good solution to this problem. In this application, you can create up to six separate pie charts in one chart. What's more, you can make the individual pie charts proportional so that the area of each represents that chart's contribution to the whole.

In Figure 7.5, there are four separate pie charts created in Harvard Graphics. Each chart shows the sales of four different products. The relative size of each pie represents the proportion of sales in each region.

There are, as you probably know, many applications you can use to create charts. Most of these can produce the types of charts you ordinarily need. However, most applications have one or two capabilities that are not present in the others. As you have seen, Harvard Graphics can create multiple proportional pie charts, an ability not found is most other applications. If you have a frequent need to create charts, you should become familiar with several applications, and add those applications to your repertoire.

There's another valuable point to mention here. The original data for the multiple pie charts shown in Figure 7.5 was created in Excel. From Excel, the

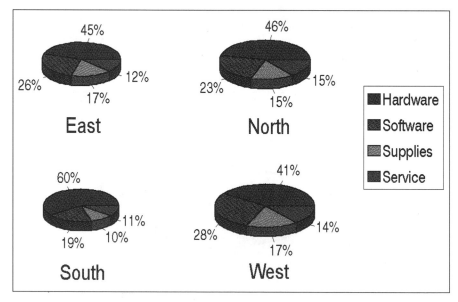

Figure 7.5 **An example of multiple pie charts created by Harvard Graphics.**

data was copied to the Clipboard, and then paste-linked into Harvard Graphics. Excel and Harvard Graphics, like many Windows applications, work so well together that it is easy to move data between applications and rarely necessary to retype data.

Using Column Charts

When there is too much data for a pie chart, you can use a column chart, such as that shown in Figure 7.6.

The chart is shown here as it is created automatically by Excel's ChartWizard. Other spreadsheet and charting applications can create similar charts.

You might prefer to make the legend, the key to what colors represent, somewhat larger. To do so, select the entire chart, then select the legend. From the Format menu, choose Selected Legend to display the Format Legend dialog box, choose the Font tab, and choose a font that is large enough to be seen clearly. When you do this, Excel increases the size of the entire legend. You can also drag the legend to a different position on the chart, as shown in Figure 7.7.

A three-dimensional effect can often make a chart more dramatic but, if you're not careful, some important data may be hidden, as it is in Figure 7.8. To change a chart from two-dimensional to three-dimensional in Excel, select the chart, open the Format menu, and choose Chart Type to display the Chart Type dialog box. Click the 3-D button and click OK to display the chart in a three-dimensional view. This view of the chart shows the category names, so there is no need for a legend.

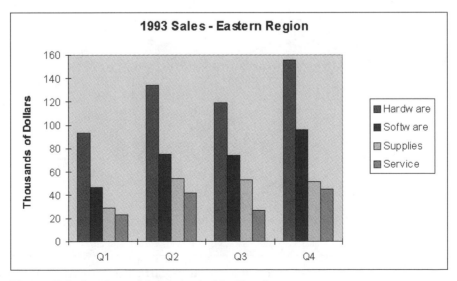

Figure 7.6 A column chart created in Excel.

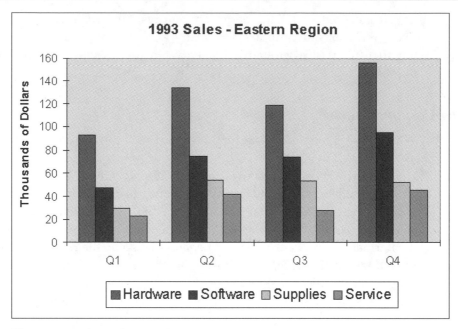

Figure 7.7 The column chart shown in Figure 7.6 with the legend enlarged and moved.

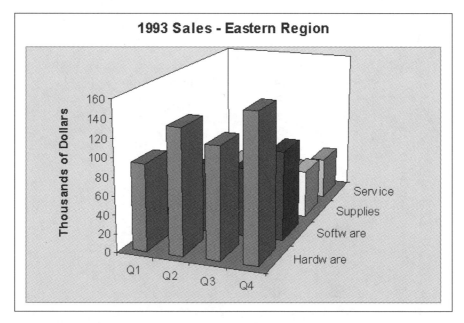

Figure 7.8 A three-dimensional column chart with some columns hidden with the same data shown in Figures 7.6 and 7.7.

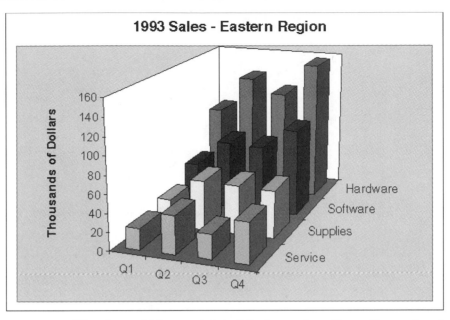

Figure 7.9 The data of Figures 7.6 to 7.8 shown in a three-dimensional chart, but with the order changed so that the smaller columns are visible.

There are several ways to deal with the problem of hidden columns in a three-dimensional chart. You can change the order of data in the chart, and you can change the angle of view. Figure 7.9 shows the same data, but with the order changed to put the smaller values at the front, so that everything is now clearly visible. To change the order of data in an Excel chart, select the chart, open the Format menu, and choose 3-D Column Group to display the Format 3-D Column Group dialog box. Click the Series Order tab, and change the order of the data series shown in the Series Order list box.

You can also rotate the chart and change the angle of view so that the data is presented in the clearest possible way. Figure 7.10 shows the chart rotated. To change the three-dimensional view, select the chart, then select the data region within the chart. Point onto one of the handles at a corner of the chart, press the mouse button, and drag. As you drag, an outline of the chart shows you the new view. Release the mouse button to show the new view of the chart.

Now a word of advice. If you are dealing with just one chart in a report, you can format that chart so that its data is presented in the clearest possible way. However, if you have several charts, you should establish a format to use with all of them, or at least with all those that are related. This may mean that some charts are shown in a less-than-ideal format. However, the alternative is to confuse the reader.

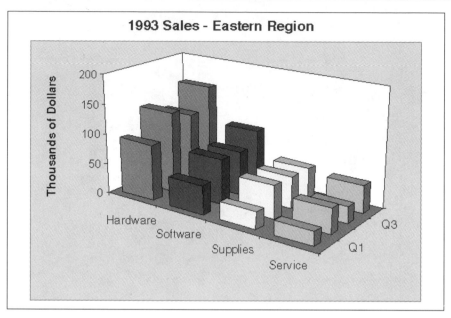

Figure 7.10 **The three-dimensional chart of Figure 7.9 shown rotated.**

The same principle applies to use of colors and shading patterns. Be consistent among all the charts in one report or presentation so that readers or viewers can easily relate data shown in all your charts. If you use green to represent Eastern Region Sales in one chart, any other chart that shows Eastern Region Sales should use green for that region.

Enhancing Charts

When you create charts, you should bear in mind that they have to, (1) *get* people's attention, (2) *keep* people's attention, and (3) *communicate* information. There are several things you can do to get people's attention; some are appropriate for use in some circumstances and others in other circumstances.

If you are preparing a chart for a widespread audience, you can afford to be informal. You see examples of such charts in news magazines, in *USA Today* and some other newspapers, and in television news and current affairs broadcasts. However, if you are preparing a chart for a technical or professional audience, you have to be careful that you do not trivialize your subject or prejudice your credibility.

One way to attract and keep people's attention is to use color effectively. Most graphics applications automatically assign colors to the various elements of a chart. The colors in the charts shown so far in this chapter are those automatically chosen by the application. You don't necessarily have to accept these colors.

Suppose, for example, you are creating a chart in which data is shown by quarter. Instead of accepting the application's default colors, it might make sense to choose ice blue for the first quarter (winter), green for the second quarter (spring), yellow for the third quarter (summer), and brown for the fourth quarter (fall). These colors would not be appropriate for people who live in the southern hemisphere.

The point here is, don't choose or accept colors for no other reason than that they distinguish between data. Try to choose colors that have some meaning, perhaps unconsciously, to the people who will see your charts.

Another way to enhance your charts is to add graphic elements. One simple, and very easy, enhancement is to add an arrow pointing to a particularly important data point in your chart. Most applications provide tools for you to do so.

For a more informal readership, you might consider replacing rectangular columns with symbols or shapes that instantly communicate the meaning of your data. Suppose you are interested in why people choose certain colors for their cars. As part of your research, you have counted the number of cars of each color in your neighborhood. Figure 7.11 shows four ways you could present this data.

Figure 7.11a shows a pie chart as Excel's ChartWizard creates it. Figure 7.11b shows the same pie chart, but with the actual car colors replacing Excel's default colors. Figures 7.11c and 7.11d show the same data presented as column charts.

If nontraditional charts appeal to you, you can replace the normal columns or bars with other graphics. In Figure 7.12, for example, columns are replaced with images of cars.

This is not intended to advocate one particular approach to chart design, but to show that your software makes it easy to choose among many approaches, and that your inkjet printer is an excellent means of printing them. It is up to you to decide which will get and keep the attention of people that matter to you.

Creating Organization Charts and Flow Charts

Next to charts that show data, charts that show organization and flow are the most frequently used. Organization charts show the relationships between departments in a company, flow charts show the relationships between steps in a process. Both consist of boxes of various shapes linked by lines.

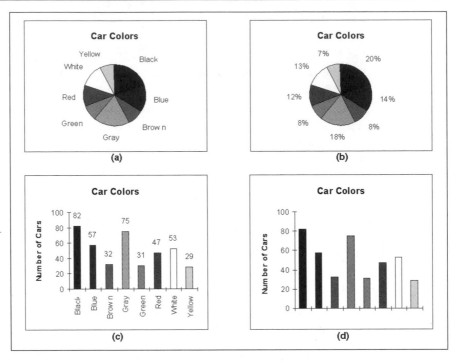

Figure 7.11 Four different ways to present data about people's choice of car colors.

Most word-processor or spreadsheet applications contain basic drawing tools you can use to create simple organization and flow charts. Word and Excel, for example, both have a Drawing toolbar that contains tools for drawing lines, rectangles, and ovals, as shown in Figure 7.13.

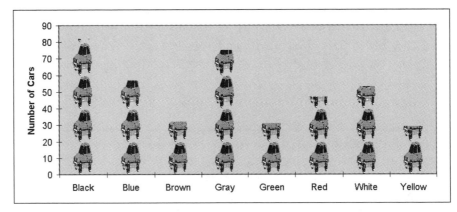

Figure 7.12 A column chart in which the normal rectangular columns have been replaced with stacked graphics.

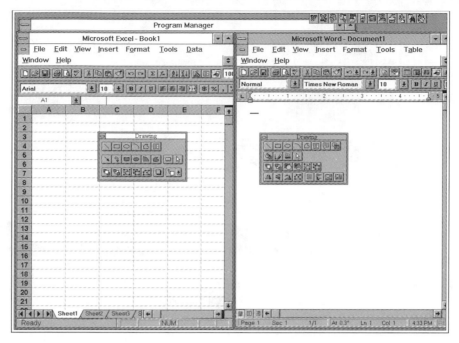

Figure 7.13 The Drawing toolbar in Excel (left) and Word (right).

While these tools are adequate for creating charts that have only a few elements, it is not easy to create the special shapes required in many charts (unless you are extremely skilled in using the Freeform drawing tool).

An alternative way to create organization and flow charts is to use a graphics application that includes standard charting symbols or for which you can purchase charting symbols as clip art. (See Chapter 8 for information about using clip art.) CorelDRAW, for example, provides many standard charting symbols as clip art.

An even better approach is to use an application, such as Visio (Windows) or IntelliDraw (Macintosh), that makes creating organization and flow charts easy.

In Visio, you can choose from many different types of symbols used for organization and flow charts, as well as other specialized types of charts and diagrams. Among those available are symbols for block diagrams, electrical diagrams, forms, maps, networks, project management, and space planning. The application's ability to place connecting lines between symbols, and to adjust those lines automatically as you move symbols, makes it very easy and fast to use.

Figure 7.14 shows a simple example of a company organization chart that was created in just a few minutes with Visio. Using a different set of Visio symbols, you can create other useful charts, such as the flow chart in Figure 7.15.

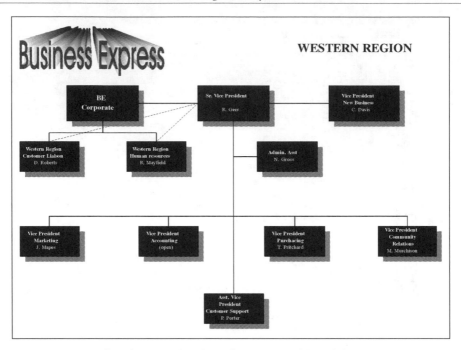

Figure 7.14 A simple organization chart created in Visio.

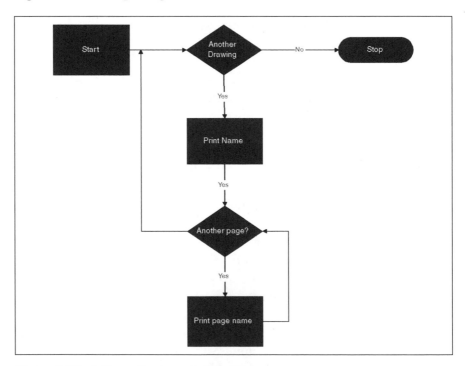

Figure 7.15 A flow chart created in Visio.

Working with Clip Art

Clip art consists of graphic images, often not copyrighted, that you can use to enhance your documents. Before the days of computer graphics, traditional artists bought books of clip-art images, cut (clipped) images they wanted to use out of the books, and pasted them into their work. You can still buy books of clip-art images in art-supply stores, scan them, and use them in your computer documents.

Now, clip art is available in electronic form on floppy disks and CD-ROMs. Word processors, such as Word and WordPerfect, include libraries of clip art, as do many graphics applications. You can also purchase clip art from companies that specialize in creating it, and you can download clip art from computer bulletin boards and communications services.

Most clip art is not copyrighted, so you are free to use it in any way you wish. Some, however, is copyrighted, so you should take care, particularly if you use clip art in material that will be published.

Each clip-art item is published as a graphics file. If you have suitable software, you can import these files, modify them to suit your needs, and paste them into your documents.

One problem with graphics is that many different file formats are in common use. While high-end applications can import most commonly used graphics formats, other applications are more limited. Appendix C lists many of the graphics file formats you are likely to come across.

Tip: You can convert a graphics file by importing it into an application and then exporting it in a different file format. You can use such applications as Collage Complete, CorelDRAW, and HiJaak for this purpose.

The following example illustrates how you can easily paste clip art into a word-processor document. Suppose you are a travel agent and you are going to send a letter to your clients suggesting travel plans they might consider for the four seasons of the year. You want to send something more attractive than just text, so you decide to use the clip-art symbols for the seasons that come with Word.

The first step is to write the text. After you've done that, you are ready to insert one of the season symbols at the beginning of each paragraph. Here's what you do:

1. Switch to the Page Layout View in Word.
2. Open the Insert menu and choose Frame.

3. Move the cross pointer to the beginning of the first paragraph, press the mouse button, drag to create a rectangle about half an inch wide and the depth of four lines of text, and release the mouse button. This creates a frame with the text wrapped around it.

4. Click the frame to select it, then click the Copy button in the Standard toolbar to copy the frame to the Clipboard.

5. Place an insertion point at the beginning of the second paragraph, then click the Paste button in the Standard toolbar to place an identical frame there.

6. Repeat step 5 to place a frame at the beginning of the third and fourth paragraphs.

7. Click the frame at the beginning of the first paragraph to select it.

8. Open the Insert menu and choose Picture to open the Insert Picture dialog box and select the Clipart directory.

9. Choose the spring.wmf file, then click OK to place it in the first frame.

10. Repeat steps 7 through 9 to place the summer, fall, and winter images at the beginning of the second, third, and fourth paragraphs.

The result is an attractive letter such as that shown in Figure 7.16.

Printing Business Graphics

The preceding sections of this chapter have offered many suggestions for creating effective business graphics. Having created these graphics on screen, you're ready to print them.

To print color graphics most effectively you should usually enable Color-Smart in the printer driver's setup dialog box. By doing so, you take advantage of the driver's ability to create highly saturated colors that make your graphics vivid and arresting. You should also make sure that the printer is loaded with the type of paper that gives the sharpest possible image.

Refer to "Creating and Printing a Document" in Chapter 6 for detailed information about printing.

Improving Print Quality

Most likely, you will be very pleased with the print quality after you follow the steps listed above. However, in some cases you may not be entirely satisfied. The following are some suggestions for solving some problems you may experience.

Quae iacta initio risum pugnantibus concitarunt, neque quare id fieret poterat intellegi. Postquam autem naves suas oppletas conspexerunt serpentibus, nova re pertetti, cum, quid potissimum vitarent, non viderent, puppes verterunt seque ad sua castra nautica rettulerunt. Sic Hanniball consilio arma Pergamenorum superavit, neque tum solum, sed saepe alias pedestribus copiis pari prudentia pepulit adversarios.

Quae dum in Asia geruntur, accidit casu ut legati Prusiae Romae apud T. Qunitium Flamininum consularem cenarent, atque ibi de Hannibale mentione facta. ex iis unus diceret eum in Prusiae rego esse. Id Postero die Flamininus senatui detulit. Patres conscripti, qui Hannibale vivo numquam se sine insidiis futuros existimarent, legatos in Bithyniam miserunt, in iis Flamininum, qui ab rege petent, ne inimicissimum suum secum haberet sibique dederet. His Prusia negare ausus non est: illud recusavit, ne id a se fieri postularent, quod adversus ius hospitii esset: opsi, si possent, comprehenderent: locum, ubi esset, facile inventuros.

Quae iacta initio risum pugnantibus concitarunt, neque quare id fieret poterat intellegi. Postquam autem naves suas oppletas conspexerunt serpentibus, nova re pertetti, cum, quid potissimum vitarent, non viderent, puppes verterunt seque ad sua castra nautica rettulerunt. Sic Hanniball consilio arma Pergamenorum superavit, neque tum solum, sed saepe alias pedestribus copiis pari prudentia pepulit adversarios.

Quae dum in Asia geruntur, accidit casu ut legati Prusiae Romae apud T. Qunitium Flamininum consularem cenarent, atque ibi de Hannibale mentione facta. ex iis unus diceret eum in Prusiae rego esse. Id Postero die Flamininus senatui detulit. Patres conscripti, qui Hannibale vivo numquam se sine insidiis futuros existimarent, legatos in Bithyniam miserunt, in iis Flamininum, qui ab rege petent, ne inimicissimum suum secum haberet sibique dederet. His Prusia negare ausus non est: illud recusavit, ne id a se fieri postularent, quod adversus ius hospitii esset: opsi, si possent, comprehenderent: locum, ubi esset, facile inventuros.

Figure 7.16 Clip art used in a Word document.

Differences between On-Screen and Printed Colors

ColorSmart does an excellent of reproducing the colors specified in your document. If there are differences between what you see on the screen and what you see on paper, the problem is probably in how your screen reproduces colors.

Chapter 5 contains information about how colors are reproduced on the screen and in print, and explains why differences exist between the two media. Chapter 13 contains information about minimizing these differences.

Uneven Color or Streaks

Uneven color or streaks of missing color are probably due to insufficient ink in print cartridges or clogged nozzles. These problems are more noticeable in printed graphics than they are in printed text.

See Chapter 3 for information about cleaning the nozzles. Replace print cartridges if necessary.

Bleeding

The term *bleeding* refers to ink of one color flowing into adjoining ink of another color. This can happen in two ways: by ink being absorbed too much into the paper (*wicking*) and by ink flowing on the surface of the paper. Both problems are more likely to be evident in printed graphics than in printed text.

Wicking should not occur if you use suitable paper. You can minimize the problem by using HP LX JetSeries paper.

Bleeding on the surface of the paper is caused by using too much ink, or not providing enough drying time. You can reduce the amount of ink used by choosing Normal instead of Presentation or High Quality in the printer driver dialog box.

Smeared Images

Ink, of course, is liquid and takes some time to dry. In normal circumstances, ink is dry enough when pages emerge from the printer that the action of dropping one sheet of paper on top of another does not cause smearing. However, if you handle printed sheets carelessly, some smearing may occur, particularly in the case of graphics that use a lot of ink.

When you print transparencies, you should always use HP Premium Transparency Film and make sure you print on the correct side. If you print on the wrong side of this film, the images will be badly smeared.

The simple solution is to handle freshly printed sheets with reasonable care. When you remove them from the printer, make sure your fingers don't touch the inked surface, and don't slide one sheet on top of another. In the case of transparencies, make sure the ink is completely dry before you put printed film into protective covers. These precautions are particularly important when you are printing on paper or transparency material that absorbs very little ink.

Optimizing Color Printing

See Chapter 13 for more information about optimizing color printing.

Introduction to Desktop Publishing

Having explored the basics of printing with inkjet printers, and looked at business graphics, we turn now to documents that combine text and graphics.

The term *desktop publishing* was first used by Paul Brainerd, the founder of Aldus Corporation, in 1985. Brainerd used it to describe the process of creating publications on a personal computer, rather than by traditional manual methods.

But what is a publication? In the sense we use the word here, a publication can be a single page, a 1000-page book, or anything in between, so it isn't size that characterizes a publication. Rather, a publication is printed material that looks as if it has been prepared professionally.

Most publications contain text and graphics. Text is printed in appropriate fonts, with proper use of established typographic conventions. A publication doesn't, for example, use a double hyphen (—) to represent a dash; instead, it uses an em-dash (—), a dash that has a length equal to the size of the font's capital M. Also, a publication uses proper opening and closing quotation marks ("like this"). Graphics may be simple rules (lines) between columns and sections, line drawings, or photographs that are integrated into pages, even, where appropriate, with text wrapping around graphics.

Publications may be printed in just one color, usually black, but more often are printed in two or more colors.

A publication can be a single-page fact sheet or flyer, a two- or four-page newsletter, a brochure or annual report, a magazine or catalog, or a book.

After you have created a desktop publication as a file on your hard disk, you can print that file directly on your color inkjet printer. Alternatively, you can have the file used to create the printing plates from which the publication will be printed by traditional methods. In the latter case, you can use your inkjet printer to print a proof copy of the publication for checking before you proceed to commercial printing.

With their capability for printing high-quality text and graphics, in black, shades of gray, and in full color, the DeskJet and DeskWriter printers are ideal desktop publishing partners.

Creating a Publication

To create a publication, you need a desktop publishing application, sometimes known as a page-layout application. It used to be that if you were working on a Macintosh computer you used PageMaker, and if you were working with a PC you used Ventura. Then, PageMaker became available in a PC version, first running directly under DOS, and then running in the Windows environment. Now, Word processors such as Ami Pro, Word, and WordPerfect have added some desktop publishing capabilities, so you can consider using your word processor for some desktop publishing projects.

To add to the wealth (or confusion) of possibilities, you can now choose from among high-end desktop publishing applications such as FrameMaker, Page-Maker, QuarkXPress, and Ventura (now reincarnated as a Corel product). You can also choose among several less powerful, and considerably less expensive, desktop publishing applications such as Microsoft Publisher and Publish It. Or, for less-demanding desktop publishing projects, you can use your word processor.

The examples in this and the next two chapters refer specifically to Page-Maker, because it is one of the two popular high-end desktop publishing applications, and almost identical versions are available for the Macintosh and Windows environments. The other popular high-end desktop publishing applications are FrameMaker and QuarkXPress, both of which are available for the Macintosh and Windows environments.

Desktop Publishing Applications

Desktop publishing originally focused on the ability to assemble text and graphics on a page, much as a traditional artist pastes art elements and galleys of text onto a board. The almost simultaneous arrival of the Macintosh computer with its graphical user interface, the PageMaker desktop publishing application, the PostScript page description language, and affordable 300-dot-per-inch laser printers put all the parts together. People soon began creating advertisements, newsletters, brochures, catalogs, and other short publications. Desktop publishing was born.

Although the original PageMaker provided most of what was needed to create short publications, it was not suitable for longer ones. The longest publication the original version could handle consisted of 128 pages. The application had no provision for creating tables of contents and indexes.

Ventura soon arrived on the scene with a different focus. This PC application focused on long documents and was quickly adopted by technical writers for use in creating manuals and also by publishers for the creation of books. Although Ventura had most of the features people needed to create long documents, it lacked some of PageMaker's ability to work with the detailed layout of individual pages.

Subsequent versions of PageMaker and Ventura have ventured more and more into each others' original territories. Now, you can use either application to create long or short documents, and you can work with detailed page layouts in either. Almost identical versions of PageMaker are available for the Macintosh and Windows environments. Although a Macintosh version of Ventura was available for a while, only a PC version now exists.

QuarkXPress jumped to popularity in the Macintosh environment because it offered more capability and precision than PageMaker. The subsequent introduction of a Windows version doesn't seem to have gained so much favor. FrameMaker, initially a UNIX application that was popular on Sun computers, is now available in compatible Macintosh and Windows versions.

At the time this book is being written, the current versions of FrameMaker, PageMaker, QuarkXPress, and Ventura are all strong contenders for desktop publishers' loyalty, offering similar capabilities and equally capable of creating outstanding publications.

The original intent of desktop publishing applications was to assemble text and graphics created in other applications into a document. While that is still those applications' primary strengths, you can now use many of the applications to create and edit text and, to a limited extent, to create graphic elements.

Computer Hardware for Desktop Publishing

Working with desktop publishing places more demands on your computer hardware than many other types of tasks. This is because publications tend to be large, often contain graphics, and use computation-intensive operations.

Also, because you want to be able to see pages in fine detail, a larger-than-normal monitor with high resolution is highly desirable.

As with most Macintosh and Windows applications, the faster your processor and the more memory you have, the better. The desktop publication itself is likely to require 10–20 megabytes or more of hard disk space, depending on which options you install. In addition, you require space for a word processor and graphics applications and, of course, for the publications you work with. Don't be surprised if 100 megabytes of disk space in total are required just for the applications you use for desktop publishing.

One of the major capabilities of desktop publishing applications is that they allow you to see text and graphics on the screen as they will appear when printed. To take advantage of this, you need a high-resolution color monitor and the graphics hardware to support it. Although these applications can work with a standard Macintosh or PC VGA monitor that displays 640 by 480 pixels, you need a monitor with a resolution of 1024 by 768 pixels or better to adequately see what your documents will look like when they are printed.

And then there's the question of color. Basic monitors can display only 256 different colors, whereas your color printer can print over 16 million colors. Whereas 256 colors are adequate when you work with desk and business graphics, you need the ability to see many more colors when you work with full-color graphics such as photographs.

Depending on the type of work you do, you may find it necessary to invest in the computer hardware (graphics board) and monitor that can display over 16 million colors at high resolution. This addition is expensive, costing considerably more than the computer itself.

Designing Publications

Creating a desktop publication starts with design. It is primarily the design of a publication that gives it a professional look that creates credibility and interest, and gets readers' attention.

Whether the publication is short or long, the design should be consistent throughout all the pages. That doesn't mean that every page should look the same as every other page but, rather, that every page of a particular type should look the same as every other page of that type.

Good design takes time and thought, but brings rewards. Every hour you spend on design before you get into the details of a publication will save you at least that amount of time throughout the entire project. What's more, the final result will be something you can be proud of.

Finding Design Ideas

There are many sources of design ideas that you can use. PageMaker and other desktop publishing applications contain templates for several types of publications. You can use these as they are, or modify them to suit your requirements.

Among the best sources for design ideas are other publications. Of course, you don't want to copy another publication to the extent that yours looks identical to the one that gave you the ideas, but you can use it to see what looks right and what doesn't. Choose what seems to fit your needs.

Get into the habit of studying published material from the point of view of design, instead of reading the content. This way, you'll soon see what works. A good way to extend your desktop publishing skills is to copy the design of other publications using dummy text and graphics in your desktop publishing application.

Design Fundamentals

Many books have been written about designing publications; a few of these are listed in Appendix B. Several magazines that cover the field are published every month; some of these are also listed in Appendix B.

It's not our intention here to provide a thorough introduction to the principles of design. Rather, we hope to draw your attention to some of the fundamentals, and to whet your appetite for more information.

Creating a Grid

Most books about publication design stress the importance of a grid that establishes the overall appearance of pages. A typical grid, shown in Figure 8.1, sets the top, bottom, left, and right margins for the main contents of each page. The grid also sets positions for items such as headers and footers.

PageMaker and other desktop publishing applications make it easy to establish a grid by providing master pages. For publications that have facing pages, you can create separate left (*verso*) and right (*recto*) master pages. As you work on the actual pages of the publication, you can use these grids to place text and graphics in position on the individual pages. The master pages can also contain text, such as headers and footers, and graphics that should appear on all, or most, pages of the publication. You can, of course, ignore what is on the master pages when you are working with pages that require special treatment.

Most publications predominantly contain text. Everything that pertains to text should be consistent throughout the entire publication and should be positioned according to the grid on the master pages.

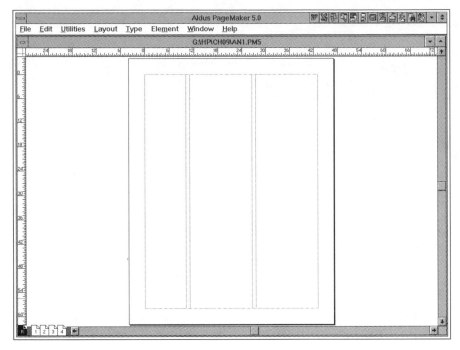

Figure 8.1 **A grid for a newsletter shown in PageMaker.**

Specifying Type

The second step in planning your publication is to decide on fonts, font sizes, line spacing, and paragraph spacing you will use.

We'll delay getting into this in detail until Chapter 9. For the present, just note that you should identify all the text elements in your publication such as:

- Body copy (text in paragraphs)
- Captions (text that identifies illustrations)
- Titles and subtitles

and decide on the type specifications for each of them.

As always, be consistent throughout your publication and throughout a series of related publications.

Specifying Colors

The third preliminary step is to decide on the colors to be used throughout the publication, including the color of the paper on which it will be printed and the colors for various text and graphics elements. This chapter deals with colors for printed publications. Chapter 11 covers the subject of colors for transparencies used in presentations.

White is usually the best choice for paper color, primarily because it provides the best contrast with other colors. To give your publication a more professional look, you may prefer to use a very light shade of another color. Reserve bright colored papers for throw-away flyers.

To make body copy (text in paragraphs) easy to read, its color should contrast strongly with the paper color. From this point of view, the best choice is black ink on white paper. To make your publication a little different, you might choose a very dark blue or brown.

Headlines and titles can be emphasized by printing them in a different color from the body copy. Be careful not to give your publication a rainbow effect. Usually, it's best to choose just one second color and keep to that for the entire publication. You can afford to use lighter colors only for text printed in large, bold fonts.

Working with Text

Most of us have learned that when we do jobs around the house, or enjoy a hobby, we get the best results in the least time, and get the most enjoyment out of the task, by using the proper tools. Yes, you can try to pound a nail into a piece of wood with the handle of a screwdriver; the result is likely to be a bent nail, spoiled wood, a broken screwdriver, and bruised and bleeding fingers. It's the same with desktop publishing. You will do your best work in the least time, and with the least frustration, if you use the right tools for each part of a desktop publishing project.

Desktop publishing applications include the capability to create and edit text. However, it's usually better to use your word processor for these tasks and then assemble the text into pages in the desktop publishing application. Use the desktop publishing application's text editing capability only for creating titles and making last-minute changes to text.

Working with a Word Processor

Leading desktop publishing applications are highly compatible with many word processing applications. PageMaker, for example, works with text created in Ami Pro, Word, and WordPerfect, as well as plain ASCII text and text in Microsoft's Rich Text Format (RTF). PageMaker does this by means of program modules known as filters. Aldus, the PageMaker supplier, sends updated filters to registered users from time to time, so that the application remains compatible with the latest versions of word processors.

One reason that you should create text for a publication with your word processor is that you are probably very familiar with it, know many of its capabilities and shortcuts, and are comfortable with it. Another reason is that if other people are involved in writing and editing text, it is easier for them to do so with the application they know than to work directly with the desktop publishing application.

Using Styles

Chapter 6 suggested that you should make a habit of using the styles capability of your word processor to maintain a consistent look for your business letters and memos. Styles are even more valuable when you are preparing text for use in a desktop publishing application.

You can create a style for each type of paragraph to define such attributes as the font name, the font size, the leading (space between lines), the space before and after paragraphs, alignment, and indentation. If you are using a word processor that is compatible with the desktop publishing application, every detail of each style is accurately reproduced when you move your text into the publication.

You will find, for example, that styles you create in Microsoft Word are highly compatible with styles in Aldus PageMaker. This compatibility exists in the Macintosh and Windows environments. For information about the style compatibility from other word processors and to other desktop publishing applications, you should refer to the product documentation. Style compatibility is a volatile issue that changes with software revisions.

Tip: If you have difficulty in sharing styles between a word processor and a desktop publishing application, you should contact the companies responsible for both. One or the other may be able to supply an improved filter (or other solution) that alleviates the problem.

Spell and Grammar Checking

Your desktop publishing application probably contains a spell checker, but doesn't have any way to check grammar. Most word processors, on the other hand, can do both.

By creating your text in a word processor, you can benefit by looking at the suggestions it makes about grammar and style. It's usually better to do spell checking at this stage as well.

Tip: You can purchase independent dictionaries and grammar checkers that you can use to check text in your word-processing and desktop publishing applications. WordStar's American Heritage Dictionary and Correct Grammar, available in Macintosh and Windows versions, are examples.

Most of us use words not in the dictionaries that come with our applications. As a result we either add words to the standard dictionaries, or create custom dictionaries. One day, perhaps, we shall be able to maintain one dictionary that all applications can reference. For the present, we have to live with the problem of dedicating disk space for several dictionaries and of maintaining those dictionaries.

By creating text for publications in a word processor and checking the spelling at that stage, you can avoid the need to update two dictionaries.

Working with Graphics

The Macintosh and Windows environments can handle two types of graphics: *bitmapped* and *vector*. You use different graphics applications to create the two types and save them as files. You can place both types of graphics into your publications.

Bitmapped Graphics

Bitmapped graphics are those in which one or more bits of computer memory represent each pixel on your monitor's screen and each dot on the printed page.

In the case of a black-and-white image, one bit is required for each pixel. The two possible states of a bit allow each pixel to be black or white.

For a *grayscale* image (one that contains shades of gray), 8 bits are used for each pixel. Because there are 256 possible combinations of 8 bits, there can be 256 shades of gray ranging from white to black. Grayscale images use 8 bits per pixel, rather than another number, for two reasons. Computers handle data in 8-bit units, called bytes. Also, 256 shades of gray provide a convincing representation of *continuous-tone* photographic images in which there are no perceptible steps between one shade of gray and the next.

Color bitmapped images usually have 24 bits for each pixel, 8 bits for each of the three primary colors, red, green, and blue. This means that each of the primary colors can be displayed in 256 shades of brightness. With the three colors combined, this results in 16,777,216 ($256 \times 256 \times 256$) possible colors. A typical person with good color vision can distinguish about 1 ½ million different colors, whereas a person who is experienced in working with color might be able to distinguish over 7 million colors. 24-bit representation of color is, therefore, more than adequate for desktop publishing.

In some high-end applications, 32 bits are used for each pixel, 8 bits for each of the three primary colors and another 8 bits (known as the alpha channel) to define the degree of transparency.

Some applications use only 8 bits for each color pixel. This scheme allows you to choose a palette of 256 colors from the total spectrum of available colors. While this is adequate for most business graphics applications, it is not adequate where you need realistic representation of many colors and where you want one color to fade smoothly into another.

> *Note:* The shades of gray or number of colors your monitor can display may be significantly less than those processed by your application because of limitations in your video card and monitor, particularly in the case of laptop computers.

Bitmapped images may be saved on disk as files in many different formats which are known by such cryptic abbeviations as EPS (Encapsulated Post-Script), TIFF (Tagged Image File Format), and PCX (PC Xchange). The same image saved in each of these formats creates files of quite different sizes. Each format has advantages and disadvantages according to the applications you are using.

One characteristic of a bitmapped graphic is that the file size, for a specific file format, is determined by the size of the image, the resolution (dots per inch) in which it is created, and the number of bits for each dot. The file size is the same whether the image is blank or has a large amount of detail.

Vector Graphics

In vector graphics, images are described mathematically. A straight line, for example, can be completely defined by the positions of its starting and ending points, and by its thickness, color, and pattern. A circle can similarly be defined by the position of its center, its radius, the thickness, color, and pattern of its perimeter, and the color and pattern with which it is filled.

Unlike a bitmapped image, the resolution of a vector image is determined by the video system used to display it or the printing system used to print it. Color is an attribute that a vector graphics application lets you define. The actual color that appears on your screen or is printed is a matter of how the application interacts with your video and printing systems.

As for bitmapped images, vector images can be saved in files having various formats. Applications such CorelDRAW that create vector images each save files in a proprietary format. Fortunately, desktop publishing applications can import files in most major formats.

The size of a vector graphic file is independent of the size of the displayed or printed graphic, and is usually much smaller than the size of the same image created as a bitmapped graphic.

Comparing Bitmapped and Vector Graphics

Bitmapped graphics have the appearance of hand-drawn or painted pictures, or even of photographs. Vector graphics have a more mechanical look because these images are based entirely on mathematical calculations. You should choose one or the other according to the effect you are trying to achieve.

In general, working with vector graphics requires less artistic skill than working with bitmapped graphics. When you use a bitmapped graphics application, you are using your mouse or other pointing device just as an artist uses a pencil, pen, or brush.

> *Note:* If you work extensively with graphics applications, particularly with bitmapped graphics applications, you will probably find it easier to use a tablet or stylus instead of a mouse.

Vector graphics images have the advantage that you can easily scale them to any size while retaining their original quality. You can magnify or reduce them in proportion, so that the height-to-width ratio remains constant, or you can shrink or stretch them vertically or horizontally.

You can change the size of bitmapped images, but only to a limited extent. You can halve the linear size of an image by eliminating alternate pixels, and you can double the size by duplicating every pixel. However, if you try to change the size to, say, 90 percent of the original, you must eliminate one pixel in every ten; this usually has the effect of creating an undesirable moiré pattern superimposed on the graphic. Also, when you enlarge a bitmapped image, the edges become jagged.

Figure 8.2 compares a vector graphic and a bitmapped graphic placed on a page in PageMaker. The circle on the left was created in CorelDRAW and saved as a vector file in WMF format (1290 bytes). The circle on the right was created in Corel PhotoPaint and saved as a bitmapped file in TIFF format (45,246 bytes). The small images at the top are shown in their original size. The large images at the bottom are enlarged in PageMaker to three times the original size.

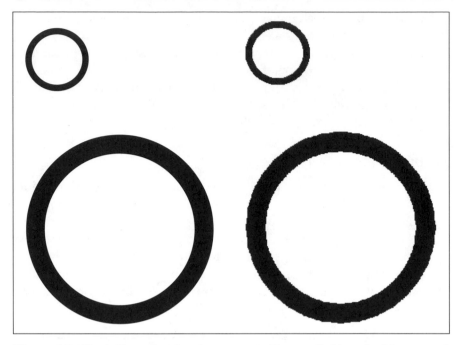

Figure 8.2 The effect of enlarging a vector image (left) and a bitmapped image (right). The jagged edges in the enlarged bitmapped image are clearly visible.

The trick with bitmapped graphics is to create them in the size at which they are going to be used. That way, you avoid any possibility of moiré patterns and jagged edges.

Vector graphics images can be rotated without distortion, often in increments of one degree or less. In contrast, bitmapped images can be flipped horizontally or vertically without distortion; rotation by any other amount is likely to cause distortion.

In summary, bitmapped images can provide greater realism than vector images. On the other hand, vector images offer, in some ways, more flexibility. Fortunately, desktop publishing applications can accept both.

You can gain some experience with bitmapped graphics using such applications as MacPaint or Windows Paintbrush. For professional-quality work, you need to use a high-end application such as Photoshop, which is available in almost identical versions for the Macintosh and Windows environments.

The Drawing module that comes with Word is a basic vector graphics application. For professional-quality work, you need an application such as Canvas, which you can use to work with bitmapped and vector graphics in the Macintosh or Windows environments. CorelDRAW is the leading Windows vector graphics application; it is supplied with Corel PhotoPaint, a separate bit-mapped graphics application. In the Macintosh environment, you can use SuperPaint to work with bitmapped and vector graphics.

Converting Between Bitmapped and Vector Graphics

You can easily convert a vector graphic image to a bitmapped image. It is somewhat more difficult to convert a bitmapped graphic to a vector graphic. The reason for this difference is apparent when you consider what a conversion involves.

The ability to display or print a vector image depends on converting mathematical information into pixels or dots, a process known as *rasterizing*. Inherent in your vector graphics application, therefore, is the ability to create a bit-mapped image. If you save the image as it appears on screen, you have a bitmapped file. Many vector graphics applications let you save images in bitmapped form with a choice of resolutions.

A bitmapped graphic exists as detailed specifications for the color of individual dots. If those dots are in a straight line, the application doesn't know that; all the application knows is that certain individual dots have certain colors. To convert a bitmapped graphic to a vector graphic, an application has to be able to detect boundaries between colors and interpret those boundaries into shapes that can be defined mathematically. The process of doing this is known as *tracing*.

Several applications are available for tracing bitmapped images to convert them into vector images. One of the more popular of these for Windows is CorelTRACE, which is included with the CorelDRAW package. Streamline provides the same capability for the Macintosh environment.

By its nature, tracing depends on recognizing boundaries between colors. For this reason, you cannot expect to convert bitmapped images, such as scanned photographs, that have gradual changes of colors. On the other hand, you can successfully convert images with strong contrast, such as scanned images of line drawings.

Using Clip Art

As mentioned in Chapter 7, a wide range of clip art is available for you to use in your publications. Some is of excellent quality, but some is of lesser quality.

One aspect of clip-art image quality is the nature of the image. Is the idea behind the image well conceived and well executed? Another aspect of quality is its resolution. Is resolution adequate for your needs? Some clip-art suppliers provide low-cost samples of their work from which you can judge its suitability before you invest in specific high-resolution images.

You don't have to use a clip-art image in its original form. Unless the copyright notice forbids, you can use a graphics application to modify the image in any way you want.

CD-ROM

CD-ROM is rapidly becoming a popular storage medium for text, graphics, and sound, as well as for applications. Its most striking feature is the ability to store in excess of 600 megabytes of data on one disk, the equivalent of more than 400 high-density floppy disks. The limitation is that CD-ROM is a read-only medium. Data can only be written once onto a CD-ROM, and this requires hardware that is much too expensive for most Macintosh and PC users.

Using CD-ROM Clip Art

CD-ROM is becoming the preferred way to distribute software, particularly software that would otherwise occupy many floppy disks. Not only is it considerably less expensive for software suppliers to use CD-ROM, but it is also a much more convenient way for users to install the software onto their computers. Another benefit, from the suppliers' point of view, is that CD-ROMs cannot be copied, so the problem of software piracy is reduced.

As mentioned previously, graphics files tend to be very large, so CD-ROM is an ideal medium for suppliers to use to distribute clip art and other graphics files.

Photo CD

Photo CD is an interesting and relatively new use of CD-ROMs. You can use your camera to take photographs as usual on negative or transparency film. A photofinisher that has a Kodak Photo Imaging Workstation can transfer up to 100 of your images onto a CD. Many graphics applications can read images from Photo CDs, allowing you to incorporate these images into desktop publications. Of course, to use Photo CD, your computer must have a CD-ROM drive.

Kodak offers five types of Photo CDs:

- Photo CD Master—the mass-market format that photo finishers support. Images on your 35-mm negative or transparency film are scanned with 24 bits per pixel, and written onto a CD. Each image is compressed and stored in a file which usually occupies 4 to 6 megabytes, depending on the detail in the image. A CD can hold up to 100 images. You can retrieve the images in up to five different resolutions:

  Base/16 — 128 by 192 pixels

  Base/4 — 256 by 384 pixels

  Base — 512 by 768 pixels

  4 Base — 1024 by 1536 pixels

  16 Base — 2048 by 3072 pixels

- Pro Photo CD Master—for professional photographers who use 120-mm or 4 by 5 inch film. Images are saved at 4096 by 6144 pixels (64 Base). In this format, each image, after compression, occupies approximately 18 megabytes.

- Photo CD Portfolio—for television-resolution images. This format can place up to 800 images on a CD.

- Photo CD Catalog—for maintaining a catalog, or database, of up to 6000 low-definition images. This format is intended to be used for indexing images only, not as a source of the images themselves.

- Photo CD Medical—for storing medical (and similar) images.

It might seem that Photo CD could eliminate the need for a scanner, but this isn't really the case. Photo CD images are bitmapped images, so you are very limited in how you can scale them to suit your publication. As with any other bitmapped image, you can reduce the size of the image by factors of 2, 4, 8, and so on, but not by any other number without introducing a patterned effect. If one of these reductions fits into your publication at the size you need, you have no problem. However, unless you plan the size of the photographed image very carefully, you are likely to find that the size of the images dictates the layout of your publication, rather than the other way around.

The benefit of using a scanner is that you can scan an image at the size and resolution you need for your publication, giving you much more flexibility than you get with Photo CDs.

Before leaving the subject of Photo CDs, we should mention that clip-art suppliers offer disks containing about 100 professional photographs each. Some of these images are royalty-free, others are not. You might find some of these images useful in your desktop publishing work.

Screen Captures

If your publication is about computer hardware or software, as this book is, you will probably need to reproduce the images a reader sees on the monitor screen. The easiest way to do this is to use an application that directly writes screen images to a file—a so-called *screen-capture* application. Using such an application eliminates the hassle of photographing screens.

Screen-capture applications let you choose the area of the screen you want to capture, the format of the file (TIF, PCX, and so on), and the type of file (black and white, grayscale, or color). You should capture screens in file formats acceptable by your desktop publishing application.

The Windows screens reproduced in this book were captured with the most versatile screen capture application we have encountered—Collage Complete. Among several screen capture applications for Macintosh computers, Baseline Publishing's Exposure Pro is highly recommended.

9

Working with Text

You can print attention-grabbing newletters on your color inkjet printer. Most newsletters combine text and graphics to communicate effectively with readers. In this chapter, we focus on the text content of newletters as we describe how to prepare text in ways that take advantage of your inkjet printer's capabilities. Chapter 10 covers graphics elements.

Although we use newsletters as examples in this chapter, you can use the information here when you work with your desktop publishing application to create many other types of publications, including flyers, brochures, catalogs, and even full-length books.

Newsletter Basics

Many organizations, large and small, find newsletters are a valuable and effective way of communicating with a target audience. Notice some key words in the preceding sentence:

- *News* (in newsletter)—People expect to find news in a newsletter, so they are motivated to read it.

- *Valuable*—Newsletters can be relatively inexpensive to produce and distribute, yet can have a big impact on readers.

- *Effective*—People do read newsletters. Some people only scan them, others read at least some of the details.

153

- *Communicating*—Well-planned and well-executed newsletters do a good job conveying ideas and information.

- *Target audience*—You can aim the contents of a newsletter directly at the people who will receive it.

Whether your organization is a social group of some sort, a manufacturer or supplier, a charity, an advocacy group, or whatever, you should consider distributing a regular newsletter to keep in touch with people and develop loyalty.

If your organization doesn't already publish a newsletter, you'll find the ideas here provide information about doing so. If you are already publishing a newsletter, you might find some information you can use to improve it.

Planning a Newsletter

To start, put together a brainstorming session to discuss what you want to achieve and to arrange your priorities. Above all, develop a clearly defined basic purpose. Is the newsletter to be for your employees or for your customers? Is it intended to be read by technical or nontechnical people?

Decide on a primary focus, and then keep that focus in mind as you create each issue of the newsletter. Be cautious about mixed purposes. You can have one or two special sections addressed to subgroups of the target audience, but always make sure the prime focus is clear to you and to the readers.

Don't be overambitious. If you haven't produced a newsletter before, you'll be surprised how much time and effort go into each issue. Be realistic about how much time and effort are available to put into each issue, and plan what is achievable on that basis.

Regular publication is essential. Newsletters are like advertisements—both must appear regularly if they are to have a significant impact. In many cases, monthly, bimonthly, or even quarterly publication works well. If you cannot schedule at least quarterly publication, you should seriously consider whether you are ready to start a newsletter.

Set a date for the distribution of each issue. Let your readers know, for example, that the newsletter will be mailed on the first Monday of every month, the last day of each quarter, or something like that. Once you have set that date, let nothing stand in your way, because the delay or absence of an issue can damage your personal reputation and your organization's. Your intention should be to build readers' interest to the extent that they look forward to each issue and, if they don't receive it on time, will call you to find out why.

Designing a Newsletter

The number-one principle to understand is that an effective newsletter, like any other publication, needs to be designed. It's not a matter of just pouring text and graphics onto pages.

Most of the overall design issues to consider are covered in Chapter 8. These include choosing an overall grid, fonts to use for various elements, and colors. Some additional detailed matters are covered later in this chapter.

It's not difficult come up with a simple, clean-looking design yourself. One easy way to do this is to look at other published newsletters and use what appeals to you, bearing in mind the limitations of your printer or, if you plan to have the newsletter printed commercially, asking your print shop for advice.

Of course, if you are untrained in graphic arts, you won't produce an award-winning newsletter by designing it yourself. If you want the best in design and have an adequate budget, consider carefully having a professional design consultant work on your newsletter. But make sure you see examples of that person's previous work and are happy with them.

Printing the Newsletter

Before you start any detailed work on your newsletter, you must make some decisions about printing. There are several possibilities.

Printing on Your Office Printer

For a newsletter that is to be printed in small quantities, perhaps less than 100 copies, consider printing it yourself on your office inkjet printer. This immediately raises the issues of your printer's capabilities and limitations.

One limitation is size. Most office printers are limited to letter- or legal-size paper. Another limitation may be not being able to print on both sides of the paper.

> *Note:* HP does not recommend using inkjet printers to print on both sides of a page. Ink from the previously printed side may accumulate within the printer resulting in inferior print quality.

Other things to consider include the printer's resolution, color capabilities, and recommended monthly throughput. HP recommends the 560C printers for printing up to 1000 pages per month and the 1200C printers for up to 8000 pages per month.

Be assured that you can print excellent, professional-quality newsletters on your DeskJet or DeskWriter printer.

Using a Color Copier

Another possibility is to print a single original on your inkjet printer, and then to have copies made on a color copier at your local copy center.

As when you use your office printer to print multiple copies, you have to be aware of the limitations of the printer you will use for the master copy and the limitations of the copier. If you go this route, evaluate the quality of sample copies before you place a quantity order.

Using a Commercial Print Shop

If you intend to print more than about 100 copies of your newsletter, you'll probably want to have a commercial print shop do the job. You'll save yourself time, money, and frustration by doing so.

There are many types of commercial print shops, ranging from instant printers that are little more than copy centers to those who specialize in large-quantity, full-color printing. The trick is to find a print shop that makes a business of doing the type of work you want and with whom you feel you can work.

If you choose this method of printing, you should use your inkjet printer to print proof copies before you hand the project over to the print shop. This way you know what the final product will look like. Also, a sample printed this way shows the print shop exactly what you intend.

Using Preprinted Paper

An alternative way to print colorful publications is to use preprinted stationery that is available from PaperDirect and other suppliers, as well as from some retailers. Paper of this sort is preprinted with borders, backgrounds, and fills. If you can find a design that suits your needs, it can save you some time and effort.

Before using preprinted paper of this type, make sure it is intended for use on an inkjet printer because some papers intended for use with laserprinters do not work well with inkjet printers. Even then, purchase a small quantity and try it out before committing to use it for a large project.

Distributing the Newsletter

Even the matter of distributing the newsletter is something to consider before you start thinking about its design in detail.

To get readers' attention, a newsletter should be addressed to people by name. If you don't do this, people tend to classify the publication as junk mail and dispose of it accordingly.

Addressing a newsletter to people by name means that you either place it in an envelope or stick a mailing label on it. You probably won't want to use envelopes due to the added cost of the envelope and the added postage required by the extra weight.

If you intend to use labels to address your newsletter, you must provide space for those labels. The neatest way to do this is to reserve a panel that appears on the outside when the newsletter is folded. A publication designed in this way is known as a *self-mailer*.

Designing a Typical Newsletter

For the remainder of this chapter, we'll concentrate on a typical newsletter that consists of four pages, uses black ink for most of the copy and a second spot color for titles and screens, and incorporates some graphics (Chapter 10 covers screens and other graphics topics).

If you're preparing a newletter or other publication that you expect to publish regularly, don't overlook your desktop-publishing application's ability to create and use templates. By creating your initial design as a template, you can easily create any number of documents based on that template. Templates used in this way can save you a great deal of time.

Choosing Page Layout Software

The process of designing a publication is quite easy if you use a desktop publishing application. The task can be done with a word processor, but with more effort and time. If I have to cut some logs, I'd rather use a chain saw than a hand saw. It's not that a hand saw can't do the job, but that a chain saw makes the job doable within a reasonable time and with a lot less sweat.

The following pages are written with PageMaker in mind because this desktop publishing application is available in very similar versions for Macintosh and Windows environments and is very widely used. If you have a different desktop publishing application, you can follow similar steps.

Laying Out the Grid

We'll assume that the newsletter will be printed on letter-size paper. If you intend to print the newsletter on your office printer, the overall size of the grid is limited by the printable area. In this case, assuming you intend to print the newsletter on a 560C printer, the minimum left and right margins are 0.25 inch, the minimum top margin is 0.26 inch, and the minimum bottom margin is 0.67 inch. The margins for a 1200C printer are different.

Before going any further, you need to make some decisions about the measurement units you are going to use in your layout. Because type is specified in points, it makes sense to use *points* and *picas* (there are approximately 72 points to an inch, one pica is equal to twelve points) as the basis for your design. In PageMaker, you can open the File menu and choose Preferences to display the Preferences dialog box in which you can choose measurement units, with different units for the horizontal and vertical rulers if you prefer. Choose Picas for both rulers so that you see the rulers marked in picas and subdivided into points.

Converted into picas, the minimum margins for the 560C printer are 1.50 (left and right), 1.56 (top), and 4.02 (bottom). In fact, you will rarely need to print as close to the margins as this.

Let's suppose you initially decide to use 4.2-pica left and right margins and 4.5-pica top and bottom margins. You can set these margins, together with the number of pages and other parameters, in the PageMaker Page Setup dialog box, as shown in Figure 9.1. You use this dialog box also to choose the page size (letter in this case), the page orientation (tall), the number of pages (4), whether or not the newsletter will be double-sided (not), and the printer you will use for printing it (HP DeskJet 560C).

After you have chosen the page setup parameters, the screen shows an outline of the page with the margin position marked, as shown in Figure 9.2. Note that the left end of the bottom line shows four numbered page icons, each representing one of the pages of the newsletter.

The next step is to decide on the number of columns and the space between the columns. You can, if you like, set the columns separately for each page, or you can use a master page to set the columns for all pages in the document. Using a master page can save a considerable amount of time when you are working with a long document, but doesn't make so much difference in the case of a four-page newsletter. When you do set the number of columns in the master page, you can change this later for individual pages if necessary.

To set the number of columns using the master page, click the page icon at the bottom left of the screen (labeled R) to show the master page.

Now, open the Layout menu and choose Column Guides to display the Column Guides dialog box shown in Figure 9.3. Notice that the measurement unit for the space between columns is picas. This is because you previously chose picas for your unit of measurement.

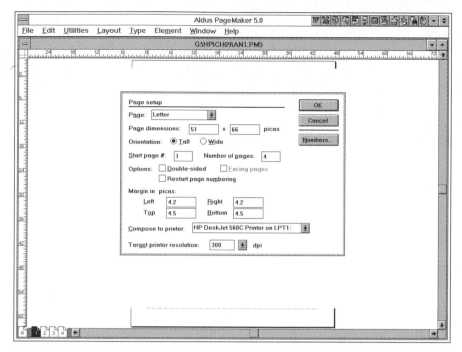

Figure 9.1 The PageMaker Page Setup dialog box with the page parameters set.

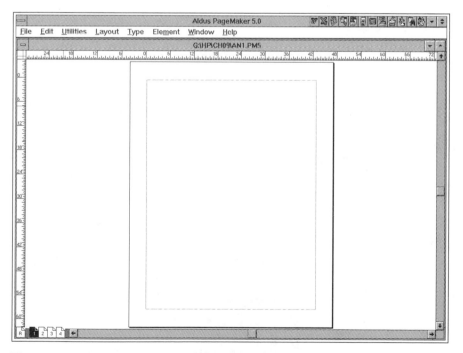

Figure 9.2 The page setup with margins shown.

159

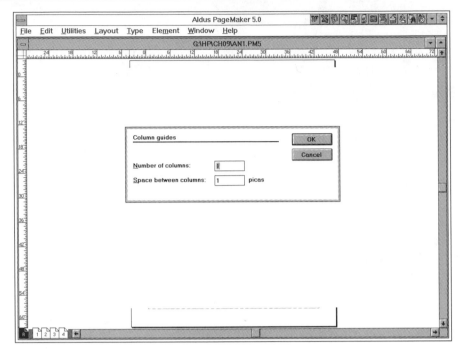

Figure 9.3 The Column Guides dialog box.

Change the number of columns to *3*, and leave the space between columns at *1* pica. When you click OK to accept these values, the master page reappears with the columns marked, as shown in Figure 9.4. Notice that the three columns are of equal width.

Three equal columns give the newsletter a somewhat formal appearance. If you want something more visually exciting, you can drag the column outlines on the master page to give a less formal appearance, as shown in Figure 9.5.

> *Note:* You can place any text or graphics on the master page that you want to appear on most pages of a document.

Choosing a Fonts and Font Sizes

The fonts you choose help to establish the character of the newsletter. You'll need a font for the body copy, a variation of that font for captions, another font for headlines, and probably one for subheads. It's important that all the fonts work together.

The predominant part of a newsletter is usually body copy, so it makes sense to start with choosing a font for that.

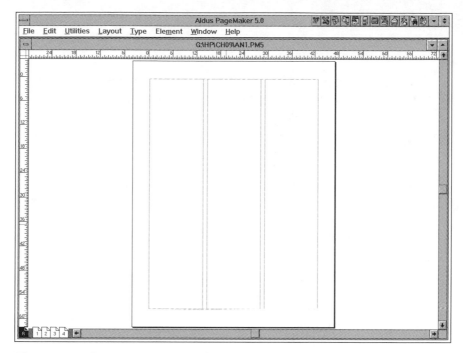

Figure 9.4 The master page with columns marked.

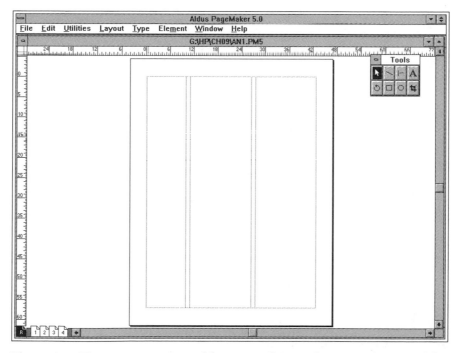

Figure 9.5 The master page with one narrow column and two wider columns.

Body Copy

The body copy should almost always be set in a simple, easy-to-read, well-proportioned serif font. There are many of these to choose from. The choice is mainly a matter of personal preference. After you choose a font, use it consistently for body copy in each issue of the newsletter. In this example, Garamond is chosen.

The next decision to be made is the size of the body copy. Chapter 5 suggested that you should choose a size so that approximately one and a half alphabets fit within the width of a column. Figure 9.6 shows that one and a half alphabets of Garamond set at 9, 10, and 11 points all come close to the ideal size. While you could use any of these type sizes, many people would consider 9-point type too small for easy reading. Ten-point type is probably a good choice.

Body Copy Leading

One of the many rules of thumb for page layout is that the leading (vertical space occupied by a line) for body copy should be approximately 120 percent of the font size. In this example, the font size is 10 points so, following this rule, the leading should be 12 points.

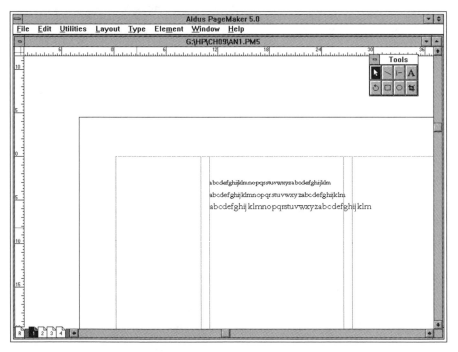

Figure 9.6 One and a half alphabets of Garamond set at 9, 10, and 11 points.

Note: The leading considered here is the space occupied by lines within a paragraph. The spacing between paragraphs is a separate matter that is dealt with later in this chapter.

By specifying the font size as 10 points, you are saying that the height of text, measured from the bottom of descenders to the top of ascenders and uppercase characters, is 10 points. By specifying the leading as 12 points, you are saying that the space occupied by each line of text is 12 points. To understand how type is aligned, you also need to know how the 10-point overall height of text is positioned within the 12-point vertical space.

By default, PageMaker uses what it calls *proportional leading*. This divides the vertical space into thirds and places the baseline of text at a level one-third of the distance from the bottom of the leading space, as shown in Figure 9.7.

There is another consideration in choosing the leading. For a professional appearance, there should be a whole number of lines between the top and bottom margins. To check whether this is so, you can calculate the distance between the top and bottom margins and divide it by the leading. In this example, the overall height of the page is 792 points (11 inches). The top and

Figure 9.7 PageMaker places text with the baseline at a level one-third the height of the leading space.

bottom margins are each 54 points (4.5 picas), so the text space is 684 points. Divide this by the tentative leading (12 points) to see how many lines fit on a page (57).

In this case, the top and bottom margins and the tentative leading result in a whole number of lines, so no adjustment is necessary. If the calculation did not result in a whole number of lines, it would be necessary to adjust the margins or the leading (or both) to obtain a whole number.

> *Note:* The top and bottom margins and leading values suggested here are only one of many possibilities.

When you have decided on the leading, you should return to the Page Setup dialog box and, if necessary, adjust the margin settings. You should also open the Preferences dialog box again and change the measurement units on the vertical ruler to correspond to the leading. In this case, change the Vertical Ruler setting to Custom with a value of 12 points.

To simplify using the horizontal and vertical rulers as you place text and graphics on the page, you should move the zero point on both rulers to mark the intersection of the top and left margin. Do this by dragging the crossed dotted lines in the small square where the rulers meet to the intersection of the top and left margins. After doing this, you can easily align any graphics, tables, or other nontext items to match the vertical position of the text.

Captions

Captions, short phrases, or sentences that identify illustrations, should be set in a font that clearly distinguishes them from body copy. One way to do this is to use the same font as that used for body copy, but somewhat smaller. You could, for example, set the captions in 8.5-point Garamond.

If you decide to use a smaller version of the body-copy font, make sure that there is sufficient difference between the body copy and the captions for readers to easily distinguish them. Also, make sure that you don't choose a font size that is difficult to read or one that your printer can't reproduce with adequate quality.

An alternative to using smaller type for captions is to use the same size as the body copy, but the italic style. Make sure, though, that you have the italic style installed on your computer; otherwise you will find yourself using a slanted version of the roman style.

Headlines

It's common practice to use a sans serif font for headlines to provide a strong contrast to body copy. In most cases, this font should be a simple, traditional design with medium-weight strokes.

As with the font for body copy, there are many possible fonts to choose from for your headlines. Arial is one possibility; Futura is somewhat heavier and seems to speak with more authority, while AvantGarde has a more exciting look. It all depends on the tone you want for your newsletter. The examples here use AvantGarde.

The size you use for headlines depends on how loud you want to shout. Usually, headlines are at least twice as large as body copy. For your lead article on the front page, you might want to go as large as three to four times as large as the body copy.

Headlines should consist of as few words as possible, but must have enough words to adequately convey what follows. You should normally limit headlines to no more than two lines of text, even if this means using a smaller font than you would otherwise prefer. If the article under the headline occupies more than one column, the headline should stretch over all the columns of body copy.

You also need to choose fonts for one or two levels of subheadings. These can be set in the same font as headlines, but in smaller sizes. Make sure the size differences you choose are sufficient to make their levels clear to the reader. Usually, there should be at least 2 points difference in size between subheading levels.

When headlines or subheads occupy more than one line of text, you have to consider the leading of those lines. The rule-of-thumb for body text does not apply to large type. If you set 36-point type with a leading of 43 points (20 percent more than the type size), the lines will seem to be much too far apart. Large type looks better if the leading is equal to the type size, or even a little less (negative leading). If you like the idea of negative leading, make sure that descenders of one line don't overlap ascenders and uppercase characters on the line below.

There should, of course, be vertical space to separate headlines and subheads from the body copy that follows them. There should also be space above subheads to separate them from the preceding body copy. This is a separate issue from the space between lines within a headline or subhead. The vertical spaces you select should be chosen to preserve the alignment of text to the vertical grid. If, as suggested above, you have chosen a 12-point vertical grid, this means that the total space occupied by a headline or subhead should be an exact multiple of 12 points.

Table 9.1 Summary of Fonts for Newsletter Example

Use	Font Name	Size	Leading	Before	After
Body copy	Garamond Book	10	12	0	0
Captions	Garamond Italic	10	12	6	6
Headline	AvantGarde Medium	36	36	15	9
Subhead 1	AvantGarde Book	20	20	12	4
Subhead 2	AvantGarde Book	16	16	6	2

Be consistent about the use of uppercase and lowercase text in your headlines. It's best to avoid using all uppercase. To make your text easy to read, just capitalize the first letters of important words in headlines. However, some people feel that all uppercase is appropriate for important headlines.

After you have made initial decisions about the fonts you intend to use, you should make a note of them. Table 9.1 summarizes the fonts to be used in this example. The Before and After columns show the vertical space between paragraphs. For each font size, the total of the leading, space before, and space after is an exact number of vertical grid increments (12 points in this case).

Tracking and Kerning

Every character in a font is allocated a certain amount of horizontal space, just a little wider than the character itself so that adjacent characters don't touch. This spacing usually works well for characters set in the sizes used for body copy. However, the built-in character spacing is often too much for larger type used in headlines and subheads. You can improve the appearance and readability of your publications by reducing the space between characters in headlines and subheads.

Tracking and *kerning* are two methods used to adjust the spacing between characters. Tracking changes the space between any number of selected characters. Kerning is used to change the space between one or more pairs of characters.

PageMaker offers six tracking choices, as shown in Figure 9.8. At the top is the standard tracking, as dictated by the font itself. Below that are the five tracking variations generated by PageMaker. These are: Very Loose, Loose, Normal, Tight, and Very Tight. For the font used in this example, Normal is just a little tighter than the standard spacing and is about right.

You can let PageMaker (and some other applications) automatically kern certain pairs of characters, but the amount of kerning is often insufficient in headlines, particularly those set in all uppercase. For this reason, you have to

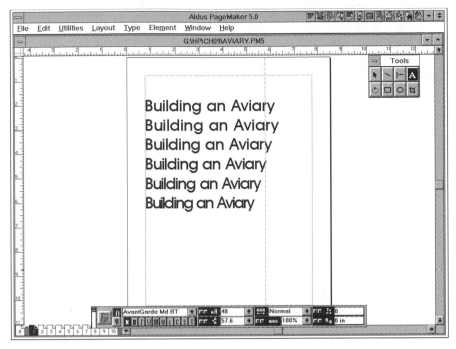

Figure 9.8 Examples of the tracking options available in PageMaker.

resort to manual kerning, which you do by placing the insertion point between two characters, then:

- PC—holding down the Ctrl key and pressing the minus key on the numeric keypad
- Macintosh—holding down the Command key and pressing the left arrow key

Changing the Font Width

In addition to changing the spacing between characters, you can also change the character width. PageMaker lets you change character width over the range from 5 to 250 percent of the standard width, in 1 percent increments.

While large changes in character width are sometimes appropriate for advertisements and flyers, in most cases you will only want to change the width slightly. It is particularly useful to be able to do this when you have a headline or subhead that is slightly too long for the space available.

Changing character width slightly is also useful when body copy is slightly too long for the available space. You might find that by reducing character width by only a few percent, you can solve otherwise impossible copy-fitting problems.

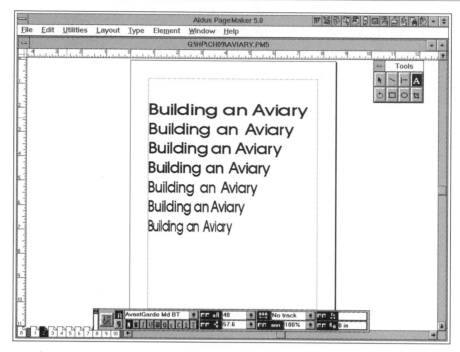

Figure 9.9 Characters set at various percentages of the normal width.

Figure 9.9 shows the effect of changing character width. From top to bottom, the illustration shows characters set at 130, 120, 110, 100, 90, 80, and 70 percent of the normal width.

Designing the MastHead

A newsletter's *masthead* identifies the publication and signifies its purpose. A masthead usually consists of the newsletter's name, set in a distinctive font, the publication date, and perhaps a volume and issue number. In most cases the masthead is at the top of the front page, although you occasionally see a vertical or even a diagonal masthead.

The masthead design should be strong and simple with no competing elements. You should not, for example, combine your organization's logo with the newsletter's logo in the masthead.

You can easily design an effective masthead based on type set in a graphic application. The DesktopNews logo shown in Figure 9.10 was created in CorelDRAW using BankGothic Medium (one of the fonts supplied with CorelDRAW) with the character spacing reduced and the characters skewed by 10 degrees. The image was copied into the Clipboard, pasted at the top of the

Figure 9.10 The masthead pasted at the top of the first page.

front page of the newsletter in PageMaker, and then stretched proportionately to fit exactly between the margins. The horizontal bar under the logo was created with PageMaker's rectangle tool. The text in the bar was also created in PageMaker. The color selected for the text is Paper, so that it appears in white (the paper color) on the colored bar.

> *Note:* Paper (as a color) refers to the color of the paper on which you are printing. Objects behind a paper-colored object are not printed; instead, the paper color shows through.

Figure 9.10 also shows the column outlines changed so that there is one narrow column and two equal, wider columns.

Having the text in white on a colored background is an example of a *reverse*, which is an attractive effect to use occasionally. When you use reverse type, you should make sure that the characters are bold and not too small. The reason for this is that ink tends to spread during printing. If you have characters with thin strokes to begin with, some parts of the strokes may partially or completely disappear. This can happen whether you print your newsletter on an inkjet printer or have it printed by a commercial print shop. If you want to use a reverse, choose a bold font and see how a printed sample looks before finalizing your design.

Creating the Body Copy

There are two ways to create body copy for a publication you are preparing in a desktop publishing application. One way is to use that application's text editing capability. The other is to create the text in a word processor and subsequently place it into the desktop publishing application. The second is usually the better approach.

There are several reasons why the second approach is better. A word-processing application such as Word has more sophisticated facilities for working with words than you are likely to find in a desktop publishing application, and, in your day-by-day work, you have probably become familiar with many of them. You probably have enough to do without learning the somewhat different way your desktop publishing application deals with editing text.

When you work with a word processor, you have access to its spell checking and grammar checking capabilities. Yes, your desktop publishing application can do spell checking, though it probably doesn't do grammar checking. If you choose to rely on your desktop publishing application for spell checking, you have two dictionaries to maintain, one in your word processor for ordinary work, and one for your publishing projects. You can eliminate the extra work by relying only on your word processor for spell checking.

Several people probably need to review your work before it gets into print. If you create your text in the word processor that most people in your organization use, they can easily review it on screen without having to install the desktop publishing application on their systems and without having to learn how to use that application. They can also use the word processor's revisions and annotations capabilities to add notes and suggestions for your consideration.

One more benefit of creating the document in a word processor relates to proofreading. However hard we try, and however many people read a document before it's printed, there always seems to be at least one error that everybody misses. We need all the help we can get in this regard. If you and others read and check the document carefully in its word-processing form, you will find most errors. Subsequently, when you place the document into the desktop publishing application, it will have a different appearance due to the change in line breaks. The chances are that you will see errors in the new format that you didn't see before.

Working with Styles

In word processing and desktop publishing, a *style* defines the overall appearance of text. You can, for example, define a style that defines the appearance of body copy. This style can define:

- The font name and size, and whether it is roman, italic, or bold
- Line spacing within paragraphs as well as any extra line spacing before or after paragraphs
- Indentation and tab positions
- Color
- How a paragraph is to be hyphenated

You can define separate styles for each type of paragraph in your document. In addition to body copy, captions, headlines, and subheads can all be defined by style, each style having a separate name.

> *Note:* In many word-processing and desktop publishing applications, a paragraph is all the text between one paragraph marker and the next. A conventional paragraph of body copy is a paragraph. Single-line headlines and subheads are, in this sense, paragraphs.

Using styles has several benefits. Styles make it easy to maintain a consistent layout within a document. Also, by copying styles from one document to another, you can make sure that several documents have the same look. Another important benefit of styles is the ease of making changes throughout a document. Suppose, for example, you want to change the font for the body copy throughout a document. If you have defined a style for the body copy, all you have to do is to make a change to the style definition. In contrast, if you did not define a style, you would have to make the required change separately for every paragraph in the document.

There's more good news about styles. If you create a document in a word processor and define styles for the various types of paragraphs, you can usually place the document in your desktop publishing application with the styles intact. This, of course, is only true if your word processor supports styles and your desktop publishing application has a filter that supports that word processor.

Documents and styles created in Word have a high degree of compatibility with PageMaker. You may need to investigate the degree of compatibility between your word processor and desktop application.

It is beyond the scope of this book to go into the details of using styles. If you work frequently with a desktop publishing application and are not already familiar with styles, you should place a high priority on learning how to use them. Your efforts will be well rewarded.

Hints and Tips

The following is a collection of hints and tips that will help you create copy for a document. Some of them will save you time and effort; others help to give your document a professional appearance.

Paragraph Separation

You should choose between two ways of marking the end of one paragraph and the beginning of the next. One way is to leave extra space, not necessarily a full line space, between paragraphs. The other is to indent the first line of each paragraph, except the first paragraph under a headline or subhead. Do *not* indent paragraphs *and* leave space between them. If you choose indentation, use less indentation than is common in typed material. One pica (one-sixth of an inch) is adequate. Using indented rather than spaced paragraphs simplifies maintaining vertical alignment between columns.

Justification

You don't have to justify the text. Many books and other publications have left-aligned text with a ragged right margin. Some studies suggest that the ragged right margin makes text easier to read. If you choose to justify the body copy, consider using ragged right for captions and notes; this can help readers separate different kinds of text.

Headline and Subhead Text

The document you prepare with your word processor should include all headlines and subheads that are to be placed within the columns of your publications. Any headlines, subheads, or other text that are not to be placed within columns should be omitted at this stage. The purpose of this is to simplify placing text in the publication.

Headline and Subhead Styles

The styles you define for headlines, subheads, and any other text that is not body copy should be defined with appropriate leading, space before, and space after so that the spaces they occupy fit your vertical grid.

Lists

Where you have a list of items or statements, consider making these bulleted or numbered items to draw readers' attention to them. Use numbering if the order has significance, such as in a sequence of operations or when the items are in a priority order. If the order has little significance, use bullets. For numbered or bulleted lists, use a hanging indent format so that the text does not flow under the number or bullet.

Placing Copy into the Publication

Don't be in too much of a hurry to place the copy you've created with a word processor into a publication. Make sure that everybody who needs to has seen the copy and given you all their corrections. Use your spell checker and grammar checker. In other words, make sure the copy is as close as possible to its final form. When it is, save it as a file to be imported into the desktop publishing application.

The actual mechanism of placing copy varies somewhat from one desktop publishing application to another. In PageMaker, you start by creating the page layout, as described earlier in this chapter. Then you open the File menu and choose Place to open a dialog box in which you select the file to be placed. When you select a file, an icon appears representing the beginning of the text. Position that icon where the text is to start and click the mouse button. PageMaker flows the text into the publication either one column at a time or automatically into the entire document.

Figure 9.11 shows the top part of the front page of the newsletter with text placed into it. The text was created in Word with styles defining the body copy, subheads, and other text elements. These styles defined the spacing before and after paragraphs in all cases, so that the spaces before and after subheads retained the overall 12-point vertical grid, with lines of body copy in adjacent columns properly aligned.

Enhancing a Page

Desktop publishing applications provide many ways for you to enhance pages. Note that we are talking about *enhancing* pages, not decorating them. Enhancements are elements that attract readers to a page and hold their attention. Decorations, on the other hand, tend to distract readers. It's not always easy to decide whether a particular element is an enhancement or a decoration. If in doubt, leave it out!

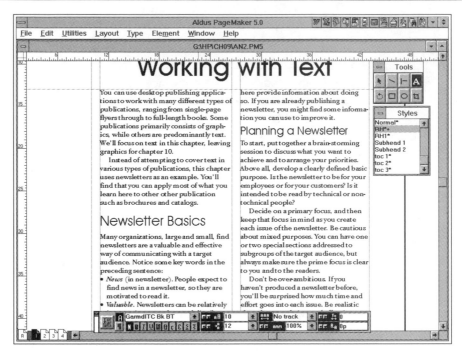

Figure 9.11 The first page of a newsletter, with text placed from a word processor.

Enhancements consist of text elements and graphic elements. We deal only with text elements here, postponing consideration of graphics to Chapter 10.

Various types of enhancements are suitable for different types of publications. Enhancements that are useful in a newsletter or consumer magazine are not appropriate for a technical publication. The enhancements described below are of the type you might use in a newsletter.

Expanding the Headline

Headlines should be short and snappy to attract readers' attention. In a few words, though, there might not be enough to convince a reader to start reading the text. That's why publications often have a short sentence, known as a *deck*, to expand on the headline.

The deck can be placed right under the headline in a font somewhat larger than that used for the body copy. An alternative is to place the deck in another prominent position on the page, such as in the narrow column at the left of our newsletter layout, as shown in Figure 9.12.

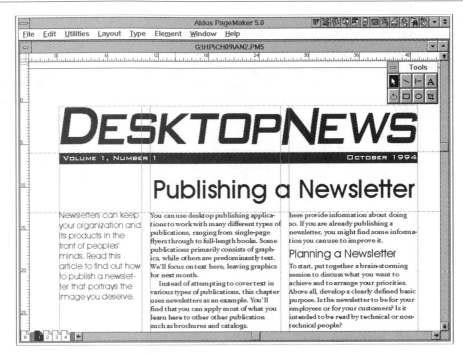

Figure 9.12 A deck in the left column of the newsletter layout.

A deck should normally consist of no more than about 20 words—enough to whet a reader's appetite.

Adding Emphasis with Pull Quotes

Pull quotes consist of text copied from the body copy and repeated in larger type on the page. Pull quotes serve three purposes:

- To emphasize important points
- To give the page a more interesting appearance
- To fill space when the available text is too short

Figure 9.13 shows an example of a pull quote on a page. In this case, the first sentence of the paragraph after the pull quote is repeated to give extra emphasis, and also to make the page more visually interesting.

Providing an Explanation in a Sidebar

A newsletter or magazine article can be made more interesting by the addition of background or supplementary information. There may be words in the article

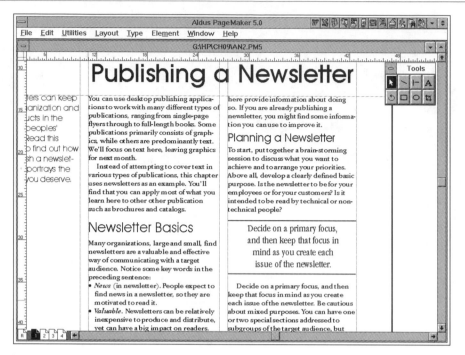

Figure 9.13 An example of a pull quote.

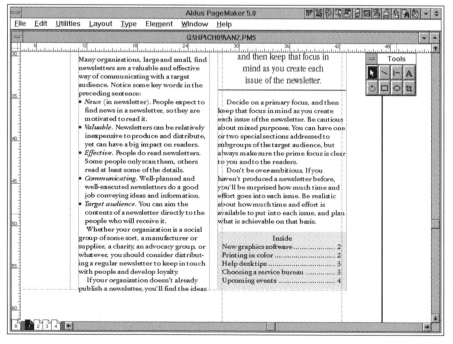

Figure 9.14 A table of contents on the front page of a newsletter.

that some readers won't understand. You want to provide this extra information, but it doesn't fit into the flow of the article. The solution is to use a *sidebar*.

A sidebar can be of almost any length. It can be set in a separate column or perhaps across the bottom of the page. Because it is separate from the body of the article, it should have some distinguishing appearance. This can be done by using a different font size or style, by enclosing it within a box, or by separating it from the rest of the page with a screen. Using boxes and screens is covered in Chapter 10.

Table of Contents

Having a table of contents on the front page is a good way of enticing readers into your newsletter. The table of contents shown in Figure 9.14 has leader dots to help the reader associate page numbers with topics. The table also has a screen to separate it from the rest of the text on the page (refer to Chapter 10 for information about screens).

10

Working with Graphics

Chapter 9 covered many aspects of working with text in documents. Now we turn to graphics, thinking particularly about preparing graphics to be printed on the 560C and 1200C printers.

The word *graphics* covers a wide range of elements that can be included in a publication, from a single straight line to a full-color photograph. How you deal with graphics depends on how the publication will be printed. If you intend to print copies of the publication on your office printer, or if you intend to print an original on your office printer and have that copied, you will use your desktop publishing application to assemble all the graphic elements. On the other hand, if a commercial print shop will print your publication, you will probably include most *line art* (images consisting of solid black with no shades of gray) in your desktop publishing file, but have the print shop assemble other graphic elements by traditional means.

As already stressed several times in this book, remember that all graphics should enhance your publication, not decorate it.

First, we'll consider some simple graphic elements you'll probably create with your desktop publishing application. In this chapter, as in the previous one, the examples used are based specifically on PageMaker. In most cases, other desktop publishing applications behave in a similar way.

Using Desktop Publishing Graphics

PageMaker and other desktop publishing applications give you the ability to draw straight lines, rectangles, and ovals that you can use to emphasize certain parts of a publication, and to separate elements on a page.

> *Note:* In the graphics world, a straight line used to separate elements on a page is known as a *rule*.

The following are some examples of how drawing tools are used.

Using a Rule to Separate Columns

The page layout for the newsletter introduced in Chapter 9 has two equal columns for text and graphics and a narrow column at the left for decks and other special items. It can be helpful to separate the narrow column from the rest of the page with a vertical rule, as shown in Figure 10.1.

You can choose a suitable width and color for the line. As with all elements, be consistent throughout your publication. If you decide to use a black line, a thickness of half a point is often a good choice. If you choose a colored line, a thickness of one point might be better. For lighter colors, use thicker lines.

Beware of using Hairline as your choice of line thickness. The reason for this caution is that it is not a precise definition and is interpreted in various ways by different applications and printer drivers. Some people interpret hairline to

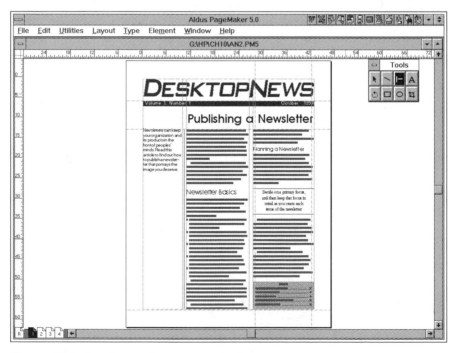

Figure 10.1 A rule used to separate columns.

mean the thinnest possible, one pixel or one dot. In some cases, the line may be so thin that it can't be seen when it's printed. Always use a specific value for line thickness.

Using a Box to Isolate Elements

Chapter 9 suggested placing a table of contents for the newsletter on the front page as a means of drawing readers into the publication. When you do so, you should make sure that the table of contents stands apart from the rest of the text on the front page. One way to do this is to enclose it in a rectangular box, as shown in Figure 10.2. Notice that the left and right edges of the box are on the column boundaries, and the width of the text has been reduced to provide a small gap between the text and the box outline.

> *Note:* Although the following information refers specifically to a rectangular box, it applies also to oval boxes.

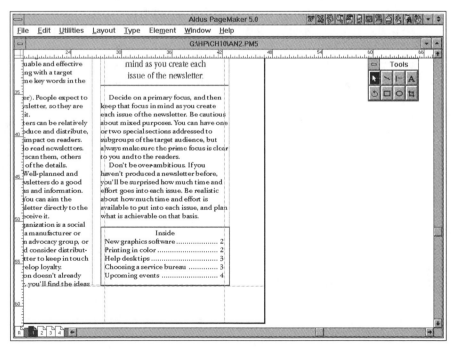

Figure 10.2 A box used to separate the table of contents from the rest of the text on a page.

By default, the interior of a box is not filled. You can think of it as a wire frame placed over the page, so that you can see everything enclosed by the box. If you choose to use one of several ways to fill the box, the interior becomes opaque so that you cannot see what it encloses. You can solve this problem by placing the box behind whatever it encloses (the way to do this is described later in this chapter).

Filling a Box

Instead of leaving the interior of a box unfilled, you can fill it with a color or with a pattern. If you choose a color, the color can be solid or screened as described below. A pattern also can be in any available color.

Adding a Screen to a Box

You can make the text enclosed in a box stand out even more by means of a uniform tint, known as a *screen*, that fills the box. The screen is formed by filling the box with dots. If the dots are black, the inside of the box appears to be gray; if the dots are colored, the box appears to have a tint.

The intensity of color in the fill depends on the spacing of the dots, which is usually specified as a percentage. For example, a 10 percent fill produces a light color by spacing dots so that only 10 percent of the space within the box is inked; a 40 percent fill produces a much more saturated color.

Choosing a screen involves some compromises. You should choose a screen that is dark enough to stand out clearly on the page, but not so dark that the text it is emphasizing is difficult to see. Also, you should not choose a screen that is so light that the separate dots of which it is composed are easily seen.

If you are using a second color in your publication, consider using that instead of black for a screen. As always, before you commit to a specific color screen, check its appearance when it is printed on the printer that will finally print your publication. Figure 9.14 shows an example of a screen used to draw attention to the table of contents on the front page of a newsletter.

Working with Layers

Earlier in this chapter, reference was made to placing a fill behind text so that the text is visible. This subject needs more explanation.

Many graphics and desktop publishing applications deal with objects in layers. You can think of layers as transparent sheets, one on top of the other. If an object on the top layer is opaque, it obscures whatever is on lower layers.

Hewlett-Packard Color Gallery

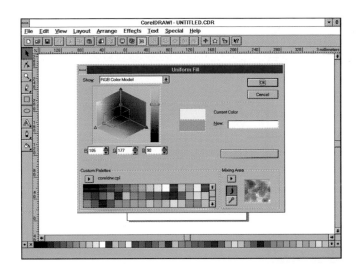

The CorelDRAW dialog box in which you can define colors using the RGB color model.

The CorelDRAW dialog box in which you can define colors using the HSB color model.

The CorelDRAW dialog box in which you can define colors using Pantone numbers.

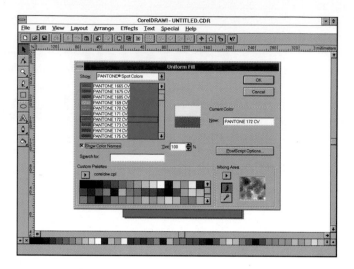

A form prepared in FormFlow and printed on a DeskJet 1200C printer.

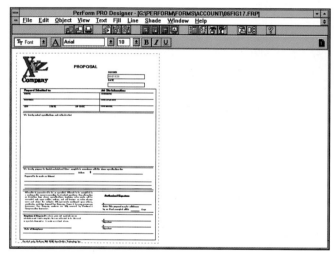

(Left) A pie chart created automatically by Excel.

(Below) A three-dimensional pie chart created in Excel.

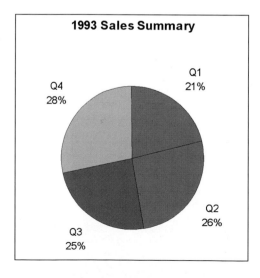

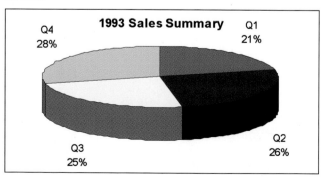

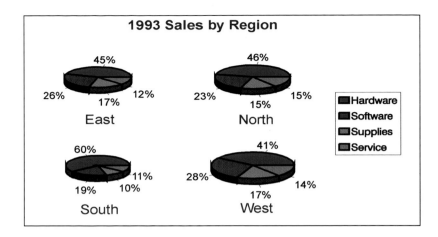

An example of multiple pie charts created by Harvard Graphics.

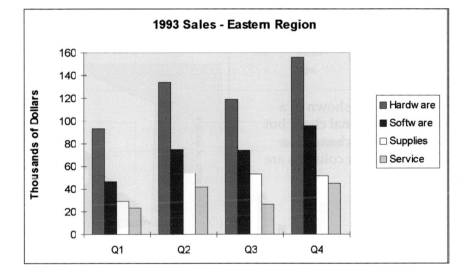

A column chart created in Excel.

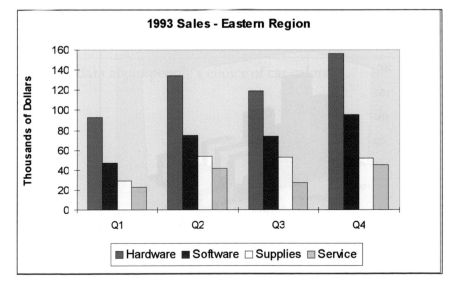

The same column chart with the legend enlarged and moved.

Some of the controls available for the ScanJet IIcx color scanner.

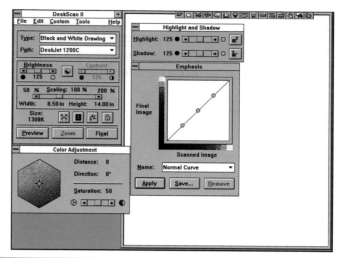

A map of the United States printed from Atlas GIS on a Deskjet 1200C printer.

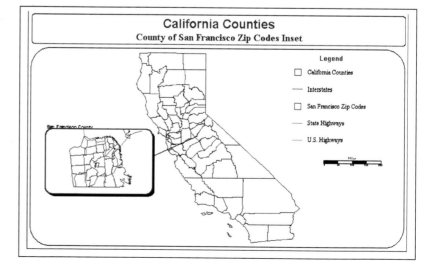

The counties in California with an inset showing zip codes in San Francisco county.

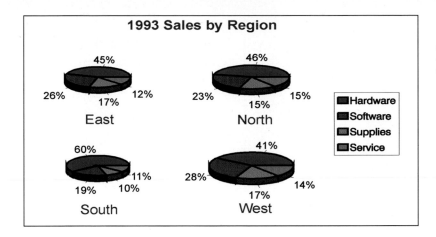

An example of multiple pie charts created by Harvard Graphics.

A column chart created in Excel.

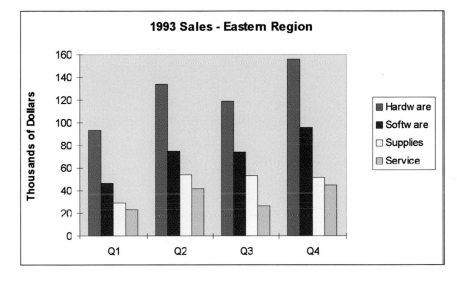

The same column chart with the legend enlarged and moved.

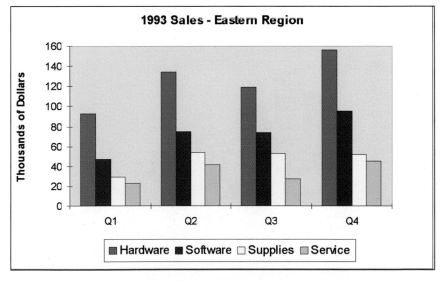

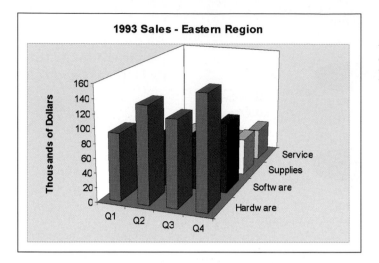

A three-dimensional column chart with some columns hidden.

The same data shown in a three-dimensional chart, but with the order changed so that the smaller columns are visible.

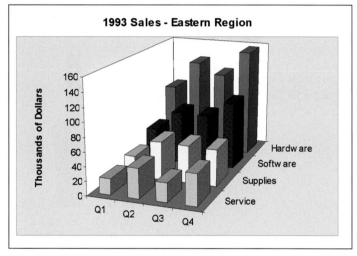

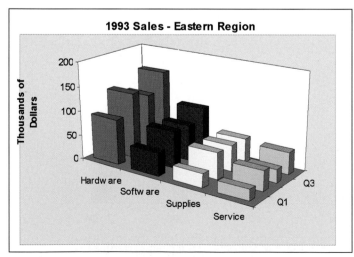

The same data shown rotated.

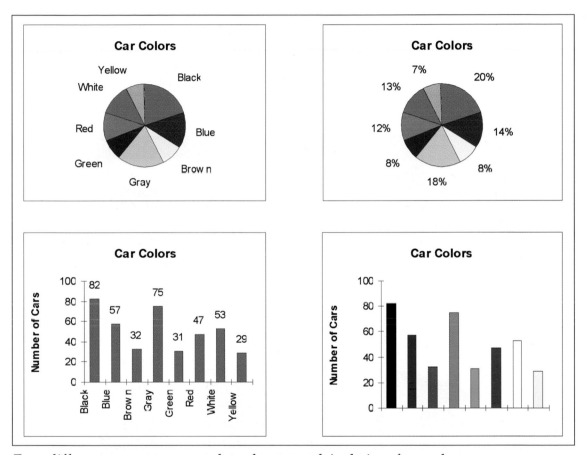

Four different ways to present data about people's choice of car colors.

A logo created from an existing font.

The effect of changing the envelope that contains text.

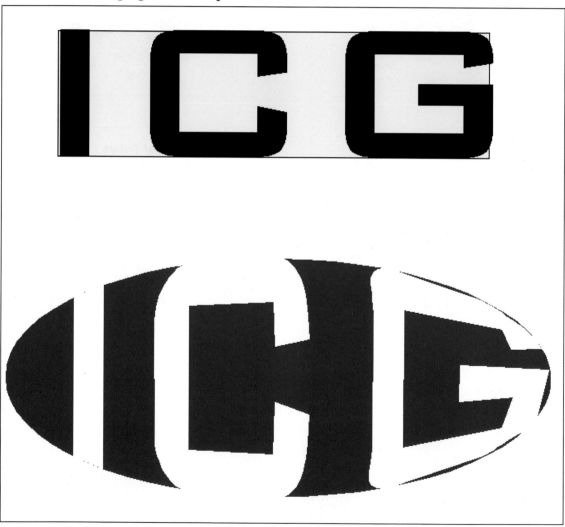

Text fitted to an oval path.

A logo created by shaping text within an envelope and fitting text.

A map created from three separate pieces of clip art, with coloring and text added.

A detailed view of a bitmap image opened in Paintbrush with each pixel visible.

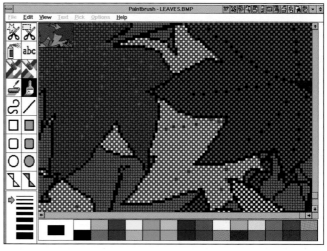

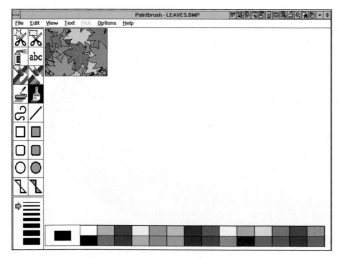

The edited bitmapped image of leaves.

A scanned image of a
Christmas ornament output
on a DeskJet printer.

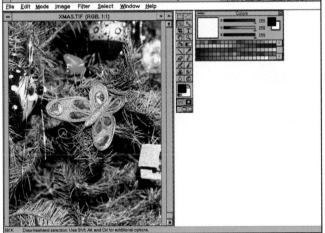

A typical Photoshop screen.

The enhanced version of the
photograph at top, with the
butterfly brightened and the
entire image sharpened.

Some of the controls available for the ScanJet IIcx color scanner.

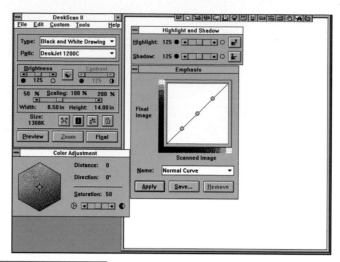

A map of the United States printed from Atlas GIS on a Deskjet 1200C printer.

The counties in California with an inset showing zip codes in San Francisco county.

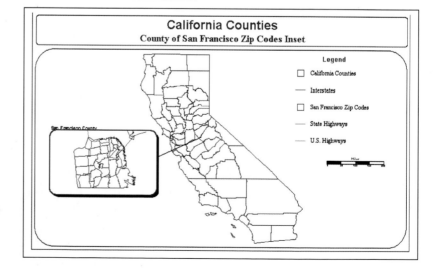

A greeting card ready to be trimmed and folded.

A photograph ready for cropping.

The Picture Window Transformation menu with Crop selected.

The Crop dialog box and the image with crop handles.

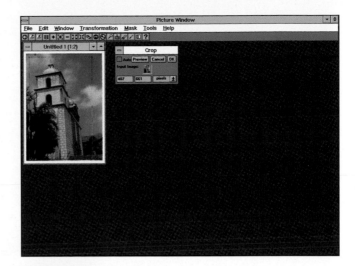

The photograph with cropping marked.

A preview of the cropped photograph.

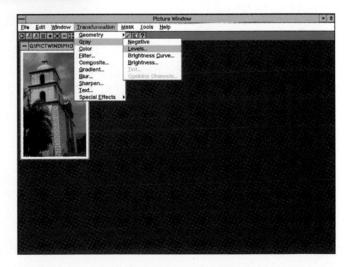

The Picture Window Transformation menu with Levels selected.

The Levels dialog box.

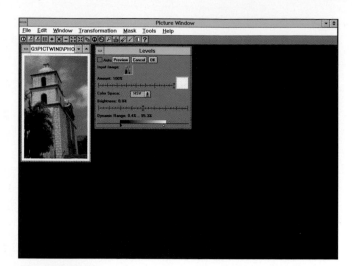

The Preview window showing the effect of brightening a photograph.

The Warp dialog box and a grid placed over the photograph.

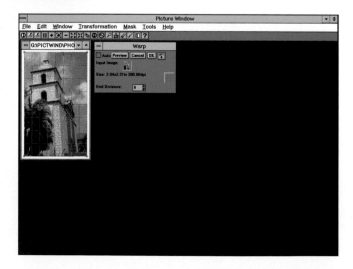

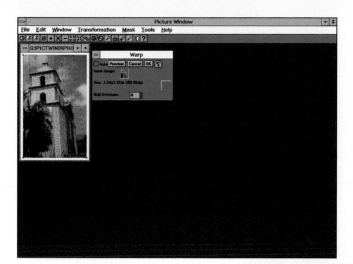

The grid set to correct a building's perspective.

A photograph of a house.

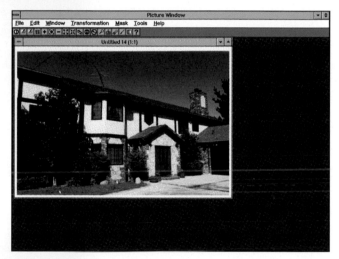

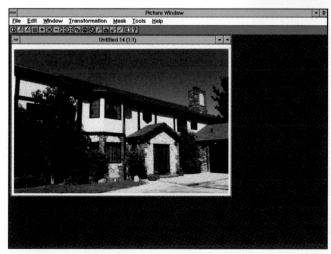

The cable and television antenna removed from the sky by cloning.

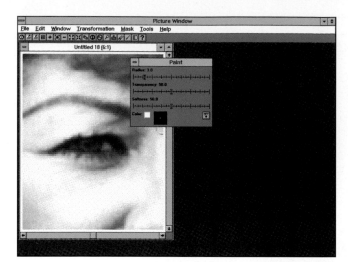

The Paint dialog box.

The Paint Color dialog box.

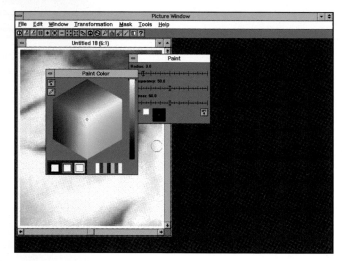

Eyes with enhanced highlights.

However, if an object on the top layer is transparent, everything on the next layer is visible.

Applications deal with layers in different ways. In PageMaker, each object you create exists on a separate layer, with the most recent object created or modified on top. CorelDRAW allows you to place as many objects as you like on each layer.

You can change the order of layers so that the appropriate ones are visible. In PageMaker, you select an object, open the Element menu, and choose Bring to Front or Send to Back. In CorelDRAW, you select an object, open the Arrange menu, and choose Order; then you can choose among To Front, To Back, Forward One, Back One, or Reverse Order.

As you work with objects in your desktop publishing application, you will sometimes seem to lose objects. This is often because the object you can't find is hidden by something on a layer above it. You can often solve this problem by sending an object you can see to the back.

Importing Graphics from Other Applications

Regard the graphics capabilities of your desktop publishing application as a bonus, not as a limitation on what you can do. Such capabilities as drawing lines and boxes are useful, but when you want more, expect to create what you need in another application and then place it in the desktop publishing document.

You can't create gradient fills and textures in PageMaker, but you can easily do so in a graphics application and then place them into a PageMaker document. Unlike the uniform fills you can create in PageMaker, a gradient fill is a fill that smoothly changes from one shade to another, or even from one color to another.

Creating Gradient Fills and Textures in CorelDRAW

You can use CorelDRAW (PC), Canvas (Macintosh and PC) or several other graphics applications to create a gradient fill that you can subsequently place in a PageMaker publication. You may find some experimentation is required before you can get this to work exactly the way you want it. Here's one technique you can use to create a gradient fill:

1. In PageMaker, decide the exact size of the box you need.

2. Open CorelDRAW and draw the box at exactly the right size.

3. Using CorelDRAW's Fill roll-up, choose gradient fill, the type of gradient fill, and the colors.

> *Note:* A roll-up in CorelDRAW is a type of dialog box that remains on the screen after you use it to make choices and selections. When you are not using a roll-up, you can roll it up, leaving only the title bar displayed.

4. Save the rectangle with its fill as a CDR file.

5. With the filled box selected, open the File menu and choose Export to display the Export dialog box.

6. In the List Files of Type drop-down list box, choose TIFF Bitmap.

7. Click the Selected Only check box so that you save only the filled box (not the complete CorelDRAW page).

8. Click OK to display the Bitmap Export dialog box.

9. At the top of this dialog box, select the number of colors you want to save and, if it is available, click the Dithered check box.

10. Click OK to save the filled box.

11. Close or minimize CorelDRAW.

12. If necessary, restore PageMaker; then place the TIFF file into the document.

> *Note:* Step 4 is necessary in case you want to modify the fill in CorelDRAW at a later time.

You will probably see some banding in the filled box as it appears on your screen. This effect should almost entirely disappear when the publication is printed. If you do see significant banding in the printed publication, it may be because you didn't select Dithered in the BitMap Export dialog box.

The steps above are specific for CorelDRAW and PageMaker. You can use other applications to produce a similar effect, although the steps may be different. In order to get optimum results, be prepared to experiment with the way you transfer the box from your graphics application to your desktop publishing application. You can try transferring by way of the Clipboard or as a file in several formats. You will find that some give significantly better results than others.

Figure 10.3 shows four examples of the many types of fills you can create with CorelDRAW: a linear fill at the top left, a conical fill at the bottom left, and two different types of textures at the right. Linear, conical, and texture fills, used judiciously, can be more attractive than solid fills.

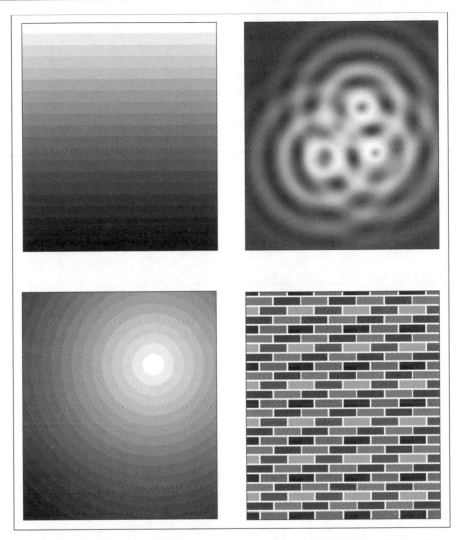

Figure 10.3 Examples of fills you can create in CorelDRAW and place into a publication.

Importing Special Kinds of Objects

The special kinds of objects we're referring to here are graphics that other applications are specifically intended to create. It's not unknown for people who want to include an organization chart or other kind of block diagram into a publication to create the diagram using their desktop publishing application's ability to draw rectangles and lines. Don't attempt that unless, of course, there is no way for you to get access to an application designed to create diagrams. You can create charts of this type far more easily in a charting application such as Visio, or in a general-purpose drawing application such as CorelDRAW, SuperPaint, or MacDraw.

The same goes for pie charts, bar charts, and line charts. Yes, you can create these types of charts in a desktop publications application if you have enough patience. But you can accomplish the same type of task much more efficiently in a spreadsheet program such as Excel.

Chapter 7 covered these types of graphics under the general heading of business graphics. Refer to that chapter for detailed information about creating them. You can move them into a desktop publishing application by way of the Clipboard or by saving them as files and then importing them. As always, when you are moving graphics from one application to another, be prepared to experiment to find the way that gives you the results you want.

Creating Custom Graphics

By custom graphics, we mean anything that is not one of the special-purpose graphics referred to in the preceding section. There are two types of graphics applications you can use: those that created bitmapped graphics, and those that create vector graphics. Refer to Chapter 5 for information about the differences between the two.

There are many type of graphics you can create, limited only by your artistic skills. These include:

- Advertising graphics
- Assembly diagrams
- Book covers
- Cartoons
- Educational illustrations
- Instruction manual illustrations
- Logos
- Product packaging
- Sketches of products
- Works of art

It is way beyond the scope of this book to suggest how you can put to good use the many capabilities included in today's graphics applications, so we'll sidestep that issue completely and, instead, concentrate on how you can modify existing images to suit your needs.

Using Vector Graphics Applications

There are endless possibilities for using vector graphics applications, such as CorelDRAW, which is used for the examples here. You can achieve similar results with Adobe Illustrator, which is available in almost identical Macintosh and Windows versions. Two of the things you can do are to modify text and clip art.

One of the big benefits of working with vector graphics—as opposed to bitmapped graphics—applications is that vector images are scalable without restriction. A logo, for example, can be scaled for use on stationery of various types, in publications, and on product packaging. A disadvantage of vector graphics is that they are not suitable for realistic images. You are not likely to have much success drawing a person's face with a vector graphics application.

Modifying Text

Creating logos is one common use of vector graphics programs. Logos are widely used to give graphic identities to corporate entities, products, events, and the like. When creating logos you should make them simple and graphically consistent with what they represent.

Many effective logos consist primarily of alphabetic characters—the HP, IBM, and AT&T logos are well-known examples. You can easily create logos of this type by using a graphics application to modify an existing font, as illustrated by Figure 10.4.

This logo was created from BankGothic medium in CorelDRAW. The characters *ComputerGraphics* have a smaller-than-normal character spacing. The characters *International* also are closer than normal, and the whole word is stretched to match the width of the bottom line. The intention here is to create a bold, strong logo that has a computer feel about it. Perhaps you could do better!

The same technique is often used to design text for product packages. You can learn a lot by looking at the packages in your local supermarket and thinking about how the lettering was created. Book covers also provide many examples of the ways fonts can be used creatively.

Figure 10.4 A logo created from an existing font.

Figure 10.5 The effect of changing the envelope that contains text.

Shaping Text Within an Envelope

Another interesting possibility you can use when creating logos is to change the shape of words. The overall shape that contains words is referred to as an envelope and is normally rectangular. You can change the shape of this envelope to create interesting effects. Figure 10.5 shows some text at the top in the rectangular envelope in which it is initially created, and below that, the same text after the envelope has been stretched in two different ways.

Fitting Text to a Curve

You can also fit text around a curve. In CorelDRAW, first draw a curve and create the text. Then, with the text and the curve selected, open the Text menu, and choose Fit Text to Path to open the Fit Text To Path roll-up. In the roll-up, click Apply and the text immediately reappears on the path, as shown in Figure 10.6. In this example, text is fitted to the same path as that was used as an envelope in the previous example.

You can combine shaping text within an envelope and fitting it to a path to create designs for logos. Figure 10.7 shows an example.

Working with Clip Art

Many applications, word processors as well as graphics applications, provide a range of copyright-free clip art you can use to enhance your publications. Each piece of clip art you use should serve two purposes: it should relieve the

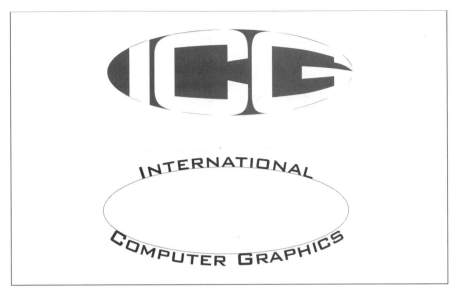

Figure 10.6 Text fitted to an oval path.

monotony of a page that would otherwise consist of solid text, and it should reinforce the message on the page. Don't fall into the trap of decorating your pages with clip art!

Remember that thousands of people have access to the clip art that comes with widely used applications such as Word and CorelDRAW. While it's usually fine to use this type of clip art in publications that have a small, local readership, you should be careful about using them in a publication that has widespread readership. You probably don't want your readers to see the art in your prestigious publication also used in the local tennis club newsletter.

Figure 10.7 A logo created by shaping text within an envelope and fitting text to curves.

One more word of caution. Just because it's clip art doesn't necessarily mean that it's not copyrighted. If it is copyrighted, you must get permission to use it in any publication.

You can make any changes you wish to noncopyrighted clip art. You can:

- Change its size or proportions
- Crop it
- Rotate or skew it
- Change its colors
- Add to it or delete from it

As an example of what you can do with vector graphics clip art, suppose your newsletter contains an article that mentions the two facilities where Hewlett-Packard inkjet printers are produced, San Diego in California and Vancouver in Washington. You could enhance the article with a map showing the locations of these cities.

Fortunately, you don't have to draw the map yourself, because the clip art that is packaged with CorelDRAW includes outlines of every state in the United States (and also of almost every country in the world). You can import the outlines of the western states into CorelDRAW, position them, color the states to clearly define each one, and mark the two cities of interest. Figure 10.8 shows the result.

An interesting effect to use sometimes is to place a shadow behind a graphics image, as in Figure 10.9. This was done by duplicating the entire image, with the exception of the city names, changing the color to black, moving the duplicate so that it is slightly offset from the colored image, and then placing the black image on a layer behind the colored image.

There is more information about working with maps later in this chapter.

Working with Bitmapped Graphics

Bitmapped graphics are images in which you work with individual pixels. With sufficient artistic skill, you can use bitmapped graphics applications to achieve effects that are close to impossible with vector graphics applications. Most bitmapped graphics applications include an airbrush tool you can use to spray paint over an area.

Although you can use bitmapped graphics applications to draw geometric shapes such as rectangles and ovals, once these objects are drawn, they exist as patterns of individual dots rather than as complete objects, as they are in vector graphics applications.

Figure 10.8 A map created from three separate pieces of clip art, with coloring and text added.

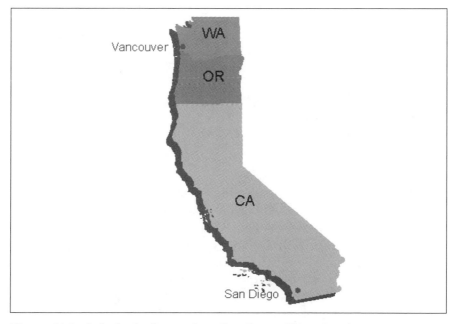

Figure 10.9 A dark shadow enhancing the outline of an image.

Note: A recently available graphics application, Altamira Composer, make it possible to work with components of bitmapped graphics as objects in the Windows environment.

Various bitmapped graphics applications are available. At the low end are MacPaint, which is packaged with some Macintosh computers, and Paintbrush, packaged with Windows. At the high end are Photoshop, available in Macintosh and Windows versions, and Corel PHOTO-PAINT (Windows).

You can use these applications in two ways: to create original art and to modify existing art.

Creating Original Art

If you are already an accomplished artist, you might like to experiment with a bitmapped graphics application. If you like to work with cartoons or other relatively simple art, a low-end application and a fairly standard computer should prove adequate. However, for more sophisticated work, you will need a high-end application and a powerful computer.

Hint: Most people find it's much easier to work with a graphics tablet rather than a mouse.

It's beyond the scope of this book (and beyond the ability of this author) to provide advice about creating original art. To keep up to date with what artists are doing in this medium, you should subscribe to a magazine such as *Computer Graphics World*.

We'll concentrate here on using bitmapped graphics applications for modifying existing graphics.

Modifying Existing Art

You can use a low-end application to edit a simple bitmapped graphics image, such as the leaves shown in Figure 10.10, open in Paintbrush.

As an example of modifying the image, you can easily lighten the dark green leaf at the right. To change the color of most of the image, just pick a lighter green from the palette at the bottom of the screen and paint over as much of the leaf as you can, without getting too close to the edge. To finalize the image, open the View menu, choose Zoom, and select the area where you want to work in detail. Now you see a detailed view of the image, as shown in Figure 10.11, with each pixel showing separately.

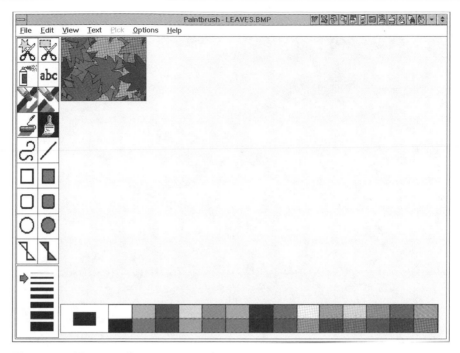

Figure 10.10 A bitmap image open in Paintbrush.

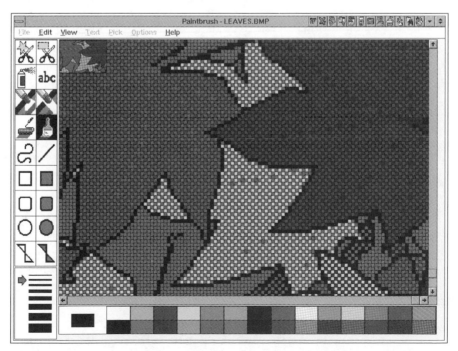

Figure 10.11 A detailed view of the image with each pixel visible.

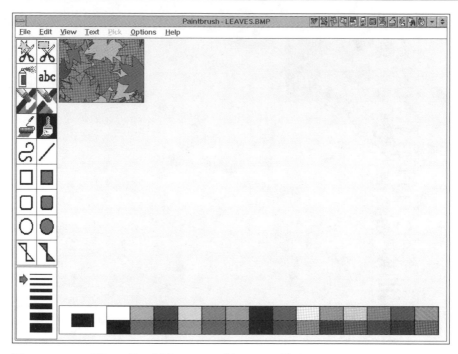

Figure 10.12 The edited bitmapped image of leaves.

In this view, you can easily change the color of individual pixels right up to the edge of the leaf. Just select the color in the palette, and click each pixel you want to change. After you've finished, open the View menu again and choose Zoom Out to see the complete image in its original size, as in Figure 10.12.

As you can see, it's quite easy to work with small images in a fairly basic bitmap graphics application. You wouldn't want to work this way, though, to attempt delicate editing tasks on an complex image such as a scanned photograph. You should use a high-end application such as Photoshop for this type of work.

To see Photoshop in action, we'll use the scanned image of a Christmas tree ornament, shown in its original form in Figure 10.13. (These photographs, reproduced from images printed by the DeskJet 560C and 1200C printers, give you a good idea of the quality these printers can produce.) The objective is to add some sparkle to the picture by sharpening it and brightening the butterfly.

You work with Photoshop in a screen somewhat similar to the one in Paintbrush, but with many more capabilities. Figure 10.14 shows a typical Photoshop screen. The toolbox, shown near the center, contains the tools available for working with the image. The color palette at the right shows the colors initially available.

Figure 10.13 Scanned images of a Christmas ornament printed on the DeskJet 560C (top) and 1200C (bottom) printers.

Figure 10.14 **A typical Photoshop screen.**

You can, of course, do much more in Photoshop than in Paintbrush. In particular, there are numerous subtle effects, including various ways to sharpen an image. One of the more useful sharpening effects is unknown as Unsharp Mask. Although the name suggests the opposite, the effect of Unsharp Mask is to increase the contrast between pixels at the edges of image elements and so give the image a sharper appearance. To sharpen the entire image, open the Filter menu, choose Sharpen, and then in the submenu choose Unsharp Mask to display the Unsharp Mask dialog box. Click OK to apply the mask to the image.

Tip: You can, if you like, select a specific region of the image by using the rectangle or ellipse section tools (or by using the lasso tool to select an irregular shape) and then apply the mask to just the selected region.

Another very useful capability when working with photographic images lets you adjust the brightness and contrast of specific regions. To do this, first select the lasso tool in the toolbox (the second tool in the left column) and use it to trace around the part of the image you want to adjust. Then open the Image menu, choose Adjust, and in the submenu choose Brightness/Contrast to display the Brightness/Contrast dialog box.

Figure 10.15 The enhanced version of the photograph in Figure 10.13, with the butterfly brightened and the entire image sharpened.

To increase the brightness of the selected part of the image, just drag the Brightness slider to the right; as you do so, you immediately see the effect on your screen. You can also drag the Contrast slider to increase or decrease the contrast within the selected area of the image. The effect of changes like this is shown in the enhanced image in Figure 10.15.

This single example provides only a small sample of what you can do with a high-end bitmapped graphics application.

Scanning Images

A *scanner*, a device that converts images on paper to bitmapped files, is a desirable, some say essential, accessory for anyone who is more than casually involved in desktop publishing.

There are three classes of scanners: hand-held, desktop, and high-definition. Hand-held scanners are the least expensive. Typically 3 or 4 inches wide, they are simply dragged over an image to convert the image to a file. Although a little difficult to use at first, after some practice they are quite satisfactory for scanning small images. Grayscale and color hand-held scanners are available.

Desktop scanners, typically about the size of a desktop copier, can accept documents up to ordinary letter or legal size, which is more than adequate for most purposes. Like hand-held scanners, desktop scanners are available in grayscale and color versions. Although originally much more expensive than hand-held scanners, the price of desktop scanners has recently dropped to the extent that their benefits far outweigh the higher cost.

Hand-held and desktop scanners are generally limited to a scanning resolution of 300 or 400 dots per inch, which is adequate for most desktop publishing work. Where higher scanning resolution is required, such as when preparing photographs for printing in high-quality publications, it is necessary to use a high-definition scanner. Scanners of this type provide a resolution of 1200 or 2400 dots per inch and cost many times more than typical desktop scanners. They are usually owned by service bureaus that provide imaging and prepress services for commercial printers.

> *Note:* Specifications for scanners often include two figures for resolution: optical and interpolated. The optical resolution specifies the maximum number of dots per inch the scanner can detect. The interpolated resolution is the maximum number of dots per inch the scanner driver can save in a file. The scanner driver adds dots by averaging the actual dots the scanner reads. It is the optical resolution that actually defines the scanner performance.

Most hand-held and desktop scanners can scan only reflective copy such as photographic prints and drawings. They cannot ordinarily scan transparencies such as 35-mm slides. It is possible to purchase a transparency adapter for some desktop scanners such as the HP ScanJet IIcx, but these accessories cost almost as much as the scanner itself. High-definition scanners, on the other hand, are primarily intended for scanning transparencies, because transparencies are the preferred medium for professional work.

Using a Desktop Scanner

We deal only with desktop scanners in the next few paragraphs, because this is the type of scanner you will probably use. A hand-held scanner is not generally adequate for serious color work. A high-definition scanner is normally the province of full-time professionals who provide support for photographers and commercial printers.

You may think of a scanner only in terms of creating a graphics file from an existing illustration. However, once you have one, you will find it has other uses.

Many people, including trained artists, find that creating a drawing or painting with a graphics application is far from easy. Quite often, a sketch that requires only a few minutes with a pencil on paper takes much longer to create on screen. The solution is to do what you have always done—create the original drawing or painting on paper, scan it, and proceed from there. You may find that this simple tip can save a lot of time.

Do you sometimes spend time retyping printed material because you need it in a file? By adding *optical character recognition* (OCR) software, you can use your scanner to read printed pages with a surprisingly high degree of accuracy. You can experiment with OCR using the bundled capability that comes with CorelDRAW and Image-In. For more sophisticated use, you may need one of the leading OCR applications such as OmniPage or WordScan.

One more use of a scanner, this time in conjunction with your printer, is as a copier. If you have a color scanner and a color printer, your scanning software probably lets you print a scanned image directly. While this process is quite slow, it saves a trip to the local copy center when you need an occasional color copy.

Calibrating a Scanner

When you are working in color, you want the colors in the final printed publication to be the same as those in the original you scanned. There are several stages between the original image that is scanned and that image as it is printed; these stages are known as the *print path*. Calibration is the process of making adjustments so that the colors of the image you see on your screen before you scan correspond to the colors in the printed publication.

For the present, we assume that your scanner is properly calibrated. Refer to Chapter 13 for more information about calibration.

Optimizing Scan Resolution

Your computer communicates with a scanner by way of a driver, similar in concept to a printer driver, that is usually provided by the scanner manufacturer. One of the functions of the driver is to allow you to choose the scanning resolution, up to the maximum of which the scanner is capable.

In choosing a scanning resolution, you should aim to scan as much detail as the printer that will print the image can reproduce. If you choose a higher scanning resolution, all you achieve is having a larger image file than necessary.

Not only does this waste disk space, but it also becomes more difficult to transport from one computer to another, and to work with the image if any modifications have to be made (which is usually the case).

The rule-of-thumb developed for scanning an image that is subsequently to be printed on an offset press is to use a scanning resolution that is twice the line screen the print shop will use to create the printing plates for an offset printing press. Inkjet printers don't use line screens to create printing plates, but an equivalent line screen figure exists. For 560C or 1200C printers, the equivalent line screen is 53. This means that the ideal scanning resolution is about 100 dots per inch. You can set this resolution in the DeskScan II's Print Path dialog box if you are using an HP scanner.

Optimizing a Scan

Your scanner driver gives you a great deal of control over a scanned image. Figure 10.16 shows some of the controls available when you use HP's DeskScan driver to control the ScanJet IIcx color scanner.

The information about optimizing a scan that follows applies specifically to the HP ScanJet IIcx. Other types of scanners have similar controls.

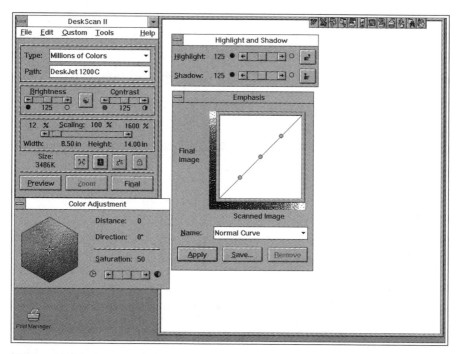

Figure 10.16 Some of the controls available for the ScanJet IIcx color scanner.

Your objective should be to get the best possible scanned image. Subsequently, you can make minor adjustments to the image with a graphics application. It is not a good idea to accept the automatic settings of your scanner and rely on the graphics application to optimize the image.

Choosing the Type of File to Save

If you have a color scanner, you can choose among several types of file formats for the scanned image. You should choose the file type that corresponds to the way you will use the file. If you are going to print the scanned image in black and white, for example, there is no point in scanning it in color.

You can choose among file types such as:

- Black-and-white drawing
- Color drawing
- Black-and-white halftone
- Color halftone
- Black-and-white photograph
- Color photo (8-bit color)
- Millions of colors (24-bit color)

You can save the scanned file in various data formats. The DeskScan application that comes with the ScanJet IIcx for the Macintosh can save files in the following formats:

- EPS (with or without an image that can be displayed on the screen)
- MacPaint
- PICT
- PICT Compressed
- TIFF
- TIFF Compressed

The DeskScan application that comes with the ScanJet IIcx for the PC can save files in the following formats:

- EPSF (with or without an image that can be displayed on the screen)
- OS/2 Bitmap
- Paintbrush (PCX)
- TIFF 5.0
- TIFF 5.0 Compressed
- Windows Bitmap

See Appendix C for information about these file formats.

You should save the scanned image in the format that works best with your application. The documentation that comes with the application may have advice about this, or you may have to experiment.

Be aware that graphics files can be quite large, particularly in the case of high-resolution 24-bit color images. You need a way to save these files so that you don't quickly run out of hard disk space. You also sometimes need to move a file from one computer to another. If your files are too large to fit on a floppy disk, some possible solutions are:

- To move a large file from one computer to another, connect the two computers to a network so that you can easily share files.
- Upload the file to a bulletin board or communications service, and then download it to the other computer.
- Use a compression utility, such as Stuffit (Macintosh) or PKZip (PC), to reduce the size of the file so that it will fit on a floppy disk.
- Copy the file onto several disks or onto magnetic tape using a backup utility.
- Use an application such as Split to divide a large file into several files.
- Use a high-capacity removable disk, such as those available from Scitex.

As you see, there are a variety of methods of dealing with very large files, some inexpensive and inconvenient, others expensive and convenient. Choose whichever makes sense for your work.

Cropping and Scaling the Image to Be Scanned

You should crop the image so that you scan only the part that will be used in your printed publication. If you scan any more than that, you get an unnecessarily large image file and you have to use your graphics or desktop publishing application to crop it later.

To crop the scanned image, click the Preview button in the DeskScan window. After a few seconds, a preview image appears on your screen. Drag the border around the preview image to mark the rectangular area that is to appear in the final scanned image file. You can see the exact size of the cropped image on the screen.

As an alternative to defining a rectangular area, you can define any irregular shape as an area to be scanned. By doing so, you can minimize the size of the image file and save yourself time later when working with the image in a graphics or desktop publishing application. To define an irregular shape on an HP DeskJet scanner, hold down the Command key (Macintosh) or Ctrl key (Windows), hold down the mouse button, and drag to draw around the part of the image you want to scan.

The scanner driver allows you to scale the scan, usually over a very wide range. You should choose a scaling factor such that the scan is exactly the size it will appear in the printed publication. This is important because the scanned image is a bitmapped graphic and, as explained earlier in this chapter, you cannot satisfactorily adjust the size of bitmapped graphics.

Scaling is usually proportional so that the horizontal and vertical sizes keep the same ratio. However, you can choose nonuniform scaling in order to change the horizontal and vertical scaling independently.

In order to calculate the scaling factor required, you must have previously planned your publication so that you know the exact size each scanned image will be when printed. Then you can calculate the scaling factor.

Adjusting the Brightness and Contrast

When the scanner previews an image, it automatically adjusts brightness and contrast to suit the range of that image. This has advantages and disadvantages similar to those of an automatic camera. It usually produces an acceptable image but almost never the best one.

You can adjust the brightness and contrast manually to improve the overall appearance of the image.

Controlling Shadows and Highlights

By default, a scanned image is adjusted so that the lightest area appears white and the darkest area appears black. You can adjust the shadow areas of the image so that lighter areas become black, which has the effect of hiding details in the shadows. You can also adjust the highlight areas so that darker areas become white, which has the effect of hiding details in the highlights. Either of these adjustments creates more contrast in the midtones.

Changing the Emphasis

By default, the tones in the scanned image are in proportion to the tones in the original image, as indicated by the straight line in the Emphasis window. You can alter this relation, choosing instead to lighten midtones, darken midtones, or show more contrast in shadows. You can also change the emphasis curve manually to obtain special effects.

Adjusting the Color

You can adjust the overall color balance of an image. This might be necessary, for example, if you have a photograph with an overall green cast, such as happens when a photograph is taken under fluorescent lights without proper filtration. You can compensate for a color cast by introducing a compensating overall color in the Color Adjustment window.

You can also change the overall color saturation, reducing the color saturation to make the image paler, or increasing the saturation to make the image more vivid.

Using Other Controls

The scanner driver may provide other controls you can use to optimize the scanned image. DeskScan, for example, lets you create a scanned image that is a mirrored or negative version of the original. You can also sharpen a scanned image to enhance details.

Scanning Images Yourself or Having Them Scanned by a Service Bureau

You can choose between scanning images yourself or having images scanned by a service bureau. If you need a high-definition scanned image, you probably don't have a choice. However, if you need a lower-definition image, there are benefits in scanning the image yourself.

This chapter has devoted a considerable amount of space to scanning because it is important for you to understand that there is a lot more to scanning than just pushing a button. By making adjustments to the scanning parameters, you can create thousands of different scanned images from one original. Of those thousands, some will be easy to work with to get the effect you want on the printed page. Other scans will be difficult, perhaps impossible, to work with.

Some scanning choices can be specified exactly. You can, for example, state the scanning resolution, indicate the cropping, and specify scaling factors. Other choices are a matter of personal judgment.

If at all possible, you should create your own scanned images so that you make the choices that best suit your needs. You can also rescan an image if your first attempt does not prove satisfactory.

If you choose to have a service bureau create scanned images, make sure you choose a bureau that understands your needs and is prepared to put the necessary amount of effort into providing the optimum image. Also, be prepared to pay extra for that level of service.

Working with Special Graphics Applications

In addition to the general-purpose bitmapped and vector graphics applications already mentioned in this book, numerous special-purpose applications are available. If you have a particular field of interest that involves working with graphics, you should look into the availability of applications targeted for that field, rather than try to use general-purpose graphics applications.

As examples of special graphics applications, the following sections refer briefly to computer-aided design and mapping.

Computer-Aided Design

One well-known category of graphics applications is *Computer-Aided Design* (CAD). These applications can be used for architectural, electrical, electronic, mechanical, and other design purposes. Printed output from these applications is usually in much larger format than can be handled by home and office printers. However, in cases where smaller printed output is adequate, your inkjet printer can do the job.

Chapter 12 contains some information about using applications of this type at the personal level for home and garden planning.

Mapping Applications

An earlier section of this chapter referred to using maps available as clip art to illustrate your work. While clip-art maps are easy to use and might be suitable for simple illustrations, these maps are inadequate for more sophisticated needs. In these cases, you need to use mapping applications, such as Atlas GIS.

With Atlas GIS and similar applications, you can create maps with virtually any level of detail. Drawing maps is only one aspect of the capabilities of Atlas GIS. The abbreviation *GIS* stands for *Geographic Information System*, a phrase that indicates the scope of the application's capabilities. You can think of the product as a database application that deals specifically with data about geographic areas. Here, though, we look at Atlas GIS only as a means of creating and printing maps.

Atlas GIS is supplied with several sample maps and accompanying data. Among these is a map of the United States, with all the states, counties, major cities, and interstate highways marked. Figure 10.17 shows this map printed on a DeskJet 1200C printer.

The color capability of the 560C and 1200C printers is particularly valuable when you need to reproduce an illustration as complex as this. With Atlas GIS, you can choose appropriate colors for each feature of the map. In this case, state boundaries are in black, county boundaries in gray, interstate highways in blue, and major cities in green. Because each type of feature is on a separate layer, you can choose which features to print.

You can easily magnify sections of the map to show more detail within specific regions. Figure 10.18, for example, shows the counties in California with an inset of San Francisco showing zip code boundaries.

Figure 10.17 A map of the United States printed from Atlas GIS on a DeskJet 1200C printer.

Figure 10.18 The counties in California with an inset showing zip codes in San Francisco county.

Placing Graphics into a Publication

Desktop publishing applications can accept graphics in many different formats.

There are two methods for copying graphics from a graphics application to a desktop publishing application: by way of the Clipboard, or by saving as a file and then placing. The quality of the imported image can sometimes vary significantly depending on the method chosen and, in the case of the second method, on the filter used, so it's worth experimenting to see which gives you the results you are looking for. What works for one application may not work so well for another.

Using the Clipboard

Copying from a graphics application is much the same in the Macintosh and Windows environments. In either case, you select the graphic in the application in which it was created, open the Edit menu, and choose Copy to place a copy of the graphic in the Clipboard. Then you open the desktop publishing application, open the Edit menu, and choose Paste to display an icon that represents the graphic. Move the icon to the position where you want the top-left corner of the graphic to be, and click the mouse button.

PageMaker can use *Object Linking and Embedding* (OLE) to link or embed graphic objects in the Macintosh and Windows environments. Many Windows applications, but not so many Macintosh applications, are compatible with this technology.

When you use Paste to place a graphic in your PageMaker publication, as described above, you embed that graphic. This means that a complete copy of the graphic exists within the PageMaker publication and that the copy is independent of the graphic in the application in which it was created. If you want to edit the graphic embedded in the PageMaker publication, double-click on the graphic to open the application in which it was created, make any changes, open the File menu, and choose Exit & Return or Update (or a command with a similar name) to return to the PageMaker publication.

Linking is an alternative to embedding. To place a linked graphic in a PageMaker publication, open the Edit menu and choose Paste Special to open the Paste Special dialog box. In that dialog box, choose Paste Link if it is available (Paste Link is dimmed and not available if the application in which the graphic was created does not support linking). The graphic appears in the publication ready for you to drag it into position.

A linked object retains a link to the object in the application in which it was created. This means you can change the object in the application in which it was created and then update any or all publications in which that object occurs.

To gain a more complete understanding of linking and embedding, you should consult your desktop publishing and graphics applications' documentation.

Placing Graphics Files

You can create graphics objects in various applications, save them as files, and then place them into PageMaker.

To place an object in a PageMaker publication, open the File menu and choose Place to display the Place Document dialog box. By default, the dialog box contains a list of all importable files in the current directory. If necessary, select the directory that contains the file you want to place, select the file name, and click OK.

If the file you select is small, PageMaker displays an icon representing the graphic. Position the icon where you want the top-left corner of the graphic to be, and click the mouse button to display the graphic. If the graphic file you select is larger than 256 kilobytes, PageMaker displays a message asking if you want to include a complete copy of the graphic in the publication. If you click Yes, the entire file is copied into the publication; if you click No, only a low-resolution version of the file, suitable for displaying an on-screen image, is copied into the publication, and a link to the original version is established. Whichever choice you make, the graphic is displayed in your publication.

> *Note:* Whether you choose to place a low-resolution or high-resolution image into your publication file, PageMaker uses the high-definition image for printing.

Resizing an Image

After you have placed an image in a PageMaker publication, either by way of the Clipboard or from a file, you can change its size.

If the image is in vector format, you can resize it without restriction and without causing any undesirable moiré patterns in the final printed image. The easiest way to resize an image is to select it and then drag a handle. Hold down the Shift key while you drag to maintain the same aspect ratio, as in the original. An alternative method of resizing an image is with the PageMaker control palette; you can change the image dimensions to specific values or to a specific percentage of the original size.

If the image is a bitmapped graphic, you can also resize it without restriction using the same methods as for vector graphics. However, to avoid moiré patterns in the final printed image, you should only choose those sizes that are exact multiples of the resolution of the printer on which the publication will be printed. To do this, make sure you have properly set the printer resolution in the Page Setup dialog box (300 dpi for 560C and 1200C printers), then hold down the Ctrl key while you drag a handle.

> *Note:* The PageMaker User Manual recommends using the above method only for resizing monochrome bitmapped images. You may not get good results if you try to use this method with color bitmapped images. The reason for this is that some color changes may occur due to the dithering used by the printer to simulate colors.

Cropping an Image

When you place a graphic object onto a page of your publication, you initially see the complete image. You can crop that image so that only a part of it is displayed and printed. When you do so, the magnification of the visible part of the image remains unchanged.

To crop an image, select the image in the PageMaker publication, choose the cropping tool from the toolbox (the bottom-right tool), and place the cropping pointer over one of the image's handles. Press the mouse button and drag to change the size of the visible part of the image.

After you have cropped an image, the publication file still retains the data for the invisible part. You can, therefore, enlarge the visible part of the image by using the cropping pointer to drag a handle away from the center of the image.

In general, you should create graphics objects that contain only what you want to appear in the publication. If you are using an existing graphic, you should create a separate file that contains only the part of the graphic to be used. In this way, you can minimize the size of your publication file and linked graphics files.

Printing a Publication

When you print a publication, you should normally select ColorSmart and High Quality in the printer setup dialog box. After you do this, the printer automatically optimizes printing for text, business graphics, and photographic images on a page.

11

Preparing a Presentation

This chapter is about preparing effective presentations. We're talking here about face-to-face presentations, in which you present your ideas to a group of people.

When you prepare a printed document for people to read, you rely entirely on what is on the printed page to get and keep readers' attention and, perhaps, to motivate them. In contrast, when you stand up in front of a group of people to present your ideas in person, there are many factors that can contribute to, or detract from, the effect you have on your audience. These include:

- Your personal appearance
- What you say and how you say it
- The visual aids you use
- The handouts you distribute

While there's little your printer can do about your personal appearance, there is much it can do to help you prepare and deliver your spoken message effectively, to prepare visual aids, and to create handouts that will help your audience remember the presentation.

The Mechanics of a Presentation

The subject of presentations is only one topic in this book, so we cannot cover all the types of presentations you might make. Instead, the focus here is on the

211

most common types of presentations, those in which one person speaks to a group of people ranging in number from a handful to a couple of hundred. These types of presentations can be classified by the method used to display visual aids: overheads, slides, or computer screen.

Using Overhead Transparencies

By far the most common type of presentation is one in which the presenter uses an overhead projector to display transparencies on a projection screen.

This type of presentation has a number of advantages over other types:

- You can create overhead transparencies quickly and inexpensively on your inkjet printer.
- You can easily change the order in which you display your transparencies.
- Overhead projectors and projection screens are readily available, can be rented, and are relatively inexpensive.
- You can make the presentation in a room that is bright enough for the audience to take notes.

Some disadvantages of overhead transparencies are that the displayed images are not as bright and dramatic as those produced by other methods, and that changing transparencies on the projector can be a somewhat clumsy and distracting process.

Overhead transparencies are suitable for use in informal presentations to a relatively small group of people, not more than about 50.

Using 35-mm Slides

Using 35-mm slides projected onto a projection screen is the hallmark of a professional, well-prepared presentation. Their main advantages are:

- They provide bright, dramatic (where appropriate) images.
- They can be used effectively for audiences of almost any size.
- Changing from one slide to the next (or the previous) is just a matter of pushing a button.

Unfortunately 35-mm slides have a number of disadvantages, including these:

- They are considerably more expensive to create than overhead transparencies.
- They take much more time than overhead transparencies to create (unless you have in-house facilities).

- It is very difficult to show slides out of order during a presentation.
- The presentation room must be almost completely dark, making it difficult for the audience to take notes.

On-Screen Presentations

By on-screen presentations, we mean using a computer monitor to display images, a technique that is becoming quite popular.

You can use an ordinary computer monitor to display your images to a very small audience. The size of the audience depends, of course, on the size of the monitor. If you have a 14- or 15-inch monitor, you can use it with an audience of about half a dozen people. For larger groups, you need one or more large display monitors or a projector. Display monitors and projectors are very expensive.

The advantages of on-screen presentations are:

- You don't need to create overhead transparencies or slides.
- You can easily change the order in which your images are displayed.
- You can easily make changes to your images.
- There is the possibility of incorporating short movie segments into a presentation.

Instead of displaying images directly on your monitor, you can use an overhead projector panel. This is a device that you place on an overhead projector and connect to your computer. The images on your computer screen are also created on the overhead projector panel and, as with a normal overhead transparency, projected onto a projection screen.

At the time this book is being written, affordable overhead projector panels provide only rather dim, 256-color images and are, therefore, only suitable for informal presentations to quite small groups. Panels that give much better images are available, but they are very expensive.

Preparing a Presentation

At the time you give your presentation, you need to have:

- Speaker's notes
- Visual images
- Audience handouts

Whether you are going to use overhead transparencies, 35-mm slides, or on-screen visuals, you should use a presentation application such as PowerPoint on your computer to coordinate preparation of these three elements of your presentation. PowerPoint is used in the examples in this book because it is one of the more popular Macintosh and Windows applications in this category.

You can, of course, prepare all the elements of a presentation without using a presentation application. For example, you can use a graphics application such as CorelDRAW or a word processor such as Word to create slides containing text and graphics. It is much easier, though, to use a presentation application.

For the present, we'll focus on a presentation that uses overhead transparencies. Some notes later in the chapter refer to the other types of presentations.

Planning a Presentation

As always, time spent planning brings rewards. When planning a presentation, bear in mind an important difference between a written document and a presentation. A person reading a written document can easily refer back or forward to other parts, can reread material that isn't initially clear, can pause to look up a reference. The reader is in total control. In contrast, a person listening to a presentation can proceed only in the order and at the speed dictated by the presenter. It is vital, therefore, that you think very carefully about the order in which you present material and about the depth in which you cover each topic.

Working with an Outline

PowerPoint and other presentation applications help you to prepare a presentation in the form of an outline. When you open PowerPoint to create a new presentation, one way to proceed is to display the outline screen shown in Figure 11.1. Initially, this screen contains an icon representing the first slide in your presentation.

> *Note:* The word *slide* used here includes images that will become overhead transparencies and on-screen displays, as well as 35-mm slides.

The outline screen is where you arrange the main points of your presentation. Whatever text you place on this screen will appear as words in your slides. For each slide, you type a title and then the topic points under that title.

Entering slide titles and topics is just like using the outlining capability in Word. In fact, if you prefer, you can create your presentation outline as a Word outline and then use that in PowerPoint.

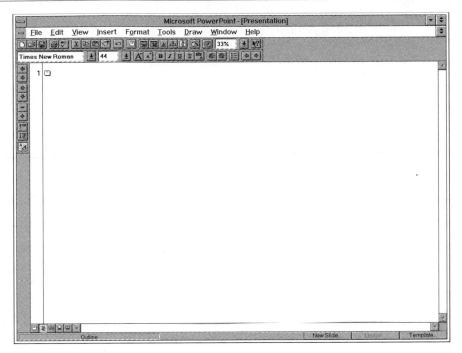

Figure 11.1 The initial PowerPoint outline screen.

Note: To import an outline from Word, open the PowerPoint File menu and choose Open to display the Open dialog box. In the List Files of Type drop-down list, choose Outlines. Select the Word outline file and click OK to open it in PowerPoint.

After you have entered the text for your slides, the outline screen looks similar to that in Figure 11.2.

One of the benefits of using the outline to create a presentation is that you can easily change the order of slides, move topics from one slide to another, split one slide into two or more separate slides, and so on.

Most good presentations have the following structure:

1. Title slide.
2. Introduction—one or two slides that tell the audience what you are going to talk about.
3. Detailed presentation—one slide for each main topic.
4. Summary—one or two slides to remind the audience what you've said.
5. Wrap-up—a slide to tell the audience what you hope they will do.

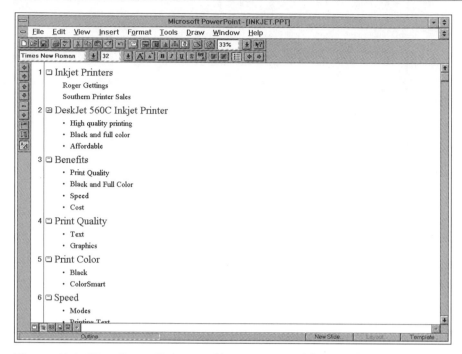

Figure 11.2 The PowerPoint outline screen with text for some slides entered.

Each slide should have no more than five or six topic points, each point with no more than five or six words. Use a new slide for each major fact you want to present.

Saving Your Presentation

As usual, you should save your presentation whenever you have completed a significant stage in its preparation, such as when you have completed the outline. To do so, open the File menu and choose Save or Save As to open the Save As dialog box. Give the presentation a file name, then click OK to open the Summary Info dialog box shown in Figure 11.3.

Notice that the Summary Info dialog box is a little different from the one you see in other applications. The area at the top shows the number of slides in the presentation and also has a space for the name of a template (we'll get to the subject of templates soon). You'll also see that the title of the first slide in the presentation appears in the Title box.

You enter information in the Subject, Keywords, and Comments sections of the dialog box as you do in other applications, then click OK to save the outline.

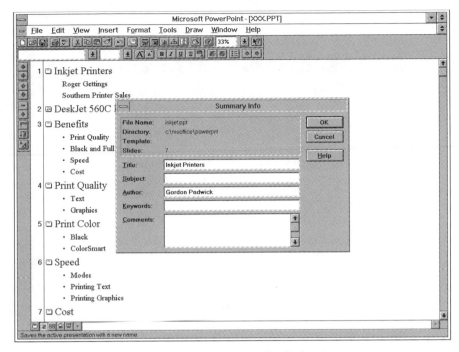

Figure 11.3 The PowerPoint Summary Info dialog box.

Choosing Slide Layouts

The next stage in designing a presentation is to choose a layout for each slide. In PowerPoint, you do this by displaying the slides one at a time.

In the outline, select a slide and then click the Slide View button (on the left at the bottom of the screen) to display that slide. Then click the Layout button (on the right at the bottom of the screen) to display the Slide Layout dialog box shown in Figure 11.4.

You can choose among 19 different layouts for each slide. The supplied layouts include designs for:

- Title slides
- Slides with one or two columns of bulleted text
- Slides that contain charts, imported graphics, tables, or other objects

For each slide, choose the layout that is closest to what you want, then click the Apply button to display the slide with that layout. If you need to, you can easily modify the layout for individual slides.

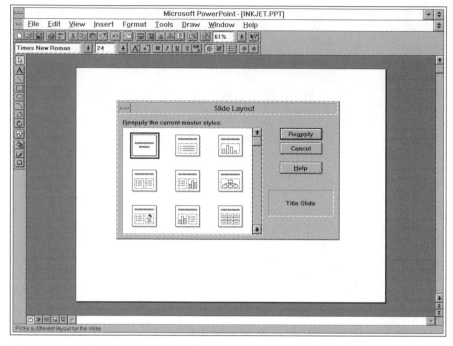

Figure 11.4 **The PowerPoint Slide Layout dialog box.**

Adding Graphics

You can add graphics to your slides from such sources as:

- Clip art
- Scanned images
- Images created in graphics applications
- Charts created in spreadsheet applications

To add graphics to a slide, display that slide in slide view. If you haven't already done so, choose one of the layouts that provides a place holder for an object.

If you want to add a graphic that already exists as a file, click the outline of the graphic place holder to select it, then open the Insert menu and choose Picture to display the Insert Picture dialog box. In that dialog box, choose the file you want to insert, and then click OK. PowerPoint scales the image and inserts it into the place holder.

To create a new graphics object to insert into the place holder, double-click the place holder to open the Insert Object dialog box. You can use this dialog box to open any graphics, spreadsheet, or other application that can create

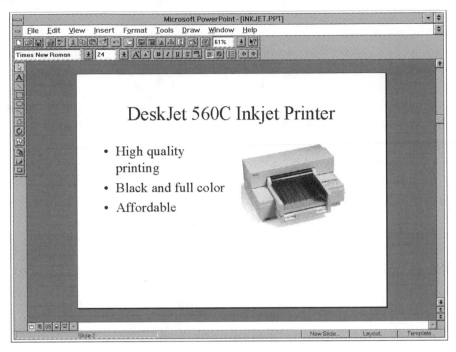

Figure 11.5 A slide with a scanned image inserted.

graphics within your environment. Create the graphics object in that application, then open the File menu and choose Exit and Return (or a similar command) to return to PowerPoint with the new graphics object inserted.

Figure 11.5 shows an example of a slide with a scanned image inserted.

After you have placed your graphics objects into the appropriate slides, you can return to the outline view if you wish to make changes to the text within the slides. When you do so, you will see that the slide icon associated with each slide that incorporates a graphic contains a small geometric design.

In PowerPoint, you can create a Master Slide and place graphics on it that will appear on every slide in the presentation. You may be tempted to add a unifying identity to your presentation by putting your company logo on every slide. Don't do it! If you are preparing a presentation on behalf of your company, put the logo on the first and last slides, but not on any others (unless the logo appears naturally as part of a product illustration). Your audience doesn't need to be reminded about your affiliation on every slide.

Selecting a Template

So far, you have prepared slides without regard for whether they are going to be printed as overhead transparencies, imaged as 35-mm slides, or shown as an on-screen presentation. Nor have you paid any attention to a background color or to the color or font for the individual items of text on each slide.

PowerPoint comes with a large number of templates from which you can select to provide a coordinating style for an entire presentation. Each template has a specific background, and specifies fonts, font sizes, and font colors for the various text regions on your slides. You choose one template for an entire presentation, though you can modify the appearance of individual slides if you need to.

The PowerPoint templates are grouped in four categories:

- Black-and-white overhead
- Color overhead
- 35-mm slide
- Video screen

In each category the templates have colors and a height-to-width ratio appropriate for the medium.

To choose a template for an entire presentation, display one of the slides and click the Template button (at the bottom-right of the screen) to display the Presentation Template dialog box that lists the categories of templates. Choose one of the displayed template categories, such as color overheads, to see a list of available templates in that category, as shown in Figure 11.6.

To see what any template looks like, click its name in the list. When you do so, a miniature representation of that template appears in the sample box at the bottom-right of the dialog box.

When you look at the supplied templates for overhead transparencies, you will see that some have white backgrounds and others have colored backgrounds. Projected overhead transparencies are usually easiest for the audience to read if the text is in black or a very dark color on a white or very light-colored background. In contrast, templates for 35-mm slides and on-screen presentations have white or light-colored text on a dark background.

To apply one of the templates to your presentation, select its name in the list, then click Apply. The selected template is applied to all the slides in the presentation. Figure 11.7 shows how the template affects a typical slide.

You can, of course, make any changes you wish to the background and fonts used in individual slides.

> *Note:* You can use a template you have designed yourself instead of using one of those supplied. If you do design your own template, keep it simple.

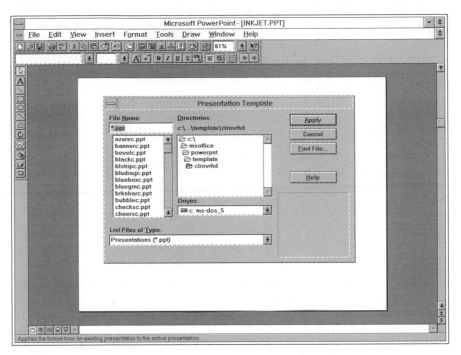

Figure 11.6 The PowerPoint Presentation Template dialog box showing the list of available color overhead templates.

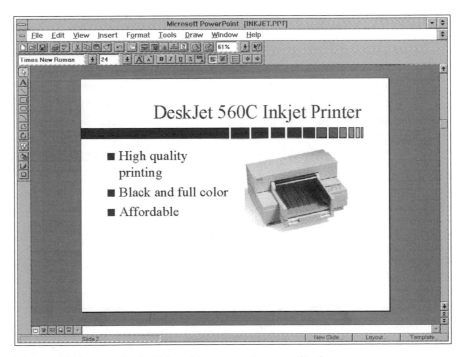

Figure 11.7 A typical slide with a template applied.

221

After you have applied a template to a presentation, the name of that template appears in the Summary Info dialog box. To see this, open the File menu and choose Summary Info.

Printing Overhead Transparencies

If you are preparing an on-screen presentation, you don't need to print transparencies. However, if you intend to use 35-mm slides, it's a good idea to use overhead transparencies for a trial run. That way, you can rehearse your presentation alone and in front of colleagues while using relatively inexpensive overhead transparencies. Then you can correct mistakes and make improvements before committing to relatively expensive 35-mm slides.

Overhead transparency material is considerably more expensive than paper. For that reason, you should check your work carefully before printing transparencies. This is a three-step process:

- Display each slide on your monitor and check it carefully.
- Print a review set of slides on ordinary paper and check them (have a colleague check them as well).
- Print the transparencies.

Printing a Review Set of Slides

The purpose of the review set of slides is to check for accuracy, so you don't need these to be in color. PowerPoint lets you select a black-and-white printing mode so that you can print the slides as fast as possible and save the ink in your color print cartridges. In this mode, all solid fills become white and all patterned fills become black and white. This mode has no effect on the color of the slide background.

If you have selected a template with a colored background, you can temporarily change the background color to white. To do so, open the Format menu and choose Slide Background to display the Slide Background dialog box shown in Figure 11.8.

Click the Change Color button at the bottom of the dialog box to display the Background Color palette, click the white sample color, and click OK to return to the Slide Background dialog box. Click Apply To All to make the backgrounds of all slides temporarily white.

> *Note:* You can easily change back to the original template background color when you are ready to print transparencies, as explained later in this chapter.

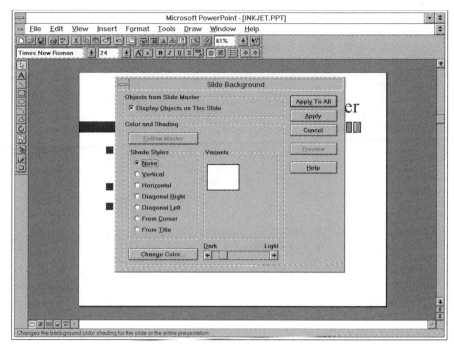

Figure 11.8   The Slide Background dialog box.

To select the black-and-white printing mode, open PowerPoint's File menu and choose Print to display the Print dialog box shown in Figure 11.9.

In this dialog box, click the Black & White check box so that all areas filled with color are printed in white.

The second line in the Print dialog box is labeled Print What. It is here that you choose whether you want to print slides, notes pages, or handouts. If necessary, open the Print What list box and choose Slides.

Select the printer you want to use if it is not already selected, then click Options to display that specific printer's Setup dialog box. Choose the appropriate options for draft printing (as explained in Chapter 3), then click OK to return to the Print Setup dialog box and again OK to return to the Print dialog box. In the Print dialog box, click OK to start printing.

Check the black-and-white paper copies of your slides and make any necessary corrections before proceeding.

After you have made all the necessary corrections, restore the slide backgrounds to their original colors if you had changed them. To do this, display any slide and click the Template button to display the Presentation Template dialog box. Choose the original template and click Apply.

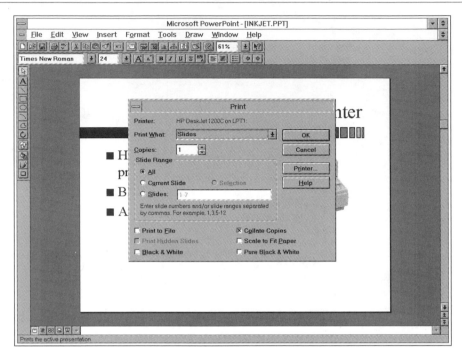

Figure 11.9 The PowerPoint Print dialog box.

Note: If you have forgotten the name of the original template, open the File menu and choose Summary Info to display the Summary Info dialog box, which shows the name of the template in the third line of the top section.

Printing Transparencies

You should use only Hewlett-Packard LX JetSeries Transparency Film for printing transparencies on your inkjet printer. Remove almost all the paper from the paper input tray and add no more than about 50 sheets of Transparency Film.

Tip: To avoid the possibility of misfeeding Transparency Film, always have a few sheets of ordinary paper at the bottom of the paper input tray.

Notice that the film has a white strip across one end and on only one side of each sheet of film. This white strip is used by the printer to sense the presence of film. Insert the film into the paper input tray with the white strip on top and on the end going into the printer first.

To print the slides:

1. Open the File menu and choose Print to open the Print dialog box.

2. If you had previously checked Black & White, click the check box again to uncheck that option.

3. Make sure the Print What box contains Slides (even though you are going to print overhead transparencies).

4. Click Printer to open the Print Setup dialog box.

5. If necessary, select the printer you want to use, then click Options to display that printer's Setup dialog box.

6. In the printer's Setup dialog box, make sure ColorSmart is selected, choose the best print quality, and select HP Transparency as the media type in order to allow time for the ink to dry between printing one transparency and the next.

> *Note:* In the case of the DeskJet 560C printer, select Transparency or, if you need additional time for the ink to dry, select Transparency (Extra Dry Time) as the media type. When you select the latter, printing stops after each transparency is printed. After printing each transparency, wait a sufficient amount of time for the ink to dry, then click OK in the Setup dialog box to print the next transparency.

7. Click OK to return to the Print Setup dialog box, and again click OK to return to the Print dialog box.

8. Click OK to start printing.

Preparing Speaker's Notes

You, the speaker, need notes to remind yourself what you intend to say while each slide is projected. If you don't have adequate notes, you will probably forget what you want to say and be tempted to read the text on each slide to your audience.

Adequate notes are not a script; they provide just enough information to prompt you. PowerPoint (and other presentation applications) make it easy to prepare notes by preparing speaker's sheets, each of which contains a miniature version of a slide and space for you to type notes.

In PowerPoint, go to the first slide of the presentation and click the Notes Page View button (the fourth from the left in the status bar) to display a notes view of the first slide, as shown in Figure 11.10.

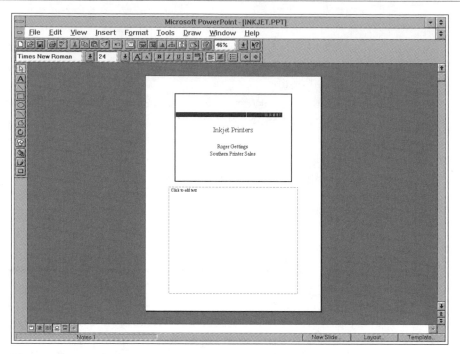

Figure 11.10   The notes view of a slide.

The upper part of each notes page shows a reduced-size version of the slide. The bottom part of the page is space for your notes.

Click the large rectangle in the lower part of the page, then type your notes, with one line for each major thought, and using as few words as possible to summarize each thought. After you've typed the notes for one slide, click the next slide button, and add notes for that slide.

The font and font size you use for your notes are very important, particularly if you have less-than-perfect eyesight. During the presentation, you must be able to see the notes and your audience clearly. If you normally wear eyeglasses or contact lenses, you need these to see the audience. This means that your notes must be large enough so that you can read them when you are wearing your normal lenses. You certainly don't want to be taking reading glasses on and off whenever you want to glance at your notes.

> *Note:* After you've printed your notes, practice with them to make sure the printing is the right size. Change to a larger font size if necessary.

After you've typed your notes, you can print them as you ordinarily print a document. In this case, open the Print dialog box, and choose Notes Pages in the drop-down Print What list box.

The advantage to using PowerPoint to generate the speaker's notes is that the slide illustrations always exactly match the actual slides. If you change slides in the presentation and generate a new set of speaker's notes, the illustrations on those notes always correspond to the slides. Any text you type as notes is, of course, not affected by changes to the slides.

Preparing Audience Handouts

The purpose of a presentation is to provide information or motivation that everyone in the audience remembers. One way to help people to remember is to give them printed versions of your slides.

PowerPoint prepares printed handouts automatically. After you have finished creating the presentation, open the File menu and choose Print to open the Print dialog box. Open the drop-down Print What list box to show a list of what can be printed. Here, you can choose among three types of handout configurations:

- Two slides per page
- Three slides per page
- Six slides per page

The second choice, three slides per page, is a good one because it shows three slides in a column on the left side of the page, with room for people to write notes on the right side of the page, as shown in Figure 11.11.

One of the benefits of having a color inkjet printer is that you can give your audience color copies of the slides they see on the screen, which is much better than giving out difficult-to-read black-and-white copies.

Preparing 35-mm Slides

Of course, your inkjet printer does not create 35-mm slides. However, it is an extremely useful tool in the process of creating these slides.

You create images for 35-mm slides in the same way that you create images for overhead transparencies, except you should use one of the templates for 35-mm slides. These templates contain colors that are suitable for slides whereas

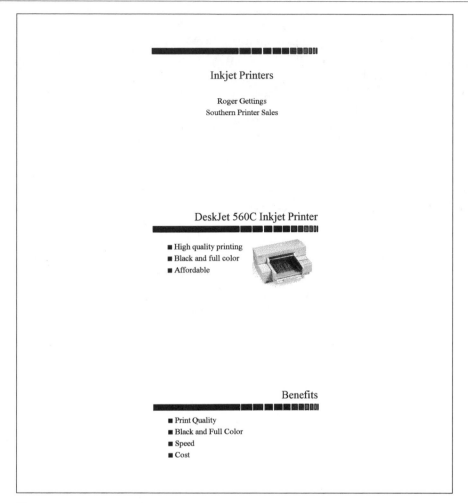

Figure 11.11 A typical handout page.

the overhead templates contain colors suitable for overheads. After you have prepared the images, you can take your PowerPoint files (or send them by modem) to a service bureau that will convert them into slides (a process known as imaging). Before you do that, though, you should be certain they are correct.

The best way to check your slides before they are imaged is, first, to print them on paper for preliminary checking and, second, to print them as overhead transparencies and use the transparencies to rehearse the presentation in front of colleagues. After taking the time to go through these two steps, you are unlikely to incur the expensive steps of having slides re-imaged.

Here's another suggestion about preparing 35-mm slides. Before you have a service bureau image a batch of files, have a representative one or two slides

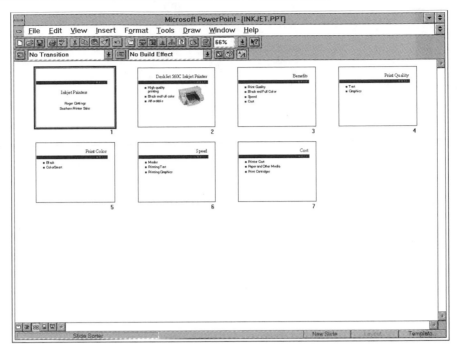

Figure 11.12 Slides in the Slider Sorter view.

imaged. By doing this, you can check that the colors that appear when the slides are projected are what you intend. This is particularly important if there are colors (such as the color of a company logo) that must be reproduced accurately.

Preparing an On-Screen Presentation

One of the benefits of on-screen presentations is that you don't have to print overhead transparencies or have 35-mm slides made. However, you still need speaker's notes, unless you're planning a very informal presentation to a small group. Also, you need to prepare handouts for your audience.

Preparing a presentation of this type is similar to preparing an overhead presentation. After you have prepared your slides, you can use the Slide Sorter view to change their order. To see the slides in order, as shown in Figure 11.12, click the Slide Sorter button (the third button from the left in the status bar).

Although the main purpose of this view is to let you change the order of slides for an on-screen presentation, it's also useful when you want to quickly review what is in a sequence of slides you are preparing for use as overheads or as 35-mm slides.

Personal Projects

The preceding chapters contain many suggestions about working with typical business projects. Here, we turn to some of the things you can do with your inkjet printer on a more personal level for your workgroup and family. Some of the specific projects covered in this chapter are greeting cards and invitations, school reports, home planning, and enhancing photographs.

Creating Greeting Cards

We'll start with a project that can be a lot of fun—creating your own greeting cards. You can use the same techniques to create other types of cards such as invitations and announcements.

Greeting cards are fun to work with because they give you an opportunity to use decorative fonts that you are advised not to use for most types of projects. You can also create some exciting effects with clip art and colors. One of the great things is that you can easily personalize your cards.

The easiest type of card to make is one that's printed on a single sheet of letter-size paper folded twice to divide the sheet into quarters. The final card, as it appears on the screen, is shown in Figure 12.1.

The bottom two panels contain what will be the back and front of the card after you fold the paper. The top two panels contain what will be the inside of the card. The unusual part is, as Figure 12.1 shows, that you have to print the

231

Figure 12.1 **A greeting card printed on a single sheet of paper.**

top two panels upside down so that after you fold the paper, these panels are correctly oriented.

If you are using Word or another word processor, there are several ways to print the top two panels upside down. One way is to create those two panels in a graphics program and rotate them before or after inserting them into the word processor document. Another way is to use a graphics application such as CorelDRAW that automatically places the four panels in the correct orientation. We'll look at both ways in detail.

Using Word to Create a Greeting Card

The following steps show how to use Word to create a birthday card printed on a single sheet of letter-size paper. The front of the card (the bottom-right panel of the paper) will have some clip art and a simple greeting. The right side of the inside of the card (the top-left panel of the paper) will have a personalized greeting. In this example, the back and inside left of the card are left blank.

In Word, start by opening the Page Setup dialog box and setting the four margins to the minimum values allowed for your printer. Select the Page Layout view of the document. If the vertical ruler is not displayed, open the Options dialog box and, in the View tab, click the Vertical Ruler option box to select it. Now you're ready to create the front of the card.

To place a graphic on the front of the card:

1. Open the Insert menu and choose Frame.

2. Using the horizontal and vertical rulers as a guide, draw a frame to outline the area for the graphic. It's not important to be precise because you can easily move and resize the frame later.

3. Open the Insert menu and choose Picture to display the Insert Picture dialog box.

4. Select the clip-art file you want to use (the example uses the JAZZ.WMF file in the clip art supplied with Word) to place the clip art in the Word document.

5. If necessary, use the handles around the clip art to change its size. You can also drag the clip art to change its position.

Now you can add a "Happy Birthday" greeting to the front of the card. In the following steps, the two words are placed into separate frames so that you can place them individually.

1. Open the Insert menu and choose Frame.

2. Create a frame of any size.

3. Type the word *Happy*.

4. Select the word, then open the Format Font dialog box and choose a font, font size, and font color (the example uses Shotgun BT, 36 point, magenta). Unfortunately, Word only allows you to choose among 16 predefined colors for text.

5. Drag the frame containing the word to where you want it to be.

6. To remove the frame outline, open the Format menu and choose Borders and Shading, select the Borders tab, and click the None option box in the Line section.

7. Repeat steps 1 through 6 to place the word *Birthday* in a frame.

This completes the front page of the card.

The following steps show how to use WordArt to create the inside page of the card and place it upside down.

1. Open the Insert menu and choose Frame.

2. Draw a frame in the top-left panel.

3. Open the Insert menu and choose Object to display the Object dialog box with a list of Object Types displayed.

4. Choose Microsoft WordArt and click OK to display the Enter Your Text Here dialog box shown in Figure 12.2.

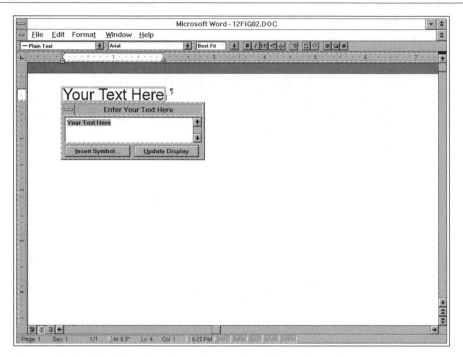

Figure 12.2   **The WordArt Enter Your Text Here dialog box.**

5. Type the text that you want to have on the inside page of the card.

6. Open the drop-down list of WordArt effects (by clicking the arrow button near the left end of the toolbar) and choose one of the effects.

7. Open the drop-down list of fonts (by clicking the second-from-left arrow button in the toolbar) and choose a font.

8. Open the Format menu and choose Rotation and Effects to open the Special Effects dialog box.

9. Change the Rotation value to 180 and click OK.

10. Open the Format menu and choose Shading to display the Shading dialog box.

11. In the Color section, choose a color for the text in the Foreground drop-down list box, then click OK.

12. Double-click the menu-control box in the title bar of the Enter Your Text Here dialog box to hide the dialog box.

13. Click anywhere outside the WordArt frame to return to Word.

14. Open the Format menu and choose Borders and Shading. In the Line section of the Borders tab, click None to hide the borders, and then click OK.

After all this, you have an image at the bottom right of the page that will be the front of the card after you fold it, and you have an upside-down image at the top left that will be the right side of the inside. Open the File menu and choose Print Preview, to see if you have the images positioned correctly. If not, return to the Page Layout view, and drag to change the image positions. You may have to do this more than once to achieve what you want.

This completes the inside of the card.

You can now go ahead and print the card on good-quality paper, fold it, and admire your handiwork. Make sure the ink is completely dry before you fold the card. To fold the card neatly, the trick is to make a light fold by hand, then place a ruler over the fold and press hard. This way, you can make a sharp fold without the risk of smudging, and without the possibility of your fingers marking the paper.

Using a Graphics Application to Create a Greeting Card

It's somewhat easier to create a greeting card when you use a graphics application. In CorelDRAW, for example, you have access to versatile graphics capabilities and you can take advantage of being able to divide a page into four sections, with each of the sections automatically oriented suitable for folding.

In CorelDRAW, do the following to set up the page for a folded greetings card:

1. Open the Layout menu, choose Page Setup to display the Page Setup dialog box, and choose the Size tab as shown in Figure 12.3.

2. In the Size tab, select Letter as the size and Portrait as the orientation.

3. In the Layout tab, select Side-Fold Card. The miniature layout at the top of the dialog box shows the page divided into four parts, as shown in Figure 12.4. Each part is a separate page in the CorelDRAW document, with the pages numbered as shown in the figure.

4. Click OK to accept the page layout.

5. Open the Layout menu again and choose Insert Page to display the Insert Page dialog box.

6. Change the number of pages to be inserted to 3 (so that you have a total of four pages) and click OK. The status bar at the bottom of the screen confirms that you have a four-page document.

This completes setting up the CorelDRAW document. Notice in Figure 12.4 that after you fold the completed card, page 1 will be the front of the card, pages 2 and 3 will be the inside pages, and page 4 will be the back. Now you can go ahead and place text and graphics on the four pages. You don't have to invert the inside pages; CorelDRAW does this for you automatically.

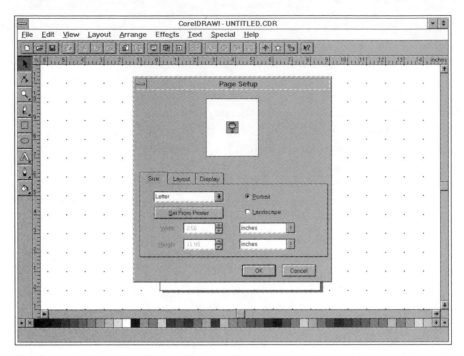

Figure 12.3 The CorelDRAW Page Setup dialog box with the Size tab selected.

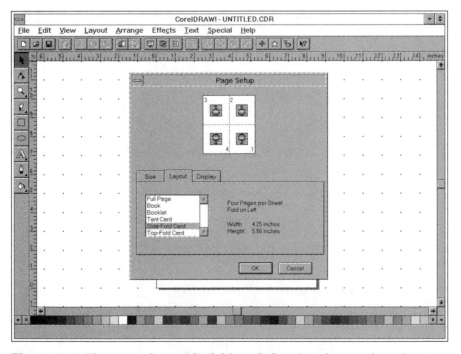

Figure 12.4 The setup for a side-fold card showing the numbered pages.

236

The front page of the card shown in Figure 12.5 consists of a photograph imported from one of Corel's Professional Photos CD-ROMs with a greeting superimposed over it. The inside contains only a simple greeting, but you can be more elaborate if you like. All the pages have one of CorelDRAW's texture fills as a background.

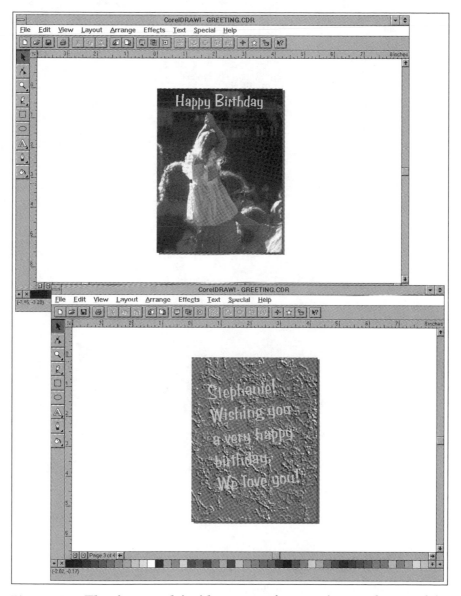

Figure 12.5 The front and inside pages of a greeting card created in CorelDRAW.

Figure 12.6 The greeting card ready to be trimmed and folded.

You should choose high-quality paper such as HP JetSeries Glossy paper to print the card, using your printer's high-quality printing mode. The final printed card is shown in Figure 12.6. All that remains to be done is to trim the edges and fold it. Make sure the ink is dry before you fold the card.

School Reports

There is virtually no limit to the ways in which you and your family can use an inkjet printer to enhance school and college reports at all grade levels. Even the youngest students can impress their teachers with computer-generated drawings and paintings. College-level students will find enormous benefits in using computer-generated charts to illustrate their work.

By encouraging young people to use a computer for their school projects, you will not only help them get better grades, but also to understand that it isn't just what you create, it's how you present it that can make a big difference in life's projects. The skills they learn while working with their school projects will put them ahead in future years.

Here are some specific suggestions for ways in which students can use a computer and color printer to enhance their school and college reports, as well as for other school activities:

- Use clip-art images of people (such as in the CorelDRAW clip art library) to illustrate all types of reports that refer to famous people, past and present

- Create drawings to illustrate science projects

- Use project management software (such as Microsoft Project) to plan and monitor team projects

- Use spreadsheet applications to maintain school and league sports statistics and to print charts

- Use clip-art maps (or draw maps) to illustrate geographical, historical, and current affairs projects

- Create presentations using overhead transparencies

- Develop drawing and painting skills

- Produce publications such as newsletters and programs for athletic events, theatrical productions, and other school activities

The techniques for using applications and printing documents is no different for these activities than for other projects explained throughout this book.

Planning Your Home

Your personal computer can be a great help in planning your home. Whether you're thinking about getting some new furniture and are wondering how it will fit into the available space, remodeling a kitchen, adding a room, or even designing your new dream house, your computer can be a great help.

You could use almost any graphics application to draw rooms and place furniture, fittings, and appliances in them. However, as we've advised before in this book, it's much easier to use an application specifically intended for home planning. The examples shown here are created with Broderbund's 3D Home Architect, a Windows application. There are several other applications you can use, such as Expert Home Design from Expert Software, which is available for the Macintosh and Windows environments.

Planning a Room Addition

For one reason or another you may be considering adding to your home. As an example, suppose you need a home office. It's a good idea to plan the project very carefully so that the room suits your needs as completely as possible. You can use 3D Home Architect to do that. After you're satisfied, you will need to have someone who is familiar with your local building codes prepare the final plans for approval.

The first stage in planning is to decide where the room should be added. In our imaginary situation, we're fortunate: there's a corner between the existing family room and garage that looks as if it would be an ideal position for the new room. Start by drawing the existing walls. Everything you do in 3D Home Architect is based on walls, so walls come first.

To draw the existing walls:

1. Open the Build menu and choose Wall.

2. In the secondary menu, choose 6 Inch Walls, because you will be drawing exterior walls.

3. Using drawing techniques as you do in other graphics applications, draw the existing walls. Notice that the separate walls are automatically joined together. You can see the length of the walls as you draw them by watching the panel in the toolbar immediately below Window and Help in the menu bar.

4. To label the existing rooms, open the Build menu and choose Text.

5. Click where you want the text to be, type the text, and click OK to place it. The result should be something like Figure 12.7.

The next step is to draw the new walls for your office. Proceed as follows:

1. Open the Build menu, choose Wall, then click 6 Inch thickness for outside walls.

2. Draw the two outside walls for the office, as shown in Figure 12.8.

You need a door into the office. To place a door in the wall between the office and the family room:

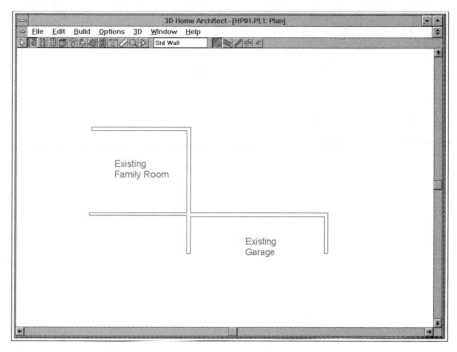

Figure 12.7 A drawing of the existing walls.

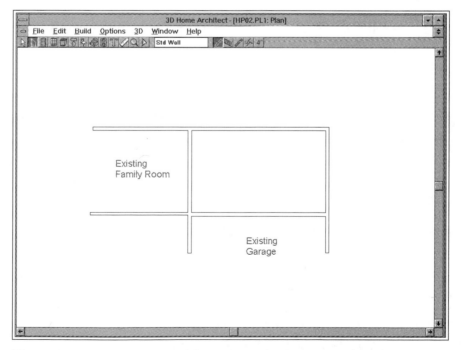

Figure 12.8 The plan after adding two walls for the new office.

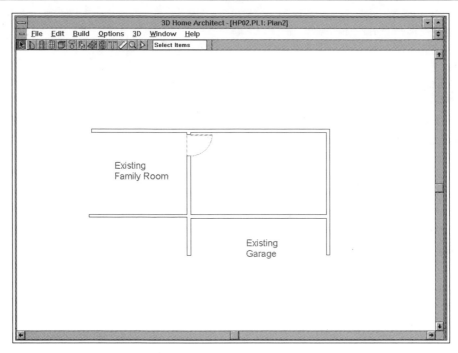

Figure 12.9 **The door added to the office.**

1. Open the Build menu, choose Door, and then choose Std Door.
2. Click in the wall between the office and the family room to place an opening for the door there.
3. Choose the selection tool at the left end of the toolbar.
4. Click in the door opening to reveal three selection handles.
5. Drag the center selection handle to position the door opening.
6. To place a door in the door opening, point onto the selection handle at the edge of the door opposite where the hinges should be, press the mouse button, drag in the direction the door should open, and release the button. The result is shown in Figure 12.9.

To add a window to your plan:

1. Open the Build menu, choose Window, and choose one of the listed window types.
2. Click in the wall where you want the window to be to place the window as shown in Figure 12.10.
3. If necessary, you can use the selection tool to change the position of the window.

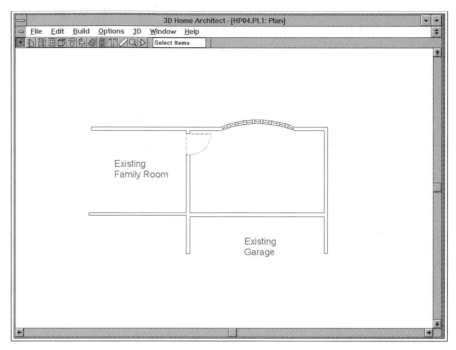

Figure 12.10 **A bow window inserted in a wall.**

Now, you need to add electrical wall outlets. To add wall outlets in what 3D Home Architect considers to be standard positions:

1. Open the Build menu and choose Place Outlets.

2. Point into the new room and click the mouse button.

3D Architect places electrical outlets around the walls as shown in Figure 12.11. You can drag these outlets to other positions now if you wish, but it's better to wait until you have planned where the furniture will go.

To place furniture in the room, open the Build menu and choose Furniture. This gives you access to a library of furniture shapes in various categories, one of which is Tables and Desks. Choose one of the desks, point where you want to place it, and click the mouse button. Select the desk and drag the center handle if you want to move it.

Continue in this way to place chairs, file cabinets, bookshelves, and whatever else you need in the room. This way you can check whether the room is an appropriate size for your needs before you go too far. Figure 12.12 shows the room with some typical office furniture in position.

You should mark the positions for electrical switches and indicate which outlets they control. Open the Build menu, choose Electrical, choose Switches,

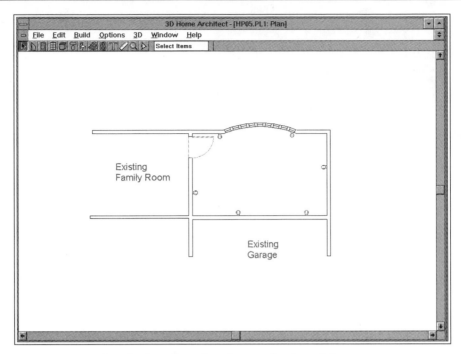

Figure 12.11 Electrical wall outlets in standard positions.

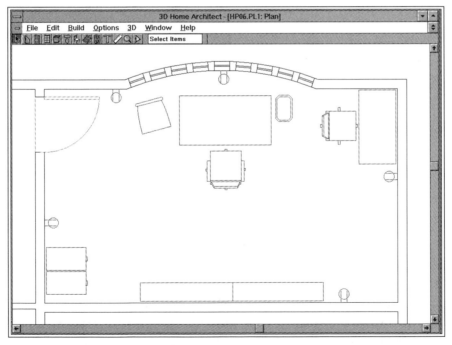

Figure 12.12 An enlarged view of furniture placed in the room.

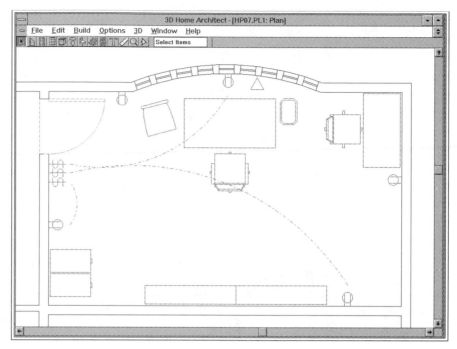

Figure 12.13 **The final plan for a home office.**

and click the switch positions in the plan. You can show which outlets each switch controls by selecting the connection tool and dragging from a switch to an outlet. Figure 12.13 shows the final plan.

You can even see a three-dimensional view of your office, as shown in Figure 12.14. To do this, click the Eye button in the toolbar, then move the camera-shaped pointer to one corner of the room and drag in the direction you want to view. Release the mouse button to see the three-dimensional view.

After you have completed all this work, you can use your inkjet printer to prepare printed copies of your plans that you can give to an architect or contractor. By taking the time to do the preliminary planning yourself, and by printing an accurate, easy-to-understand copy, you are likely to get what you want without having to pay for repeated revisions to drawings.

Working with Photography Projects

Working with photography projects is one of the most fascinating things you can do on your computer. With the help of your color inkjet printer, you can achieve exciting results.

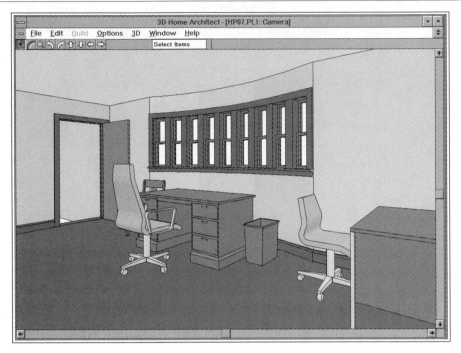

Figure 12.14 A three-dimensional view of the home office.

In common with almost everybody else who reads this book, you probably have a camera and use it to take family pictures, to help you remember vacation highlights, and for various other purposes. If you're like most people, you shoot a roll of film, have it processed, and get back a stack of small prints. You glance through the prints a few times and then stuff them into a drawer, making a mental note that you ought to put them in an album with labels indicating the date and place on which each was shot, as well as the names of the people in the pictures. If you're like me, that's as far as you get!

The most likely reason you are not very interested in your photographs after you've had them printed is that many of them are disappointing. They don't turn out the way you expected. You probably know that you can take your negatives to a professional photo lab for retouching and other improvements, but that's very expensive, something most of us do only for very special photographs.

Now, if you have a reasonably powerful computer and a good color monitor, you can retouch and enhance your photographs yourself. As you work, you can see the results of everything you do on the screen. After you're satisfied with your efforts, you can print the photographs on your inkjet printer.

> *Note:* We're dealing here with personal photographic projects. Techniques similar to those described here are used to create publication-quality photographs, the main difference being that the image definition used is much higher than can be handled on most home and office computer equipment.

You may already have the software you need to work with photographs. Corel PHOTO-PAINT, one of the applications packaged with CorelDRAW, contains many tools that are intended for manipulating photographic images. If you don't already have a suitable application, you might consider purchasing Picture Window, the $199 application available from Digital Light & Color that is used for the examples in this section. If you intend to get seriously into manipulating photographic images, you should consider using Adobe Photoshop or Aldus PhotoStyler, both of which have very sophisticated capabilities.

The three main steps involved in working with a photograph are:

- Converting the photograph to a file
- Retouching and enhancing the image in the file
- Converting the file to a viewable image

The steps are dealt with separately in the following pages.

Converting a Photograph to a File

It's necessary to scan a photograph to convert it to a file before you can work with it. You can do this in three ways:

- Using a desktop scanner
- Having a service bureau scan the photograph to create a file on disk
- Having a service bureau scan the photograph to create a Photo CD

Whether you scan an image yourself or have it scanned by a service bureau, you have a choice of file formats. See the information later in this chapter about file formats.

Using a Desktop Scanner

If you have a color scanner capable of creating 24-bit scans and have an original color print at least as large as the final printed image you intend to create, you can create a file that will give good results for ordinary purposes. You can, of course, scan a photograph that is smaller than the final one you intend to create, but you might not be entirely pleased with the enlarged result.

Use your scanner's facilities to make preliminary corrections to the photograph, as explained in Chapter 10. Crop the photograph so that the scanned file contains only a little more than you want in the final printed image. You can also make preliminary corrections to brightness and contrast, and correct any overall color cast at this stage.

You should always set the magnification on your scanner so that the scanned file corresponds to the size of the final image you want to print. By doing this, you can get the best possible results without handling files that are much bigger than necessary.

Set the scanner resolution to the minimum value that gives adequate resolution to avoid creating unnecessarily large image files. For most purposes, 100 dots per inch is satisfactory. See Chapter 10 for more information about scanning.

One important benefit of scanning the photograph yourself is that you can easily repeat the scan if your initial try causes problems later.

Scanning by a Service Bureau

There are several reasons why you may want to have your photograph scanned by a service bureau, rather than do it yourself.

Your scanner is likely to be capable of scanning only reflective images—those you see by light reflected from the surface—such as printed photographs. Scanners of this type cannot scan transparencies such as 35-mm slides without the addition of an expensive option. If you are starting with slides or other transparencies, therefore, you need the help of a service bureau.

One other reason to consider using a service bureau is if you are preparing photographs for use in high-quality publications that require a higher resolution than is available from most desktop scanners. This subject is beyond the scope of this book.

If you do decide to ask a service bureau to scan images for you, be sure that you specify exactly what you want and that the people there understand how you will use the scanned image. Bureau charges for scanning tend to be quite high, so make sure you understand what the charges will be before you place your order.

Using Photo CDs

Photo CDs are convenient if you plan to work on many photographs. You can have up to 100 photographs transferred from 35-mm transparencies or negatives onto a single CD at much less expense than having them individually scanned. This service is provided by companies that specialize in Photo CDs and by some photographic processing companies. You can take your original transparencies or negatives (or unprocessed film) to almost any retail store that offers photo processing and ask for Photo CD service.

As mentioned in Chapter 8, each image on a Photo CD is recorded at several resolutions, the best being 2048 by 3072 pixels. With this resolution, you can achieve excellent results when creating quite large final prints.

> *Note:* The higher definition Pro Photo CD, used for transparencies up to 4 by 5 inches, provides images containing up to 4096 by 6144 pixels.

File Formats

Scanner drivers, the software that controls scanners, can write a scanned image to disk in several formats. The most common of these is TIFF (Tag Image File Format); you may find that your scanner allows you to choose among several other formats. The applications you use to work with scanned images can accept files in various formats, usually including TIFF.

As a starting point, you should probably adopt TIFF as your personal standard unless, of course, your scanner (or the service bureau's scanner) and graphics software cannot work with this format. Be aware, though, that TIFF is rather like the word "red"—it doesn't mean exactly the same thing to everyone. TIFF is an evolving standard to which various companies add enhancements from time to time. This means that TIFF files written by one application cannot always be read correctly by another. You need to experiment to be sure that the TIFF files written by the scanner you are using are completely compatible with your graphics application.

TIFF files tend to be quite large. You may find that a TIFF file is too large to fit on a floppy disk. To solve this problem, you can use the Compressed TIFF format. Depending on the nature of the scanned photograph, the compressed file may be considerably smaller than the uncompressed version. The disadvantage of compression is that details can be lost. Usually the lost detail is too insignificant to be noticed. Again, you have to experiment to see how well compression works in your circumstances.

Formats other than TIFF may work well for you and may result in considerably smaller files than equivalent TIFF files. Try them and see what happens.

Photo CD files use the PCD format developed by Kodak, so you have no choice about format in this case. Most, though not all, recent versions of graphics applications can accept PCD files. If your graphics application does not accept PCD, one option is to purchase an application such as Kodak PhotoEdge that can open these files and save them in other formats.

> *Note:* You can also use PhotoEdge to retouch and manipulate your photographs.

Retouching Photographs

You can easily improve every photograph you take by using some of the techniques mentioned in the following pages. Some improvements are easy and require very little time; others are difficult, require you to develop specific skills, and are time-consuming.

The improvements covered here are:

- Cropping to eliminate unnecessary background and foreground distractions
- Changing the brightness to compensate for over- and underexposure
- Improving the contrast to add sparkle to flat images
- Correcting perspective of buildings that appear to be falling
- Changing angles when you didn't hold the camera quite straight
- Removing objects that spoil the mood
- Improving portraits

The following pages describe many of the techniques you can use to improve your photographs, using the application Picture Window as an example. You can achieve similar results with other applications.

To get optimum results when retouching a photograph, you should make sure your monitor is properly calibrated before you start work. Refer to Chapter 13 for information about calibrating a monitor.

Cropping

Cropping is the process of cutting unnecessary and distracting parts from the edges of a photograph. This is very simple to do and can add dramatically to the photograph's impact.

In Picture Window, open the file containing the photograph to be cropped, as shown in Figure 12.15.

Proceed as follows to crop the photograph:

1. Open the Transformation menu, choose Geometry, and then in the submenu choose Crop, as shown in Figure 12.16. The Crop dialog box that appears shows the size of the image in pixels (or other units if you prefer), as shown in Figure 12.17. Also, small crop handles appear at the corners of the image.

Figure 12.15 A photograph ready for cropping.

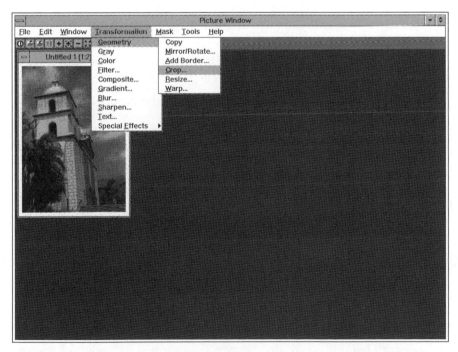

Figure 12.16 The Picture Window Transformation menu with Crop selected.

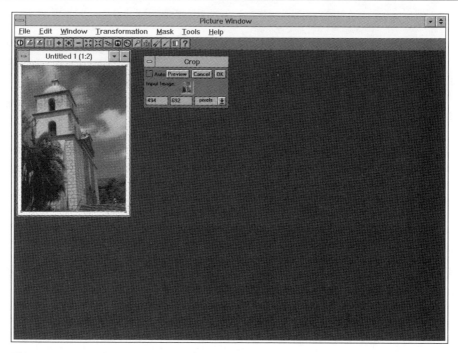

Figure 12.17 **The Crop dialog box and the image with crop handles.**

2. Drag the crop handles to create a rectangle that contains the part of the photograph you want to retain, as shown in Figure 12.18. As you drag the handles, the Crop dialog box shows the size of the photograph.

3. Click Preview to create a preview of the cropped photograph, shown in Figure 12.19.

4. Repeat steps 2 and 3 if you want to change the cropping.

5. When you are satisfied, click OK in the dialog box to create a new image, close the dialog box, and close the Preview image.

6. Open the File menu, choose Save As to open the File Save dialog box, name the new file, and choose OK to save it to disk.

As you would expect, the cropped image file is considerably smaller than the original file.

Changing the Image Brightness

If the photograph on your screen is too dark or too light, you can change the overall brightness. To do so, open the cropped image and proceed as follows:

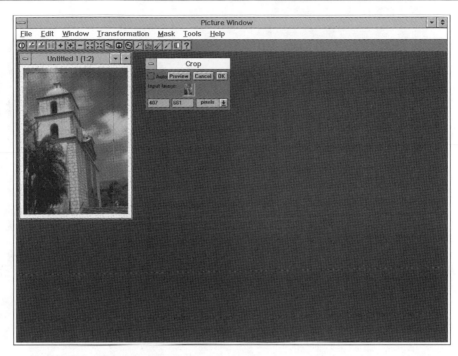

Figure 12.18 The photograph with cropping marked.

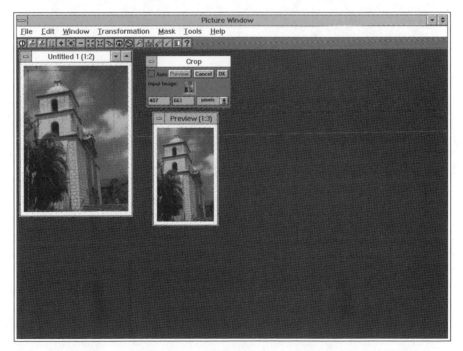

Figure 12.19 A preview of the cropped photograph.

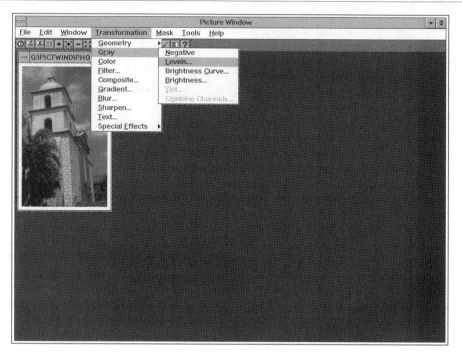

Figure 12.20 **The Picture Window Transformation menu with Levels selected.**

1. Open the Picture Window Transformation menu, choose Gray, and choose Levels as shown in Figure 12.20. After a few seconds' delay, the Levels dialog box appears, as shown in Figure 12.21.

2. Drag the Brightness slider to the right to increase the overall brightness of the picture, or to the left to decrease the brightness, then click Preview to see the effect of the change, as shown in Figure 12.22.

3. When you are satisfied, click OK in the Levels dialog box to create the new photograph, then save the image to disk.

Improving the Contrast

Many photographs look best when they use the whole tonal range of which a print is capable. The darkest shadows in the image should be completely black and the brightest highlights should be completely white.

If the image tones do not occupy the maximum range, you can improve matters by using the Dynamic Range control in the Levels dialog box shown in Figure 12.21. With the image displayed, drag the black triangle under the Dynamic Range scale to the left until it is under the darkest point on the scale, and drag the white triangle until it is under the whitest point on the scale. As

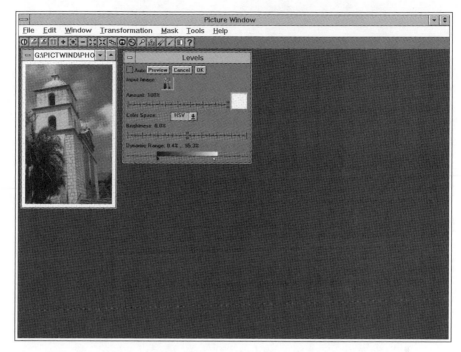

Figure 12.21 The Levels dialog box.

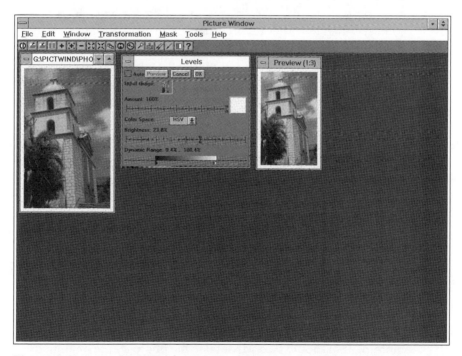

Figure 12.22 The Preview window showing the effect of brightening a photograph.

before, click Preview to see the effect of the change, and then click OK to make the change permanent.

Correcting Perspective and Angles

When you take a photograph of a building, particularly a tall one, you have to point the camera up in order to get the top into the picture. The resulting photograph shows the building with verticals leaning toward the center. If you don't hold the camera horizontal from side to side, the whole building appears to be falling over. The photograph we have been working with, a picture of Mission Santa Barbara, shows this problem.

You can easily correct perspective and angle problems with Picture Window. Display the photograph and proceed as follows:

1. Open the Transformation menu, choose Geometry, and then choose Warp to open the Warp dialog box and place a grid of horizontal and vertical lines on the photograph, as shown in Figure 12.23. Notice the handles at the corners of the photograph.

2. Point onto one of the four handles at the corner of the grid that is superimposed over the photograph and drag. As you do so, that one corner moves and the other three corners of the grid remain stationary. The effect is to change the angles of the vertical and horizontal grid lines. To correct the perspective of a building, start with the top-right corner of the grid and drag until the vertical grid lines at the right side of the grid are parallel to vertical lines at the right side of the building. Then drag the top-left corner of the grid until the vertical lines at the left of the grid are parallel to vertical lines at the left side of the building, as shown in Figure 12.24.

3. Click Preview to see a preview of the perspective correction.

4. If necessary, repeat steps 3 and 4, then click OK to make the perspective correction permanent. To get the perspective exactly correct, you'll probably have to repeat these steps several times. Depending on the effect you want, you may decide to leave the photograph with some perspective distortion.

You can use a similar technique to correct the angle of a photograph. With the Warp dialog box displayed, point onto the Opt button, press the mouse button, and drag to select Rigid. After that, when you drag the grid superimposed over the photograph, the entire grid swivels. Align the horizontal grid lines to something that should be horizontal in the photograph, or align the vertical grid lines to something that should be vertical. This causes the entire photograph to change its angle.

Figure 12.23 The Warp dialog box and a grid placed over the photograph.

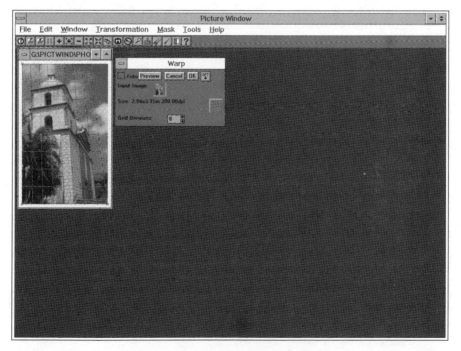

Figure 12.24 The grid set to correct a building's perspective.

Removing Distracting Objects

Many photographs are spoiled by unwanted elements that detract from the overall effect. In some cases, these elements are caused by dust that got in the way during photographic processing. In other cases, they are such things as power cables that ruin an otherwise excellent landscape, reflections of an electronic flash from a polished surface, or something behind a person's head that looks as if it is growing out of the head. All these can be corrected with Picture Window, some easily, but others with quite a lot of painstaking work.

The Clone tool is one of the most useful tools for correcting minor blemishes in a photograph. Cloning allows you to copy pixels from one place in a picture to another place. As an example, the photograph of a house, shown in a Picture Window screen in Figure 12.25, is spoiled by the television antenna on the roof and a power line in the sky in the top-left corner. We can correct these problems by using the Clone tool to copy areas of blue sky over the cable and antenna.

Here's how you can easily remove the antenna and the power line:

1. Magnify the photograph and display the part with the power line that you want to remove.

2. Open the Picture Window Tools menu and choose Clone to open the Clone dialog box shown in Figure 12.26.

3. Drag the Radius slider to choose the radius of the area you want to copy. In this case a fairly small radius is appropriate.

4. Drag the Transparency slider to choose how transparent the copied image should be. Because you want to completely obliterate the power line, you want zero transparency.

5. Drag the Softness slider to choose the degree of softness with which the copied image fades into its surroundings. In this case the default value of 50 is a good starting point.

5. Point onto the part of the photograph you want to copy, hold down the Shift key, and click the mouse button. In this case, you would point onto a clear part of the sky. A circle with a radius corresponding to the value you set in the Radius slider appears.

6. Point onto the power cable you want to eliminate.

7. Press and hold down the mouse button while you drag slowly along the cable. As you drag, the clear sky replaces the sky that is marred by the power cable.

You can remove the television antenna in the same way, with the result shown in Figure 12.27.

There are, of course, many ways you can use cloning, not only to remove objects but to add them. Perhaps you have a picture of a house with only one

Figure 12.25 A photograph of a house.

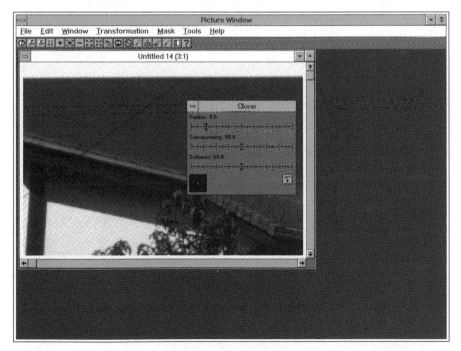

Figure 12.26 The Clone dialog box.

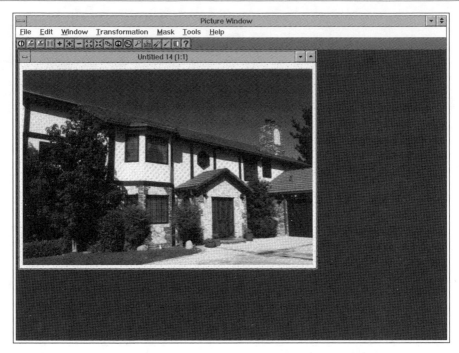

Figure 12.27 **The same photograph shown in Figure 12.25 with the cable and television antenna removed from the sky by cloning.**

window in an otherwise blank wall. You could easily create a second window by cloning the existing one.

Improving Portraits

Skilled portrait photographers know how to position their cameras and set their lights so that their photographs are as complimentary as possible to their subjects. But even so, retouching artists improve the final images by subtly reducing the prominence of blemishes that, for some reason, always seem more obvious in a photograph than they do on the person.

You can use the Clone tool to soften blemishes. When you do, remember that you get the best effect by toning down a blemish rather than by attempting to completely remove it.

Eyes are very important in a portrait. Unless you are skilled in arranging your lighting, eyes get hidden by shadows, making the person look dull and uninteresting. It's beyond the scope of what can be covered here, but you can learn to use Picture Window to lighten the shadows so that eyes become more alive, making the person look alert and friendly.

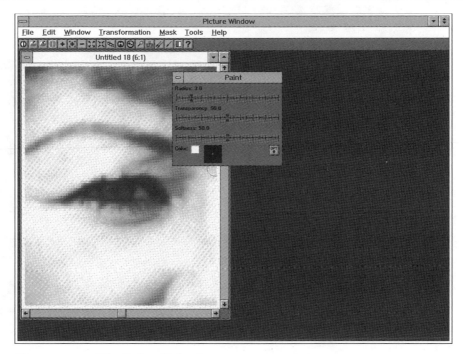

Figure 12.28 The Paint dialog box.

One professional photography trick is to arrange lights so that there is a highlight in the pupils, an effect that adds to the contact we feel with the person in a portrait. If your photographs of people lack this professional touch, you can easily remedy this with Picture Window's Paint tool. You can use the same technique to remove the red-eye that happens when you use an on-camera electronic flash to photograph a person.

You can use the Paint tool to increase the sparkle in the eyes by enlarging the existing highlight. To do this:

1. Open the Tools menu and choose Zoom.

2. Move the mouse pointer onto the photograph. Notice that the pointer changes to a cross inside a circle.

3. Point onto the eyes in your portrait and click the mouse button several times. Each time you click the button, the photograph is enlarged. Click until the detail within the eye is clearly visible.

4. Open the Tools menu again and choose Paint to open the Paint dialog box shown in Figure 12.28.

5. Click the square at the right of the word Color to open the Paint Color dialog box shown in Figure 12.29.

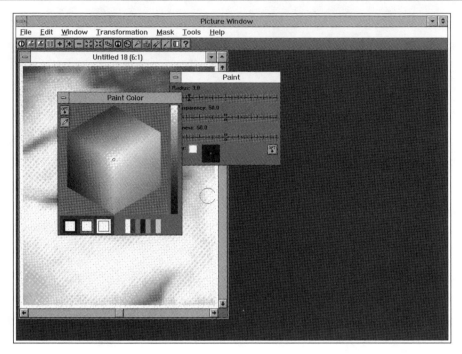

Figure 12.29 The Paint Color dialog box.

6. Click the Eyedropper tool in the Paint Color dialog box (the lower of the two buttons on the top left).

7. Click the existing highlight in an eye to pick this as the color to use. The color appears in the Color box in the Paint dialog box.

8. Click the Color box in the Paint dialog box to select it.

9. Move the mouse pointer onto the eye and drag over the part of the pupil to which you want to add the highlight.

10. Click the Zoom out button in the toolbar to reduce the photograph to its original magnification and see the result shown in Figure 12.30.

Other Enhancements

There are many other ways in which you can change and improve photographs using an application such as Picture Window. Among these are:

- Sharpening and blurring images
- Using masks so that changes can be limited to certain areas of a photograph
- Creating special effects such as posterization and embossing

Figure 12.30 Eyes with enhanced highlights.

- Adding text to an image
- Creating composite images

Using these techniques is a lot of fun, but it's quite time-consuming.

Printing Photographic Images

You can make surprisingly good printed photographic images on your 560C or 1200C inkjet printer. Of course, you should normally select ColorSmart and Presentation (560C) or High Quality (1200C) to get the best possible results. Also, you should print on HP Glossy Paper to get really sparkling photographs.

As an alternative to using ColorSmart, you might like to experiment with the Manual Color options available for the DeskJet 1200C printer to investigate the effects of the various options you can choose. If you are using a DeskJet 560C printer, compare the results you get by choosing the Automatic and Color Photo Printout modes. See Chapter 13 for information about this.

Part III

Part III contains advanced information about working with inkjet printers.

Chapter 13 deals with some of the significant issues about getting correct colors on the printed page. In this chapter, you will learn about ColorSmart, and also about how you can optimize the match of colors between those you see on your screen and eventually get on the printed page. The chapter also covers using PANTONE colors on the DeskJet 1200C color printer.

Chapter 14 provides an introduction to Printer Control Language (PCL) commands. When you are working outside the Macintosh or Windows environments, you have to know how to use these commands in order to take advantage of your printer's capabilities. The chapter shows you how to create PCL commands and how to send them to your printer.

13
CHAPTER

Optimizing Color Printing

Color is a highly subjective matter. Each of us perceives color differently, and perceives the same color differently under different circumstances. Color combinations that some people like are unpleasant to other people. It's not uncommon to choose an item of clothing in a store and, when we get home, to find that the color looks different because the store lighting is not the same as the home lighting.

Because we can't define how people react to color, it's difficult to agree about what we mean by optimizing color printing. For the purpose of this chapter, we'll assume that color printing is optimized when the colors you see on a monitor are consistently the same as the colors you see on the printed page. While this is not a precise definition, it does clarify our intent.

Notice the word "consistently" in the previous paragraph. Because of the fundamental difference between the ways in which colors are created on screen (additive) and on paper (subtractive), we can't expect to completely achieve the objective of matching colors. Where differences do exist, consistency makes it possible to compensate for them.

When you scan an image to use in a publication, optimizing colors goes one step further. In this case, you want the colors you see on the screen to match the colors of the original image, and you want the colors in the printed image to match the colors on the screen.

Controlling the Path

The stages an image passes through in order to be printed are known as its path. When you create a printed publication containing a scanned image, the path can consist of the following steps:

1. Scanning the image and saving it as a file
2. Importing the image into a graphics application, applying some corrections to it, and saving it as a file
3. Importing the image into a desktop publishing application and placing it in position on a page
4. Printing the page

At each step you deal with the positions, shapes, sizes, and colors of images. Positions, shapes, and sizes are relatively easy to deal with and shouldn't give you too many problems; those in the printed image should match the shape and size of the original image unless, of course, you deliberately make changes.

Scanning an Image

Color is a more complex matter than position. At the first stage, the scanner measures the amount of light (usually red, green, and blue components of the light) reflected from, or transmitted through, the original image. Unfortunately, the color sensing devices used in scanners suffer from various imperfections, all of which means that the color detected is not exactly what is in the original. Another result of these imperfections is that the color detected by one scanner is not exactly the same as the color detected by another scanner. This is true to a certain extent among scanners of the same model from the same supplier, and is true to a greater extent among scanners from different manufacturers.

Scanner manufacturers try to correct for these deficiencies in two ways. They calibrate each scanner so that all scanners of a specific model detect colors from a specific image as the same to within quite close tolerances. However, various manufacturers have different ideas about how the ideal scanner should perform, so this doesn't eliminate differences between various models.

The second way that manufacturers compensate for deficiencies is by providing software, a scanner driver, that allows you to adjust the scanner's response to colors. When you do this, you create a color map—a mathematical model that relates detected colors to colors in the file created by the scanner.

In addition to changing the way a scanner recognizes colors, you can also use the scanner driver's capabilities to compensate, to some extent, for deficiencies in the original image. For example, you might want to change the overall brightness, change the contrast, or add or reduce emphasis over certain tonal ranges. Be careful that what you do here does not remove any detail that you might subsequently want to work with.

Improving the Image

Learning to use the scanner's controls is your first line of attack to get an optimized image on paper. The next stage is to bring the image into a graphics application such as Photoshop, PHOTO-PAINT, or Picture Window and use that application's controls to improve the image, as described in Chapter 12.

Graphics applications such as these allow you to control how colors appear on the screen. Almost certainly, the colors you see when you first import a scanned image will not be exactly the same as those in the original image. Also, if you import the scanned image into two different graphics applications, the colors on the screen might be somewhat different.

You usually calibrate your screen to the application by choosing your monitor from a list, or by defining certain parameters of the monitor. Unfortunately, the parameters necessary are not usually listed in the monitor's specifications or known by the dealer from whom you bought the monitor; they can often only be obtained directly from the manufacturer, a process that might require persistence and patience.

Laying Out the Page

After you have done whatever optimizing is necessary in the graphics application, you save the file and then import it into your desktop publishing application. Depending on the application you are using, the image you see may be of poorer quality than you expect. This is because the purpose of the desktop application is primarily to position the graphic, not to work with its details.

> *Note:* Your desktop publishing application may allow you to display a graphic at various resolutions. PageMaker, for example, lets you display a graphic in Normal or High Resolution. In Preferences, choose Normal to simply position graphics quickly, or choose High Resolution to display more detail with better color but more slowly.

The desktop application accurately positions the graphic on the page and either keeps a copy of the graphics file or creates a link to that file. When you print the page, you are actually printing the file that was created at the time you scanned the image, or the file that you modified in your graphics application. For this reason, the detailed appearance of the graphic displayed by the desktop publishing application isn't too important. It would be nice if it were displayed as it will print, but you can live without that feature.

Printing the Page

The final stage is printing the page, either directly from the scanner, or as modified by your graphics application, or as positioned by your desktop publishing application. This is where your printer driver takes over.

While you are displaying a graphic on your monitor, you are working in the RGB world. Your eyes are seeing red, green, and blue light, and your brain is combining these colors to give you the sensation of many different colors. Your printer sees the world differently—in CMYK terms. The only thing your printer can do is to print dots of transparent cyan, magenta, yellow, and black ink, attempting to do so in such a way that the light reflected by the paper gives you the same sensation as the image you see on the screen. Quite a formidable task!

Your graphics application and printer driver have the task of converting colors that are defined by mixing various levels of red, green, and blue light, into a printed image that consists of dots of cyan, magenta, yellow, and black ink that can be either printed or not printed—they can't be printed at different intensities.

The task of converting RGB colors that you see on the screen to CMYK colors that can be printed occurs at two stages: in your graphics application and in the printer driver.

Some graphics applications offer a comprehensive, perhaps overwhelming, array of tools for optimizing printed colors; others offer none. Photoshop, Photo-Paint, and Picture Window are among the applications that provide tools for matching the colors that you see on screen to the colors that print.

In some—but not all—cases, the printer driver also provides calibration tools. The PCL driver for the DeskJet 1200C printer contains such a calibration tool; the PCL drivers for the DeskJet and DeskWriter 560C printer, and the PostScript drivers for the DeskJet 560C and 1200C printers, do not offer a color calibration capability.

Minimizing the Variables

Colors on the screen and colors on paper depend on several variables you can control. Colors you see on the screen depend on the settings of the brightness and contrast controls on your monitor. You should set these controls, and any others your monitor may have, to what you consider the best position, and then tape them so that they cannot be moved. It is vital that you do this before proceeding any further with optimizing color printing.

The next point is more difficult to control in many working situations. The colors you see on your screen are highly dependent on the room lighting. The ideal situation is that no direct light falls on the screen or into your eyes, that the room is dimly lit, and that the room lighting is always the same. Most people find it easier to judge on-screen colors if the room lighting is somewhat dim. If you can't have these conditions all the time, you should at least have them when you are doing color-critical work.

You might also find that the colors on your screen are slightly different when you first turn the monitor on from what they are after it has been on for 10 or 20 minutes (or even more), so it's a good idea to let the monitor warm up for about 30 minutes before looking carefully at colors.

The ink your printer uses is transparent. For this reason, the appearance of color depends on the color of the paper you use. Naturally, you should use white paper, but there are many different types of white paper. Inexpensive copier paper tends to be slightly gray, for example. Other types of paper may have a slight yellow or blue color cast. For consistent results, you should always use the same paper for high-quality color work. For the 560C and 1200C inkjet printers, HP's LX JetSeries Glossy Paper gives the best results. HP's CX JetSeries CutSheet Paper gives somewhat less brilliant colors.

The ambient light under which you view printed colors has a great effect on the colors you perceive. As you read in Chapter 2, when you look at a printed page you are seeing reflected light. Only those colors that fall on the printed material can be reflected. Light from ordinary tungsten light bulbs is deficient in blue light, so any blues in your printed material seen in this light appear more gray than they really are. Various types of fluorescent lamps used in most offices contain different distributions of light in the spectrum, so these affect your perception of printed color.

Again, the main point is to be consistent. Always evaluate printed colors under the same ambient light. Avoid having light fall directly on the paper, so that the glossy surface does not reflect the light source.

Matching Screen and Printer Colors

It's always encouraging when you start a task to know that it can be done, and that all you have to do is to develop the necessary skills and have enough patience. This is *not* the case when your task is to match screen and printer colors. The laws of physics don't allow you to exactly and completely match screen colors to printed colors. Having said that, at least we can assure you that you can make adjustments that provide much better matching than you get initially.

Most monitors, other than the most expensive ones, have a slight blue color cast. You can easily see this if you hold a sheet of plain white paper up to the screen. Also, most monitors do not create a true cyan.

Despite these problems, there are things you can do to improve the match between your screen and monitor.

When you work with color printing and want to evaluate the quality of your results, you need to have a high-quality image on screen to start with. If your objective is to print photo-quality pictures, you should have a high-definition monitor capable of displaying many colors. Don't be discouraged, though, if you have less than the ideal. You can do a lot of good work with a less-than-ideal monitor that has a definition of 1024 by 768 pixels and can display 256 colors. If you are serious about color work, you need a definition of 1280 by 1024 pixels and the ability to display 16.7 million colors.

Using ColorSmart

ColorSmart is a technology built into the PCL drivers for the 560C and 1200C inkjet printers. At the time this book is being written, ColorSmart is not available with PostScript drivers. ColorSmart analyzes each page to be printed, identifies separate regions that contain text, graphics, and photographs, and chooses the best way to print each region. If you wish, you can use a manual mode in which you choose how text, graphics, and photographs in your document are to be printed.

As we continue to stress in this book, color printing is not a perfect process. As a result, some choices have to be made. You can, for example:

- Optimize printing for text by giving high priority to sharp outlines of small details, even if this means some sacrifice of color fidelity.
- Optimize printing for business graphics (graphs and charts) by giving high priority to strong, vivid colors.
- Optimize printing for photographs by giving high priority to color fidelity, particularly delicate tones such as human skin colors.

This is not too much of a problem when a page contains only text, only business graphics, or only photographs. But the chances are that many of your pages contain two or three of these elements, and that's where ColorSmart can make all the difference. ColorSmart identifies each region and then chooses, or lets you choose, how each is to be printed.

You select ColorSmart or manually control how a document is printed in a somewhat different manner for the 560C and the 1200C printer, so each is described separately on the following pages.

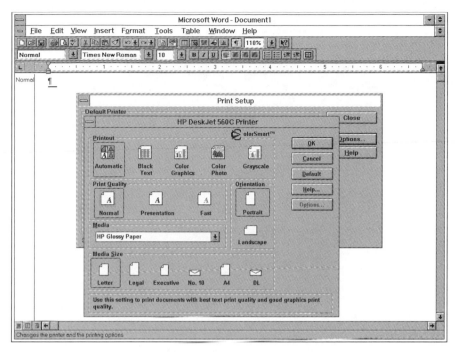

Figure 13.1   The DeskJet 560C Setup dialog box with Automatic selected.

Optimizing the DeskJet 560C Printer

For most purposes, you can get excellent printed text, business graphics, and photographs by simply letting ColorSmart take charge. When you are ready to print, open the printer Setup dialog box from your application (Figure 13.1) and, in the Printout section, choose Automatic.

When you select Automatic, ColorSmart automatically analyzes your document and identifies text, graphics, and photographic regions on each page. ColorSmart chooses appropriate color control and halftone options for each region.

For final copies of your work, you should normally choose Presentation in the Print Quality section of the dialog box and choose the type of paper in the Media section. For best results, you should use HP Special or HP Glossy paper.

If you want to take control yourself, you can choose Color Graphics or Color Photo in the Printout section of the dialog box, and then click the Options button to display the HP Printer Options dialog box shown in Figure 13.2.

You can use the controls in this dialog box to optimize printing in several ways.

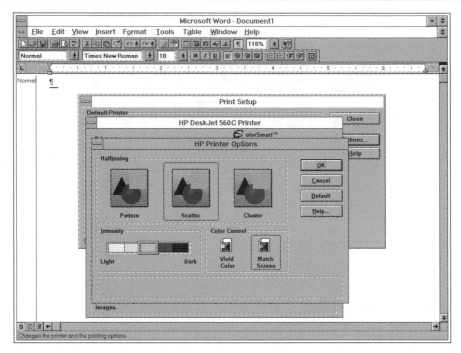

Figure 13.2 The HP Printer Options dialog box.

Choosing a Halftoning Method

In this dialog box, you can choose among three halftoning methods. Halftoning is the technique used to group cyan, yellow, magenta, and black dots to simulate millions of possible colors. The choices are:

- Pattern—provides uniform distribution of ink that is good for text, line art, freehand graphics, and business charts.

- Scatter—provides a random distribution of ink that works well for photographic images.

- Cluster—clusters dots of ink, which works well with some photographic images; also good for images that will be copied on a xerographic copier.

Controlling Lightness

The slider at the bottom left of the dialog box allows you to choose among five levels of lightness for your printed pages. You can use this control to adjust the match between the lightness of colors on your screen and the lightness on your printed pages.

Controlling Color

You can choose between two methods of printing color by clicking options in the Color Control section of the dialog box:

- Vivid Color—works best for business graphics and other types of graphics that have bright, solid colors.

- Match Screen—works best for photographs and other images that have a wide range of colors.

Match Screen assumes you are using a monitor that displays colors accurately. If your monitor has a color cast, as some do, you may have to use color controls in your graphics application to get the most realistic printed colors.

Optimizing the DeskJet 1200C Printer

For most purposes, you can get excellent printed text, business graphics, and photographs by simply letting ColorSmart take charge. When you are ready to print, open the printer Setup dialog box from your application (Figure 13.3) and, in the Color section, choose ColorSmart.

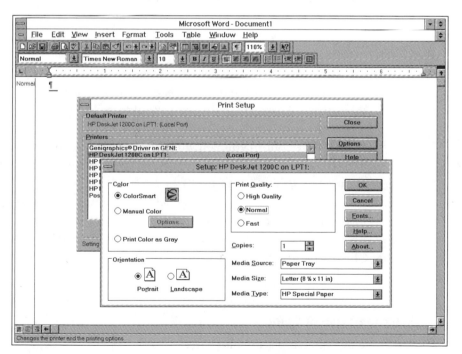

Figure 13.3 The DeskJet 1200C Setup dialog box with ColorSmart selected.

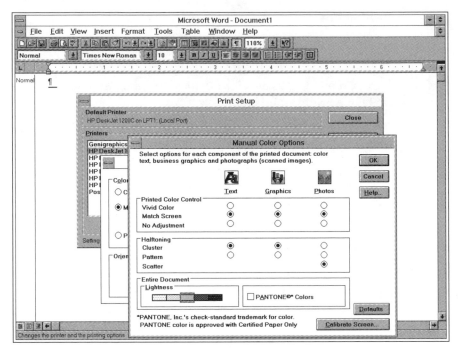

Figure 13.4 The Manual Color Options dialog box.

For final copies of your work, you should normally choose High Quality in the Print Quality section of the dialog box and choose the type of paper in the Media Type section. For best results, you should use HP Special or HP Glossy paper.

If you want to take control yourself, you can choose Manual Color in the Color section of the dialog box. You can then click Options to display the Manual Color Options dialog box shown in Figure 13.4.

When this dialog box first appears, click the Default button to show how ColorSmart selects colors and halftoning. ColorSmart automatically detects text, graphics, and photographs on each page and uses Vivid Color for all three. It uses Cluster halftoning for text and graphics, and Scatter halftoning for photographs.

Selecting Types of Colors

The three available types of colors are:

- Vivid—provides clear and vivid printed colors with some sacrifice of hue in some cases.

- Match Screen—provides the closest match between screen and printed colors (provided you have calibrated your screen as described below).
- No Adjustment—prints colors as set by the application.

You can click the buttons in the Printed Color Control section of the dialog box to change how you want the three types of images (text, graphics, and photographs) printed.

Selecting the Halftoning Method

Halftoning is the use of patterns of cyan, yellow, magenta, black, and white (paper) dots to simulate millions of different colors on the printed page. The three available types of halftoning are:

- Pattern—uses a constant uniform distribution of dots; used for freehand drawings, clip art, and color text, in some cases produces noticeable patterns.
- Scatter—gives a smooth appearance by randomly distributing dots of ink; used primarily for printing scanned images.
- Cluster—uses groups of dots; good for text and for business graphics with areas of solid color.

You can click the buttons in the Halftoning section of the dialog box to change the halftoning method for the three types of images (text, graphics, and photographs).

Controlling Lightness

The slider at the bottom left of the dialog box allows you to choose among five levels of lightness for your printed pages. You can use this control to adjust the match between color lightness on your screen and on your printed pages.

Using PANTONE colors

The PANTONE Colors check box at the bottom center of the screen allows you to choose colors from the PANTONE standard provided, of course, your application supports PANTONE colors. This subject is covered separately later in this chapter.

Calibrating Your Screen

The process of calibrating your screen provides information about what you see on your monitor to the printer driver. This allows the printer driver to better match the printed output with what you see.

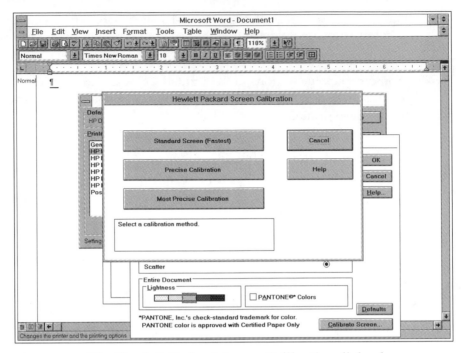

Figure 13.5 The Hewlett-Packard Screen Calibration dialog box.

It is important to understand that the printer driver only uses the results of screen calibration when the Printed Color Control is set to Match Screen in the Manual Color Options dialog box. If you want to take advantage of calibrating your screen, you must select Manual Color in the Color section of the printer Setup dialog box, choose Options, and set one or more of the print components to Match Screen.

When you go through the screen calibration process, the printer driver creates a color map, which is a table that converts the red, green, and blue values displayed on your monitor to cyan, yellow, magenta, and black dots to be printed.

To proceed with calibrating your screen, click the Calibrate Screen button in the Manual Color Options dialog box to display the Hewlett-Packard Screen Calibration dialog box shown in Figure 13.5.

This dialog box offers three types of calibration:

- Standard Screen—a fast, noninteractive method of building a color map based on typical screen characteristics.

- Precise Calibration—an interactive method of building a color map based on matching shades of gray.

- Most Precise Calibration—an interactive method of building a color map based on matching red, green, hue, and black.

The following paragraphs describe the Most Precise Calibration method. Before you start, do the following:

1. Set the room lighting to the conditions under which you will be working, making sure that there is no light source behind the monitor and that no light source is shining directly on the screen.

2. Turn on your monitor and allow about half an hour for it to stabilize.

3. Adjust the brightness and contrast controls on your monitor and tape them so that they cannot be moved.

To make sure that the printer is working correctly and that your print cartridges contain sufficient ink, press the Shift key on the printer control panel and, with the Shift key down, press the Test key to perform a self-test. If the test print is not perfect, clear any clogged print cartridge nozzles or replace print cartridges.

During the calibration process, you will print a sample color. This should be printed on the type of paper you intend to use for your high-quality printed work. Place a sheet of this paper in the paper input tray, ready to be printed (remember to have the print surface face down).

Now, you can start the calibration process:

1. Click the Most Precise Calibration button to display the first calibration screen in which you set the red level of your screen.

2. Move the slider until you can only just see the difference between the center colored part of the black rectangle and the black edges, then click Continue to display the next calibration screen.

3. Repeat step 2 for the next two screens.

4. In screen four, drag the slider until the center and outer part of the rectangle are balanced. You can do this by squinting at the screen so that the image is fuzzy. Press Continue to proceed to the next screen.

5. Repeat step 4 for the next five screens.

6. After making the adjustments on the first six screens, click the Print button to print a sample color patch. This should be on the type of paper you plan to use for your quality work.

You are now ready to make the final color adjustment. In step 6 above, you printed a color patch that you will match to a similar color patch on the screen. When you look at the printed color patch, you need to see it entirely by reflected light. One way to do this is to cut out the color patch and attach it to a piece of thick white card. After you've done that, proceed to step 7.

7. Click Continue to display a color patch, similar to the printed one, on your screen.

8. Use the scroll bar under the color patch on the screen to look at the seven available shades, ranging from one that is quite blue to one that has a pronounced amount of red. Choose the shade that most closely corresponds to the printed color patch. Match the shades, not the brightness of the colors. When you have found the best match, click OK to display the Calibration Completed dialog box.

9. Click OK to create color maps that represent the calibration.

> *Note:* To match shades in step 8, first find an on-screen shade that is a little too red, and then find one that is a little too blue. The correct shade is the one between those two.

After you have calibrated your screen, the calibration is saved in a file with a name like HPPCL5C3.HPM in your Windows directory.

To see the effect of color calibration, try printing a color photograph using ColorSmart, and compare it with the same photograph printed with Manual Color and Match Screen selected. While you are making comparisons, you might also like to try the effect of using various Halftoning types and of adjusting the Lightness control. If you have a color scanner, you can directly print a color photograph to make these tests. Otherwise, you can use a color photograph from one of the Corel Professional Photos CD ROMs or a color photograph file included in one of your graphics applications. In each case, compare the printed result with the on-screen image.

Using PANTONE Colors

PANTONE is an international standard for color communication in the graphic arts industry. Its purpose is to ensure effective color selection, specification, and control among clients, graphic designers, printers, and ink manufacturers.

At the heart of the system are color reference manuals that display colors with the precise printing formulas for achieving those colors. Each PANTONE color is identified by a number or name.

The PANTONE License

The DeskJet 1200C printer is a licensed PANTONE color printer. This means that there is a PANTONE Color Lookup Table that PANTONE-approved applications can use to print approved simulations of PANTONE colors on this printer. PANTONE colors are only licensed under the following conditions:

- Printing is on plain paper (Champion Datacopy or KYMCOPY LUX paper is recommended).
- Print Quality is set to Normal or High Quality.
- Hewlett-Packard DeskJet 1200C print cartridges are used.

PANTONE colors printed by halftoning methods on the DeskJet 1200C are approximations that should be used for proofing and are not necessarily accurate for final copy or for use in reproducing logos and other color-critical work. Only by mixing PANTONE inks can you get true PANTONE colors.

Printing from Applications

You can print PANTONE colors from applications that support these colors. Most leading graphics and desktop publishing applications do support PANTONE colors. Applications mentioned in this book that support PANTONE colors include:

- Canvas
- CorelDRAW
- Corel PHOTO-PAINT
- FrameMaker
- PageMaker
- Photoshop

After creating a typical document that includes PANTONE colors, do the following to print those colors:

1. Open the application's File menu and choose Print to open the Print dialog box.
2. Choose Printer to open the Setup dialog box.
3. Select the DeskJet 1200C, then click Setup to open the 1200C Setup dialog box.
4. Choose Plain Paper.
5. Choose Manual Color, and then click Options to open the Manual Color Options dialog box.

6. If necessary, choose Cluster halftoning for Text and Graphics.
7. Click PANTONE Colors to enable the use of the PANTONE Color Map.
8. Click OK to return to the 1200C Setup dialog box.
9. Click OK to return to the Print dialog box.
10. Click Print to print the document.

> *Note:* Any colors in the document other than PANTONE colors are printed according to the settings in the normal Color Map.

14

Controlling Your Printer

To produce the printed documents you want, you have to tell the printer what you want it to do. You do this by means of printer commands that control such things as:

- Margins
- Line spacing (for text)
- Where to start new pages
- Fonts
- Colors

There are three ways to issue these commands to the printer:

- By making choices within an application
- By pressing buttons on the printer's control panel
- By including printer commands within your document

The preceding chapters of this book have assumed that you can control the printer by making choices within an application. If, as is usually the case, your application provides all the printer controls you need, you can ignore this chapter. However, if you sometimes use an older application that does not directly support your inkjet printer, read this chapter to learn how to work with printer control commands.

Using Printer Drivers

A printer driver is a software module that knows how to talk to your printer. By using a printer driver, you can respond to on-screen choices and the driver

283

takes care of sending commands to your printer so that you get the printed document you expect.

Printer control is simple if you are working in the Macintosh or Windows environments. You install the driver supplied with your printer, and then all your applications work with the printer in the same way. For example, in the Windows environment, you can choose the Print command from most applications to display a Print dialog box. From that dialog box, you can choose Printer to display a Print Setup dialog box in which you choose the printer you want to use. In fact, when you choose a printer, you are selecting a printer driver. Then you choose Options to display that printer driver's setup dialog box, which is where you choose the printing options you want to use.

> *Note:* The exact route to the printer driver's setup dialog box varies somewhat among applications, but once you get to that dialog box, you are dealing with the printer driver that is common to all Windows applications.

If you use DOS versions of applications such as Lotus 1-2-3, Word, WordPerfect, or a text editor, you don't have the benefit of a printer driver that is shared between applications. Instead, you need to use a separate printer driver for each application or embed printer-control commands within your documents.

Many DOS applications are supplied with several disks containing printer drivers. You have to install the drivers for the printers you expect to use. When the time comes to print, you select a printer so that the driver associated with that printer can send commands to the printer in the language the selected printer understands.

If your DOS application doesn't provide a printer driver for your printer, what do you do? One solution to this problem is to search for a suitable printer driver. You might be able to download a driver from a bulletin board. Another solution is to embed printer control commands within the application.

Embedding Printer Control Commands

Many DOS applications allow you to embed printer control commands. By using these commands, you can use a printer that is not directly supported by your application; or, if your printer is partly supported, you can gain more control over your printer's capabilities.

Each application has a different way of allowing you to embed printer control commands. Following are just two examples. Consult the application documentation for information about how to use printer control commands in a specific application.

Printer Control Commands in WordPerfect 5.1

You can insert a printer control command anywhere in a WordPerfect document. To do so:

1. Place the cursor where you want to insert a printer control command.
2. Press Shift+F8 (Format) and then press 4 (Other).
3. Press 6 (Printer Functions), 2 (Printer Command), and 1 (Command).
4. Type the commands to be sent to the printer.
5. Press F7 to return to the editing screen.

Printer Control Commands in Lotus 1-2-3

If you use an older DOS version of Lotus 1-2-3, you have to use printer commands, known as setup strings, to select some options such as paper orientation and compressed printing. To do this:

1. Press /WGDP (Worksheet Global Default Printer) to display a list of printer options.
2. Select the Setup option.
3. Type the printer codes in decimal, using the format in the following example.

To set the printer for landscape orientation, compressed printing, use the setup string:

\027E\027&*l*1O\027(s16.66H

Note: The "*l*" (lowercase ell) is shown in script here so that you do not mistake it for a 1 (one).

This setup string consists of three separate commands:

- Reset — \027E
- Landscape orientation — \027&*l*1O
- Compressed printing — \027(s16.66H.

Lotus 1-2-3 uses \027 to represent the escape character.

Experimenting with Printer Control Commands

To gain an understanding of printer control commands, you can try some experiments based entirely on DOS. The following is a practical example that shows you how to print a directory listing that is better than what you ordinarily get.

You probably already know that you can display a list of files in a directory by typing **DIR** and pressing Enter. To print the listing, you type **DIR>PRN** and press Enter. The problem is that your printer uses its default settings, resulting in there being no left margin, so that you cannot three-hole punch the printed pages and place them in a binder.

> *Note:* The preceding paragraph applies to DeskJet 560C printers, and to DeskJet 1200C/PS printers when the language is set to PCL by the printer's rear-panel switches. If you send a DOS command such as DIR>PRN to a 1200C/PS printer set to PostScript, the printer tries to interpret that command as a PostScript command, fails to do so, and prints an error message. See later in this chapter for information about how to print a list of DOS files on a DeskJet 1200C/PS printer set to PostScript.

Another problem is that your printer only ejects a page when that page is full. To eject the page, you have to use the printer's control panel buttons, which can be inconvenient, particularly if you can't reach the printer from your desk.

You can solve both these problems by sending a command to set the printer margin before you ask for the directory listing, and sending a command to eject the page after you ask for the listing.

HP printers are controlled by Printer Control Language (PCL) commands. There are three types of PCL commands:

- Control codes
- Two-character escape sequences
- Parameterized escape sequences

Control Codes

Control codes are characters that initiate a printer action, such as carriage return (CR), line feed (LF), or form feed (FF).

Two-Character Escape Sequences

Two-character escape sequences consist of the escape character followed by a single character such as:

<Esc>E (reset the printer to its default settings)

<Esc>9 (reset the left and right margins to their default settings)

Note: In these examples and throughout this chapter, <Esc> represents the Escape character.

Parameterized Escape Sequences

Simple parameterized escape sequences have the format

<Esc>Xy#Z

where:

X represents a character with an ASCII value in the range 33 through 47 (! through /). The presence of this character indicates that the escape sequence is parameterized.

y represents a character with an ASCII value in the range 96 through 126 (' through ~). This is the group character that specifies the type of action caused by the command.

is a decimal number. The number may be preceded by + or -, and may include a decimal point. This is the value field that is used to specify an amount.

Z represents a character with an ASCII value in the range 64 through 94 (@ through ^). This character specifies the parameter to which the previous value applies and terminates the escape sequence.

Examples of parameterized escape sequences are:

<Esc>&a5L (set the left margin to 5)

Note: By default, margin measurements are in $\frac{1}{10}$ -inch increments. Setting the left margin to 5 produces a $\frac{1}{2}$ -inch margin.

<Esc>&*l* 0O (set portrait orientation)

<Esc>&*l* 1O (set landscape orientation)

Note: PCL commands are case sensitive. To avoid confusion between the digit one (1) and a lowercase ell (l), PCL commands traditionally show lowercase ells in script, as in the above example. It is also important not to confuse a zero (0) with an uppercase O.

There are more elaborate types of parameterized escape sequences, but these are beyond the scope of this book.

Creating and Using PCL Commands

DOS versions 5 and later come with MS-DOS Edit, which you can easily use to create PCL commands to send to your printer. Alternatively, you can use your word processor to create these commands.

Creating PCL Commands with MS-DOS Edit

If you've used Edit, you know that you can type any ordinary text and save that text as an ASCII file. You might not know how to use Edit to enter an escape character. To enter an escape character in Edit, press Ctrl+P and then press the Esc key. On screen, the escape character is represented by a small arrow pointing to the left.

To create a PCL command that ejects a page, do the following:

1. At the DOS prompt, type Edit and press Enter to open the MS-DOS Editor.
2. Press <Esc> to close the initial dialog box.
3. Type Ctrl+P and then press <Esc> to place the escape character into your document. You should see a left-pointing arrow at the top-left corner of your screen.
4. Type an ampersand (&), a lowercase ell (*ℓ*), a zero (0), and an uppercase **H**. There must be no spaces between the characters.
5. Press Enter to terminate the line.
6. Open the File menu and choose Save.
7. Name the file EJECT.TXT (or any other appropriate name), then click OK.
8. Open the File menu and choose Exit to close Edit.

This completes creating a PCL command that ejects a page from the printer. Now create a PCL command that changes the left margin from the default of 0 (zero) to 5. Repeat steps 1 through 3 in the preceding procedure; then, after the escape character, type **&a5L** and press Enter. Save the file as MARGIN.TXT.

> *Note:* By default, margin measurements are in ¹⁄₁₀ -inch increments. Setting the left margin to 5, for example, produces a ½ -inch margin.

Creating PCL Commands with Word

As an example of using a word processor to create a PCL command, use the following steps to create the Reset command (<Esc>E).

> *Note:* The reset command clears all data from the printer's memory, including downloaded fonts.

1. In Word, open the File menu and choose New to start a new document.
2. To enter the escape character, press and hold down the Alt key while you type 027 on the numeric keypad, then release the Alt key. A small square on your monitor represents the escape character.

> *Note:* You must type **027** on the numeric keypad with NUM LOCK turned on, not on the top row of number keys.

3. Type **E** and then press Enter.
4. To save the command as ASCII text rather than in word-processing format, open the File menu and choose Save As to display the Save As dialog box.
5. In the drop-down Save File As Type list box, choose Text Only.
6. Name the file RESET.TXT, then click OK to save it.

> *Note:* You must save the file as text only.

This completes creating the Reset PCL command. For convenience, you might want to move the four PCL commands you have created to a separate directory.

Using PCL Commands

After you have created these commands, you can use them to print a directory listing with a ½ -inch left margin:

1. At the DOS prompt, type **COPY MARGIN.TXT PRN** to send the command that changes the left margin to the printer.
2. Type **DIR>PRN** to send the directory listing to the printer.
3. Type **COPY EJECT.TXT PRN** to eject the last page of the printed listing.
4. Type **COPY RESET.TXT PRN** to restore the default left margin.

If you often want to print a directory listing like this, you can create a batch file such as:

```
COPY MARGIN.TXT PRN
DIR>PRN
COPY EJECT.TXT PRN
COPY RESET.TXT PRN
```

You can create this batch file using DOS Edit and save it with a name such as PRINTDIR.BAT. To execute the batch file, type PRINTDIR and press Enter.

> *Note:* This method of printing a list of DOS files can be used with a DeskJet 1200C/PS printer set to PostScript, as well as to DeskJet 560C and 1200C printers. This method works with printers set to PostScript because you start by transmitting a PCL command to the printer by sending the MARGIN.TXT file. The printer recognizes the PCL command and automatically switches to the PCL mode. In the PCL mode, it can recognize DIR>PRN. Subsequently, when you next send a PostScript command, the printer recognizes it as such and switches back to the PostScript mode.

The Printer Environment

PCL commands cause two types of actions. Some commands, such as the command to change the left margin, set a condition that remains in effect until a subsequent command changes that setting. Other commands, such as the command to eject a page, cause an immediate, one-time action.

The printer environment is the cumulative effect of all the commands that change the printer settings. When you first turn on the printer it has the default environment. Whenever the printer receives a PCL command, that environment changes and the change remains in effect until one of three things happens:

- The printer receives a command that changes the current environment.
- You turn the printer off.
- The printer receives a reset command that restores the default environment.

The reset command is the two-character escape sequence:

<Esc>E

If you change the environment—for example, changing the left margin before you print a listing—it is good practice to immediately restore the default environment by sending the reset command to the printer. This is particularly important if you are sharing a printer on a network, so that the change doesn't affect other people's printing.

Following are some of the more important default settings that are in effect when you turn the printer on:

- 10-pitch (10 characters per inch horizontally)
- Courier font
- Black text
- 80 characters per line

- 6 lines per inch vertically
- 60 lines per page
- Perforation skip on
- Autowrap off
- Manual feed off
- Print mode plain paper (unless some other print mode is selected on front panel)
- Symbol set PC-8 or Roman-8 (as set by rear-panel switches)

Using Printer Drivers

Printer drivers control a printer by sending PCL commands. As far as a printer is concerned, it makes no difference whether the PCL commands come from files you write, as described above, or from a printer driver.

Most printer drivers start by sending a reset command to the printer. This provides the benefit that you don't have to be concerned about any PCL commands previously sent to the printer. However, it does mean that you cannot send PCL commands that override or supplement the printer control provided by the printer driver.

PCL Levels

Hewlett-Packard has designed PCL to be suitable for a wide range of printers. At present, five levels of PCL are defined. Level I contains the most basic printing commands. Level II is a superset of Level I—that is, it contains all the commands in Level I—plus some additional ones. Levels III, IV, and V contain progressively more commands.

Printers are specified according to which level of PCL they support. The DeskJet and Deskwriter 560C are Level III PCL printers; The DeskJet 1200C is a Level V PCL printer.

PCL Commands

The following tables contain the commands supported by the HP DeskJet 1200C and 1200C/PS printers and by the DeskJet and DeskWriter 560C printers.

See the Software Developer's Guide for HP's DeskJet 500 Series Printer Driver (for information about using PCL commands with the DeskJet 560C printer) and The PCL5 Printer Language Technical Reference Manual (for information about using PCL commands with the DeskJet 1200C printer).

Table 14.1 DeskJet 1200C PCL Commands

Current Active Position (CAP) Movement

Command	Code	Range
Clear Margins	<Esc>9	
Horizontal Motion Index (HMI)	<Esc>&k#H	0–32767
Move CAP Horizontal (Columns)	<Esc>&a#C	(-32767)–(+32767)
Move CAP Horizontal (Decipoints)	<Esc>&a#H	(-32767)–(+32767)
Move CAP Horizontal (Dots)	<Esc>*p#X	(-32767)–(+32767)
Move CAP Vertical (Rows)	<Esc>&a#R	(-32767)–(+32767)
Move CAP Vertical (Decipoints)	<Esc>&a#V	(-32767)–(+32767)
Move CAP Vertical (Dots)	<Esc>*p#Y	(-32767)–(+32767)
Print Direction	<Esc>&a#P	0, 90, 180, 270
Push/Pop CAP	<Esc>&f#S	0–1
Space	SP	

Control Codes

Command	Code
Back Space	BS
Carriage Return	CR
Escape	ESC
Formfeed	FF
Horizontal Tab	HT
Line Feed	LF
Null	NUL

Fonts

Command	Code	Range
Character ID	<Esc>*c#E	0–32767
Character Set	<Esc>(f#W[data]	0–32767
Character Set Control	<Esc>*c#S	0–5
Character Set ID	<Esc>*c#R	0–32767
Designate Download Font as Primary	<Esc>(#X	0–32767
Designate Download Font as Secondary	<Esc>)#X	0–32767
Download Character Descriptor	<Esc>(s#W	0–32767
Download Font Descriptor	<Esc>)s#W	0–32767
Font Control	<Esc>*c#F	0–6
Font ID	<Esc>*c#D	0–32767
Primary Font Character Set	<Esc>(ID,	
Primary Font Designation	<Esc>(#@	0–3

Fonts (continued)

Command	Code	Range
Primary Font Height	<Esc>(s#V	>0 (valid to 2 decimal places)
Primary Font Pitch	<Esc>(s#H	>0 (valid to 2 decimal places)
Primary Font Spacing	<Esc>(s#P	0, 1
Primary Font Stroke Weight	<Esc>(s#B	-7 to 7
Primary Font Style	<Esc>(s#S	0–32767
Primary Font Typeface	<Esc>(s#T	0–32767
Secondary Font Character Set	<Esc>)ID	
Secondary Font Designation	<Esc>)#@	0–3
Secondary Font Height	<Esc>)s#V	>0 (valid to 2 decimal places)
Secondary Font Pitch	<Esc>)s#H	>0 (valid to 2 decimal places)
Secondary Font Spacing	<Esc>)s#P	0, 1
Secondary Font Stroke Weight	<Esc>)s#B	-7 to 7
Secondary Font Style	<Esc>)s#S	0–32767
Secondary Font Typeface	<Esc>)s#T	0–32767
Shift In	SI	
Shift Out	SO	
Underline Mode Off	<Esc>&d@	
Underline Mode On	<Esc>&d#D	0, 3

Job Control

Command	Code	Range
AppleTalk Configuration	<Esc>&b#W[data]	0–32767
Mechanical Print Quality	<Esc>*o#Q	-1, 0, 1
Negative Motion	<Esc>&a#N	0, 1
Number of Copies	<Esc>&l#X	1–99
Presentation Mode	<Esc>*r#F	0, 3
Registration (Left)	<Esc>&l#U	(-32767)–(+32767)
Registration (Top)	<Esc>&l#Z	(-32767)–(+32767)
Reset	<Esc>E	

Language Switching

Command	Code	Range
Comment (PJL)	@PJL COMMENT <comment text>	
Enter Language (PJL)	@PJL ENTER LANGUAGE = PCL	
	@PJL ENTER LANGUAGE = POSTSCRIPT	
	@PJL ENTER LANGUAGE = HPGL2	
Enter HP–GL/2 mode	<Esc>%#B	-1, 0-2
Enter PCL mode	<Esc>%#A	0, 1

Language Switching (continued)

Command	Code	Range
Exit Language/Start PJL	<Esc>%#X	-12345
Picture Frame Anchor Point	<Esc>*c#T	0
Picture Frame Horizontal Size (Decipoints)	<Esc>*c#X	0–32767
Picture Frame Vertical Size (Decipoints)	<Esc>*c#Y	0–32767
Plot Horizontal Size	<Esc>*c#K	0–32767
Plot Vertical Size	<Esc>*c#L	0–32767

Macros

Command	Code	Range
Macro Control	<Esc>&f#X	0–10
Macro ID	<Esc>&f#Y	0–32767

Page Control

Command	Code	Range
End-of-Line Wrap	<Esc>&s#C	0–1
Line Spacing	<Esc>&*l*#D	0–(Page Length)
Line Termination	<Esc>&k#G	0–3
Margin (Left)	<Esc>&a#L	0–(Right Margin)
Margin (Right)	<Esc>&a#M	Left Margin to right logical page bound
Margin (Top)	<Esc>&*l*#E	0–(Page Length)
Media Source	<Esc>&*l*#H	0–2
Media Type	<Esc>&*l*#M	0–4
Orientation	<Esc>&*l*#O	0–3
Page Length	<Esc>&*l*#P	0–(maximum supported page size)
Paper Size	<Esc>&*l*#A	2, 3, 6, 26, 27, 46
Perforation Skip Mode	<Esc>&*l*#L	0–1
Text Length	<Esc>&*l*#F	0–(Page Length Top Margin)
Vertical Motion Index (VMI)	<Esc>&*l*#C	0–(Page Length)

Print Model Imaging

Command	Code	Range
Download Pattern	<Esc>*c#W[data]	0–(23
Fill Rectangle	<Esc>*c#P	0–5
Foreground Color	<Esc>*v#S	$0 (2^{\#bits/index})-1$
Logical Op	<Esc>*l#O	0–255

Print Model Imaging (continued)

Command	Code	Range
Pattern Control	<Esc>*c#O	0, 1, 2, 4, 5
Pattern ID	<Esc>*c#G	0–32767
Pattern Reference Point	<Esc>*p#R	0–1
Pattern Type	<Esc>*v#T	0–4
Rectangle Size, Horizontal (Decipoints)	<Esc>*c#H	0–32767
Rectangle Size, Horizontal (Dots)	<Esc>*c#A	0–32767
Rectangle Size, Vertical (Decipoints)	<Esc>*c#V	0–32767
Rectangle Size, Vertical (Dots)	<Esc>*c#B	0–32767
Transparency Mode (Pattern)	<Esc>*v#O	0–1
Transparency Mode (Source)	<Esc>*v#N	0–1

Raster Color

Command	Code	Range
Color Component (First)	<Esc>*v#A	0–32767
Color Component (Second)	<Esc>*v#B	0–32767
Color Component (Third)	<Esc>*v#C	0–32767
Color Index	<Esc>*v#I	$0-(2^{\#bits/index})$
Configure Image Data	<Esc>*v#W	6, 18
Download Dither Matrix	<Esc>*m#W[data]	6–32767
Gamma Number	<Esc>*t#I	0–32767
Number of Planes per Row	<Esc>*r#U	-3, 1, 3
Push/Pop Palette	<Esc>&p#P	0–1
Render Algorithm	<Esc>*t#J	0–10
Y Offset	<Esc>*b#Y	0–Logical Page Bound

Raster Graphics

Command	Code	Range
Compression Method	<Esc>*b#M	W3, 5
End Raster Graphics	<Esc>*r#C	
Graphics Resolution	<Esc>*t#R	75, 100, 150, 300
Raster Height (Destination)	<Esc>*t#V	0–32767
Raster Height (Source)	<Esc>*r#T	0–32767
Raster Width (Destination)	<Esc>*t#H	0–32767
Raster Width (Source)	<Esc>*r#S	0–32767
Scale Algorithm	<Esc>*t#K	0–1
Start Raster Graphics	<Esc>*r#A	0–3
Transfer Raster Data by Plane	<Esc>*b#V	0–32767
Transfer Raster Data by Row	<Esc>*b#W	0–32767

Status

Command	Code	Range
Display Functions Mode Off	<Esc>Z	
Display Functions Mode On	<Esc>Y	
Flush All Pages	<Esc>&r#F	0–1
Free Memory Space	<Esc>*s#M	1
Self Test	<Esc>z	
Transparent Print Mode	<Esc>&p#X	0–32767

Table 14.2 DeskJet and DeskWriter 560C PCL Commands

Current Active Position (CAP) Movement

Command	Code	Range
Clear Margins	<Esc>9	
Half Line Feed	<Esc>=	
Horizontal Motion Index (HMI)	<Esc>&k#H	0-32767
Move CAP Horizontal (Columns)	<Esc>&a#C	(-32767)–(+32767)
Move CAP Horizontal (Decipoints)	<Esc>&a#H	(-32767)–(+32767)
Move CAP Horizontal (Dots)	<Esc>*p#X	(-32767)–(+32767)
Move CAP Vertical (Rows)	<Esc>&a#R	(-32767)–(+32767)
Move CAP Vertical (Decipoints)	<Esc>&a#V	(-32767)–(+32767)
Move CAP Vertical (Dots)	<Esc>*p#Y	(-32767)–(+32767)
Space	SP	

Control Codes

Command	Code
Back Space	BS
Carriage Return	CR
Escape	ESC
Formfeed	FF
Horizontal Tab	HT
Line Feed	LF
Null	NUL

Fonts

Command	Code	Range
Character ID	<Esc>*c#E	0–32767
Compressed Type	<Esc>&k2S	

Fonts (continued)

Command	Code	Range
Download Character Descriptor	<Esc>(s#W	0–32767
Download Font Descriptor	<Esc>)s#W	0–32767
Elite Type	<Esc>&k4S	
Font Control	<Esc>*c#F	0–6
Font ID	<Esc>*c#D	0–32767
Primary Font Character Set	<Esc>(ID,	
Primary Font Height	<Esc>(s#V	>0 (valid to 2 decimal places)
Primary Font Pitch	<Esc>(s#H	>0 (valid to 2 decimal places)
Primary Font Spacing	<Esc>(s#P	0, 1
Primary Font Stroke Weight	<Esc>(s#B	-7 to 7
Primary Font Style	<Esc>(s#S	0–32767
Primary Font Typeface	<Esc>(s#T	0–32767
Shift In	SI	
Shift Out	SO	
Underline Mode Off	<Esc>&d@	
Underline Mode On	<Esc>&d#D	0, 3

Job Control

Command	Code
Reset	<Esc>E

Page Control

Command	Code	Range
End-of-Line Wrap	<Esc>&s#C	0–1
Line Spacing	<Esc>&ℓ#D	0–(Page Length)
Line Termination	<Esc>&k#G	0–3
Margin (Left)	<Esc>&a#L	0–(Right Margin)
Margin (Right)	<Esc>&a#M	Left Margin to right logical page bound
Margin (Top)	<Esc>&ℓ#E	0–(Page Length)
Media Source	<Esc>&ℓ#H	0–2
Orientation	<Esc>&ℓ#O	0–3
Page Length	<Esc>&ℓ#P	0–(maximum supported page size)
Paper Size	<Esc>&ℓ#	1O, 1A, 2A, 3A
Perforation Skip Mode	<Esc>&ℓ#L	0–1
Print Direction	<Esc>&k#W	0–2
Text Length	<Esc>&ℓ#F	0–(Page Length Top Margin)

Page Control (continued)

Command	Code	Range
Text Print Quality	<Esc>(s#Q	1–2
Text Scale	<Esc>&k#W	5–6
Vertical Motion Index (VMI)	<Esc>&ℓ#C	0–(Page Length)

Print Model Imaging

Command	Code	Range
Foreground Color	<Esc>*v#S	$0(2^{\#bits/index})-1$

Raster Color

Command	Code	Range
Number of Planes per Row	<Esc>*r#U	-3, 1, 3
Y Offset	<Esc>*b#Y	0–Logical Page Bound

Raster Graphics

Command	Code	Range
End Raster Graphics	<Esc>*r#C	
Graphics Resolution	<Esc>*t#R	75, 100, 150, 300
Raster Graphics Depletion	<Esc>*o#D	0–32767
Raster Graphics Shingling	<Esc>*o#Q	0–32767
Raster Width (Source)	<Esc>*r#S	0–32767
Relative Vertical Pixel Movement	<Esc>*r#Q	1–2
Start Raster Graphics	<Esc>*r#A	0–3
Transfer Raster Data by Plane	<Esc>*b#V	0–32767
Transfer Raster Data by Row	<Esc>*b#W	0–32767

Status

Command	Code	Range
Display Functions Mode Off	<Esc>Z	
Display Functions Mode On	<Esc>Y	
Self Test	<Esc>z	
Transparent Print Mode	<Esc>&p#X	0–32767

Appendixes

There are four Appendixes to this book:

Appendix A provides some helpful hints and tips about using HP 560C and 1200C inkjet printers.

Appendix B consists of a list of resources from which you can obtain additional information about HP 560C and 1200C inkjet printers.

Appendix C lists many of the file formats used by applications you can use to create color printed documents.

Appendix D is a list of names and addresses of companies whose products are mentioned in this book. Many of these companies have been generous in providing help to the author.

Following is a Glossary of terms related to computer printers in general and color printing in particular.

A

APPENDIX

Hints and Tricks

Cables

Always use the cables recommended by HP to connect your printer to a computer or network.

Make sure the cable between your computer and printer is properly plugged in at both ends. Tighten the screws and snap the clips.

Media

If you experience a paper jam, remove all paper from the in tray, fan the pages, put them back in the tray, and try again.

For best results, use paper and transparency material recommended by HP. You can use ordinary copier paper for less important work.

The two surfaces of many types of paper and other print media are different. One side is intended for printing; the other is not. Always print on the print side. Load the paper into your DeskJet or DeskWriter printer with the print side down.

Print Cartridges

Always have at least one extra print cartridge of each type available. Cartridges last a long time if you print mainly text, but run out quite suddenly. This advice is particularly important if you print a lot of graphics.

To save on the cost of print cartridges, print draft copies at the lightest intensity setting.

Printer Drivers

If your printer behaves strangely, check to make sure that your application knows what printer you are using. Always use the latest version of the correct printer driver.

Use the drivers supplied by HP for Macintosh and Windows applications. Drivers for many DOS applications are available from the applications supplier.

Printing

If your application permits, print pages in reverse order so that they are stacked in the correct order in the output tray.

Get into the habit of using Print Preview (if your application permits) so that you can see how your document will look before you print it. This will save you time and money.

Select grayscale to print draft copies of color documents. It's faster than printing in color.

If colors run into each other, try reducing the print intensity, using a better quality paper, or changing the print quality setting.

To obtain the best print quality, select the High Quality print mode.

The best way to give your work a glossy look is to use LX JetSeries Glossy Paper. An alternative is to print on a good-quality smooth paper such as LX JetSeries CutSheet paper, wait for the ink to dry, then spray the page with a transparent spray. You can buy suitable sprays from art supply stores.

If you have problems printing from certain applications, consult the README.TXT file on the driver installation disk and similarly named files on your application installation disks.

If you send data to the printer and the Busy light blinks but paper does not eject, this may be because your computer is still sending information to the Print Manager or spooler, or because the printer has not finished processing the information to be printed. If you are printing from DOS, the printer may not have received a formfeed command, in which case you can press the Load/Eject button (560C) or Formfeed button (1200C) to print the page.

Printer Language

The DeskJet and DeskWriter 560C printers accept only HP PCL 3 commands.

The DeskJet 1200C printer accepts HP PCL 5 and HP-GL/2 commands. In addition, if the PostScript option is installed, the printer can accept PostScript commands. Drivers supplied by HP automatically send commands to the printer so that it accepts whichever language is being employed. These commands override the setting of rear-panel switches 1 and 2. If you are not using an HP driver, such as when you are printing from DOS, you must set the switches to the PCL position (switches 1 and 2 both down).

APPENDIX

Information and Resources

Hewlett-Packard Publications

HP DeskJet 500 Series Printer Software Guide for Microsoft Windows

HP DeskJet 560C Setup Guide

HP DeskJet 560C User's Guide

HP DeskJet 1200C and 1200C/PS Printer User's Guide

HP DeskJet 1200C and 1200C/PS Printer User's Reference

PCL 5 Printer Language Technical Reference Manual

Software Developer's Guide for HP's DeskJet 500 Series Printer Driver

HP-GL/2 Reference Guide

PostScript Software for the HP DeskWriter Family

A Guide to Using Color

Resolution: News for Hewlett-Packard Customers

Other Sources of Support for Hewlett-Packard Products

AppleLink

CompuServe

HP Peripherals Forum. Type GO HPPER

HP Audio Tips

An automated support service. Call 800-333-1917.

HP BBS

Bulletin board for information and drivers. Call 208-344-1691.

HP First FAX Retrieval System

Call 800-333-1917.

HP CPO Customer Support Center

Call 208-323-2551.

HP Driver Distribution Center

Call 303-339-7009.

Internet

192.6.71.2 or ftp-boi.external.hp

Any authorized Hewlett-Packard dealer

Other publications

Books

PostScript Language Tutorial and Cookbook, Adobe Systems, Inc.

Roger Parker, *Looking Good in Print*, Ventana Press

Harald Mante, *Color Design in Photography*, Van Nostrand Reinhold

J.D. Foley and A. Van Dam, *Fundamentals of Interactive Computer Graphics*, Addison Wesley

An Introduction to Digital Color Prepress, Agfa Compugraphic Division

Pocket Pal, International Paper

Kim and Sunny Baker, *Color Publishing on the PC*, Random House Electronic Publishing

Periodicals

Computer Graphics World, monthly, PennWell Publishing Company

PC Graphics & Video, monthly, Advanstar Communications

Presentations, monthly, Lakewood Publications

Publish, monthly, Integrated Media

APPENDIX

Common File Formats

The following is a list of file formats and the applications that support them.

Abbreviation	Description	Used In
ADI	AutoCAD plot file	1
AI	Adobe Illustrator graphic	3, 4
BAK	Backup file	Most applications
BMP	Windows bitmap	1, 2, 3, 4, 5, 6
CCI I	CorelCHART	3
CDR	CorelDRAW graphic	1, 3
CGM	Computer graphics metafile	1, 2, 3
CMX	Corel presentation exchange	3
DCX	Multiple PCX image	5
DIB	Windows DIB	1, 3
DOC	Word document	1, 2
DRW	Micrografx Designer	1, 2, 3
DXF	AutoCAD file transfer	1, 2, 3
EPS	Encapsulated PostScript	1, 2, 3, 4, 6
GIF	CompuServe graphic	1, 3, 4, 5
GEM	Graphic environment manager	3
HGL	HP graphic language	1
HPG	HP graphics	2
JPG	JPEG graphic	3, 4, 5

307

MAC	Macintosh graphic	4
MPT	Macintosh graphic	4
MST	WordPerfect master	2
PCD	Kodak photo-CD image	1, 3, 4
PCT	Macintosh graphic	1, 2, 3, 5
PCX	Paintbrush	1, 2, 3, 4, 5, 6
PIC	Lotus graphic	1, 2, 3
PIF	IBM graphic	3
PLT	HP plotter print file	1, 3
PM5	PageMaker publication	6
PSD	Photoshop graphic	4
PXI	PixelPaint graphic	4
PXR	Pixar graphic	4
RLE	Run-length encoded	3, 4
RTF	Rich text format	2, 3, 6
SAM	Ami Professional	2, 3
SCT	Scitex graphic	3, 4
SHO	WordPerfect presentation	2
TGA	Targa graphic	1, 2, 3, 4, 5
TIF	Tagged image file format	1, 2, 3, 4, 5, 6
TXT	ASCII text	1, 2, 3, 6
WK?	Lotus worksheet	3
WMF	Windows metafile	1, 2, 3, 5
WPG	WordPerfect graphic	1, 2, 3, 5
XLS	Excel workbook	3

Applications

1   Word for Windows
2   WordPerfect
3   CorelDRAW
4   Photoshop
5   Collage
6   PageMaker

Use this list only as a starting point in considering the compatibility of files between applications. In many cases, file formats have evolved over several generations. For this reason, applications that supported an older version of a file format may not support a newer version.

Some file formats are proprietary, so they are controlled by the organization that created them. Other formats are open, with the result that various organizations use somewhat different versions that are not completely compatible.

Several utilities are available for converting files from one format to another, of which the best known is HiJaak from Inset Systems.

When you import a graphics file into a different application from the one in which it was created, you may not always be satisfied with the result. The same is true when you convert a graphics file from one format to another. It is not uncommon to find that the aspect ratios change during either of these processes.

APPENDIX

Companies and Organizations

The following is a list of companies and organizations, together with some of their products and services, mentioned in this book.

Adobe System Incorporated
1585 Charleston Road
Mountain View, CA 94039

    Illustrator, Photoshop, PostScript, Streamline

Aldus Corporation
411 First Avenue South
Seattle, WA 98104

    PageMaker

Aldus Consumer Division (formerly Silicon Beach)
9770 Carrol Center Road #J
San Diego, CA 92126

    SuperPaint

Avery Dennison
20955 Pathfinder Road
Diamond Bar, CA 91765

    LabelPro, MacLabelPro, adhesive labels, card stock

Baseline Publishing
1770 Moriah Woods Boulevard, Suite 14
Memphis, TN 38117

    Exposure Pro

Broderbund Software, Inc.
500 Redwood Boulevard
Novato, CA 94948

    3D Home Architect

Caere Corporation
100 Cooper Court
Los Gatos, CA 95030

    OmniPage Professional

Calera Recognition Systems
475 Potrero Avenue
Sunnyvale, CA 94086

    WordScan

Corel Corporation
1600 Carling Avenue
Ottawa, Ontario K1Z 8R7, Canada

    CorelDRAW, CorelCHART, PhotoPaint, Ventura

CPI, Inc.
1953 Landings Drive
Mountain View, CA 94043

    Image-In

Delrina Corporation
895 Don Mills Road
500-2 Park Center
Toronto, Ontario M3C 1W3, Canada

    FormFlow

Deneba Software
7400 SW 87th Avenue
Miami, FL 33173

    Canvas

Digital Light & Color, Inc.
36 JFK Street, Suite G
PO Box 382908
Cambridge, MA 02238

    Picture Window

Eastman Kodak Company
343 State Street
Rochester, NY 14650

    Photo CD equipment and software

Expert Software
820 Douglas Road
Coral Gables, FL 33134

Expert Home Design

Hewlett-Packard Company
San Diego Printer Division
16399 West Bernardo Drive
San Diego, CA 92127

1200C and 1200C/PS DeskJet printers

Hewlett-Packard Company
Vancouver Division
18110 SE 34th Street
Camas, WA 98670

560C DeskJet and DeskWriter printers

Image Club Graphics, Inc.
c/o Publisher's Mail Service
10545 West Donges Court
Wilwaukee, WI 53224

Clip art and photo images

Inner Media
60 Plain Road
Hollis, NH 03049

Collage Complete

Inset Systems
71 Commerce Drive
Brookfield, CT 06804

Hijaak

Lotus Development Corporation
55 Cambridge Parkway
Cambridge, MA 02142

Ami Pro, 1-2-3

Microsoft Corporation
One Microsoft Way
Redmond, WA 98052

Excel, PowerPoint, Word

Page Works
3090 Fernheath
Costa Mesa, CA 92626

PageWave

Paper Direct
205 Chubb Avenue
Lyndhurst, NJ 07071

    Paper, etc.

PKWare, Inc.
9025 North Deerwood Drive
Brown Deer, WI 53223

    PKZip

Quill Laser Supplies
100 Schelter Road
Lincolnshire, IL 60069

    Paper, labels, print cartridges for inkjet printers

Shapeware Corporation
1601 Fifth Avenue, Suite 800
Seattle, WA 98101

    Visio

Software Publishing Corporation
3165 Kifer Road
Santa Clara, CA 95056

    Harvard Graphics

Starving Programmer
589 Oxford Street
Winnipeg, Manitoba R3M 3J2, Canada

    Split

Strategic Mapping, Inc.
3135 Kifer Road
Santa Clara, CA 95051

    Atlas GIS

WordPerfect Corporation
1555 North Technology Way
Orem, UT 84057

    WordPerfect

WordStar International
201 Alameda Del Prado
Novato, CA 94949

    Correct Grammar, Correct Quotes, American Heritage Dictionary

Glossary

The following is a list of terms, together with brief definitions, that you might come across while you prepare documents to be printed from your computer.

The definitions given here are those that seem to be most widely accepted. However, some terms are used with other meanings in certain publications.

Many of the terms used in computer graphics are derived from long-standing acceptance in the worlds of art, typography, graphics design, and printing. Others are from the newer disciplines of computer science and telecommunications. With these varied backgrounds, it's not surprising that some words mean different things to different people.

Additive Colors   A color produced by mixing the additive primary colors (red, green, and blue). Colors on a monitor screen are created by mixing primary colors. See also *Primary Color*.

Adobe ATM Font   A scalable outline font available from Adobe that can be used to generate screen and printer fonts on Macintosh computers and PCs. ATM is an abbreviation for Adobe Type Manager.

Alignment   The relative position of elements on a page. In the case of text, characters may be left aligned, center aligned, or right aligned. This means that the left ends of lines of text, centers of lines of text, or right ends of lines of text lie on a vertical line. In the case of graphics, objects may be left, center, or right aligned horizontally, or top, center, or bottom aligned vertically. Do not confuse justification with alignment. See also *Justify*.

Alley   The space between columns.

Alpha Channel   Information specifying the degree of transparency of an image. See also *Channel*.

ANSI   Abbreviation for American National Standards Institute.

ANSI Character Set   A code in which 256 alphabetic and numeric characters, punctuation marks, and other symbols are represented by combinations of 8 bits. The first 128 characters in this set are the same as those in the ASCII character set.

Anti-Aliasing   Smoothing the rough edges of images to minimize jaggedness.

AppleTalk   A network protocol for Macintosh computers. Macintosh computers are normally interconnected by the LocalTalk cabling system, but can be interconnected by the EtherTalk cabling system if appropriate network interface cards are installed.

Application   Software used to accomplish a specific task such as word processing, drawing, or data management.

Ascender   The portion of a lowercase character such as *b*, *d*, or *h* that extends above the height of most characters. See also *Descender*.

ASCII   Abbreviation for American Standard Code for Information Interchange.

ASCII Character Set   A character set in which 128 alphabetic and numeric characters, punctuation marks, and other symbols are represented by combinations of 7 bits.

Aspect Ratio   The height-to-width ratio of an image.

Background Printing   Printing that occurs while a computer is being used for other purposes.

Banding   The undesirable effect in a displayed or printed blend in which there are perceivable steps between shades. See also *Blending*.

Baseline   An imaginary horizontal line on which characters are aligned. See also *Descender*.

Basis Weight   The weight in pounds of a ream (500 sheets) of paper of standard size. Standard sizes are different for different types of paper.

Bezier Curve   A mathematical representation of a complex curved line used in vector-based graphics applications. The shape of a bezier curve is determined by nodes (through which the curve passes) and control points (that determine the curvature).

Bit   Abbreviation for *binary digit*. The fundamental unit of information processed and stored in a computer.

Bitmapped Graphic   A graphic image in which each pixel within the image area is represented by one or more bits. A bitmapped graphic file contains each bit in the image. A bitmapped graphic is also known as a raster graphic. See also *Vector Graphic*.

Bitmapped Font   A character set in which each character is represented by bits that define its shape. Each bitmapped font can display or print characters in only one size and style.

Bleed   Printing that extends beyond the trim edge of a page.

Bleeding   The mixing of colors that occurs on a printed page when inks of different colors blend into each other.

Blending   The capability of graphics applications to produce a smooth transition from one color to another.

Blooming   Spreading of color that occurs on a printed page due to ink spreading as it is absorbed by the paper.

Blurb   See *Pull Quote*.

Body Copy   The text on a page formatted in paragraphs, as opposed to headings. See also *Display Type*.

Bold   The style of a font that has heavier weight strokes than the roman (normal) style.

Bond   A type of paper used for correspondence.

Book   In desktop publishing, a publication consisting of two or more separate files. As a grade of paper, the type of paper used for commercially printed books.

Bounding Box   The smallest rectangle required to contain a graphics object.

Breakout   See *Pull Quote*.

Brightness   One of the three dimensions of color, the others being hue and saturation. The term is used to describe the amount of black in a color. See also *Hue* and *Saturation*.

Buffer   An area of computer memory in which data is temporarily stored.

Bullet   A symbol used on a page to draw attention to items in a list. Often a small filled circle or square.

Business Graphics   Graphs and charts of the type used in business documents and presentations. Column charts, bar charts, pie charts, organization charts, and flow charts are examples of business graphics.

Busy   When a device, such as a printer, is processing information and cannot at that time communicate with a computer, it is said to be busy.

Byline   The name (and sometimes the affiliation) of the author of an article. Usually appears at the beginning or end of the article.

Byte   A unit of information consisting of 8 bits. One byte can store one printable character. Computer memory size and disk size are specified in kilobytes (1024 bytes) or megabytes (1,048,576 bytes).

Cable   The wires used to connect a computer to a device such as a monitor or printer.

Cache   High-speed memory in a computer that reduces the time required to read data from and write data to a hard disk.

CAD   See *Computer-Aided Design*.

Calibration   The process of setting graphics software, printer drivers, and scanner drivers so that colors displayed on the screen match the colors of original graphics and the colors of printed graphics.

Callout   Label that identifies an item in an illustration. A line, known as a leader, often connects a callout to the item it refers to.

Cap Height   The height of uppercase characters.

Caption   Text that identifies an illustration on a page.

Cast   An undesirable overall color in a graphic. A cast may occur in conventional photography due to a mismatch between the color sensitivity of the film and the lighting conditions, or by processing errors. A cast can also occur during scanning. A cast can be corrected by adjustment of a scanner driver or by applying a filter in a graphics application.

CD-ROM   Abbreviation for Compact Disk Read-Only Memory. A large-capacity storage device often used for font libraries, clip art, and stock collections of photographs. A computer must have a CD-ROM drive in order to read data from a CD-ROM.

Centronics Parallel Interface   A standard method of connecting computers with printers. This standard is used by IBM-compatible computers.

Channel   The data that represents one color in an image. A channel is analogous to a plate used in a multicolor printing process. In addition to color channels, a channel, known as the alpha channel, can be used to represent the degree of transparency of an image.

Character   One of the alphabetic, numeric, punctuation, or symbols that can be displayed and printed.

Character Set   The characters available in a font.

Characters per Inch (CPI)   Used to define the size of monospaced fonts. Also known as the pitch.

Chromaticity   The definition of a color in terms of primaries, as specified by the Commission Internationale de l'Eclairage (CIE).

CIE   See *Commission Internationale de l'Eclairage*.

Clear   (1) To remove something displayed on a monitor. (2) To remove air bubbles or other obstructions that hinder the flow of ink in an inkjet printer.

Client   A computer connected to a LAN that receives data or services from another computer. The computer that provides data or services is known as a server. See also *Server*.

Clip Art   Graphics supplied on disk that you can use in your work. Some clip art can be used without payment of a royalty fee; other clip art is copyrighted.

Clipboard   Memory in which text and graphics objects can be temporarily stored. Often used as a means of moving or copying objects between applications.

Cluster   A group of pixels that, when viewed from a distance so that they blend, represent colors or shades of gray.

CMYK   Abbreviation for Cyan, Magenta, Yellow, and blacK (or Key). A model used for specifying colors. See also *Process Color*.

Color   The sensation experienced when light waves of certain frequencies impinge on the retina.

Color Blending   Using clusters of pixels so that cyan, magenta, yellow, and black inks can be used to represent millions of colors.

Color Correction   The process of modifying colors to achieve the desired printed or displayed image.

Color Gamut   The range of colors that can be recognized by, or created by, a device. The gamut of the human eye is larger than that of scanners and monitors which, in turn, is larger than that of printers.

Color Management System   A technique used to match colors between devices, such as between a scanned image, the image displayed by a monitor, and the image printed on paper.

Color Map   A table or mathematical formula that defines the relationship between the digital representation of color and the detected (scanner), displayed (monitor), or printed (printer) color. A color map is created during calibration. See also *Calibration*.

Color Matching System   A set of standard colors. Designers can specify colors by reference to a color matching system. PANTONE, TRUEMATCH, and FOCOL-TONE are examples of commercial color matching systems.

Color Model   A method of defining colors in such a way that a color in one environment matches a color in another environment.

Color Monitor   A device that displays color images. Colors are reproduced by red (R), green (G), and blue (B) phosphors.

Color Separation   Separating a color image into cyan, magenta, yellow, and black components in preparation for printing on a conventional four-color press.

Color Wheel   A circular chart showing primary and secondary colors, used by artists to determine complementary and harmonious colors.

ColorSmart   A Hewlett-Packard proprietary method of optimizing the color of images printed by DeskJet printers.

Commission Internationale de l'Eclairage   An international organization that has defined color standards in terms of chromaticity.

Complementary Color   The color that is opposite another in the color wheel. Green and red, for example, are complementary colors.

Composite Black   Black created by combining cyan, magenta, and yellow ink, rather than by black ink. In practice, composite black has a somewhat brownish appearance due to impurities in the ink colors.

Compression   (1) Reducing the dynamic range of an image so that highlight and shadow detail are visible when the image is reproduced by a device with a limited dynamic range. (2) Reducing the size of the file required to store an image on disk. See also *JPEG*.

Computer-Aided Design (CAD)   The process of using a computer to design products. Various applications are available for use in architectural, electrical, electronic, and mechanical design.

Configure   To change a device's settings so that it can communicate with a computer.

Configuration   A specific combination of a device's settings.

Configuration Switches   Switches used to configure a device such as a printer. Configuration switches are sometimes referred to as DIP switches (*DIP* is an abbreviation for Dual-Inline Package).

Continuous-Tone Image   An image in which a smooth change between tones shows no perceptible steps. Conventional photography creates continuous-tone images.

Contrast   The degree of difference between a dark area and a light area of the same color, or between areas of different colors.

Control Code   An instruction that changes a device's settings or causes a device to perform an operation.

Copy   Another word for text. See also *Body Copy* and *Copy Fitting*.

Copy Fitting   Making adjustments to text (copy) so that it fits into the available space on a page.

Copyright   Ownership of a work by its creator or by an organization that purchased the work from its creator.

Counter   The enclosed white space inside such characters as *a*, *e*, and *o*.

CPI   See *Characters per Inch*.

CPS   Abbreviation for characters per second. Used to define printing speed.

Crop   To select a part of an image.

Deck   A short sentence at the beginning of an article that elaborates on the title.

Default   A value or condition that occurs when an application is launched or a device is turned on.

Density   The ability of an image to block or absorb light. A high-density object blocks or absorbs most light.

Descender   The portion of lowercase characters such as *g*, *j*, and *y* that extends below the baseline.

Desktop Publishing   Preparing pages containing text and graphics for printing. Desktop publishing applications are also known as page layout applications.

Detail   A part of an image in which adjacent areas have very little contrast.

Device   A hardware unit that is part of, or attached to, a computer. Disk drives, printers, and monitors are referred to as devices.

Didot   A traditional unit of measurement used in typography and page layout in Europe. One millimeter is equivalent to 2.66 didot points. See also *Point*.

Dingbat   A symbol or decorative character used to separate or mark items on a page.

Display Type   Headings and titles on a page, as opposed to body copy. Display type is usually larger than body copy. See also *Body Copy*.

Dither   To represent colors or shades of gray by clusters of pixels in a displayed image or clusters of dots in a printed image. A monitor that displays 256 colors uses dithering to simulate other colors. A printer uses dithering to create many colors with only four colors of ink.

DOS   Abbreviation for disk operating system. DOS is the software that controls the overall operation of most IBM-compatible personal computers.

Dot   The smallest unit of a printed image. Also known as a Pixel.

Dots per Inch   The number of dots a printer is capable of printing in an inch. A printer actually prints the number of dots necessary to produce the best print quality based on other settings you have requested.

Download   The process of transmitting data from a main storage unit to another unit or from a higher level computer to a local computer. Font data can be downloaded from a computer's hard disk to the memory within a printer. The opposite of *upload*.

DPI   See *Dots per Inch*.

Drawing   An image in which shapes are displayed and printed mathematically, as opposed to a painting, in which an image consists of descriptions of individual dots.

Driver   A file, usually stored on a computer's hard disk, that controls the operation of a device. Drivers are required to control monitors, scanners, and printers.

Duplex   Printing on both sides of the paper.

Dynamic Range   The range between the darkest black and the lightest white in an image. The dynamic range of a photograph is greater than the dynamic range of a displayed or printed image. Also known as Tonal Range.

EconoMode   A printing mode available in the Hewlett-Packard 560C DeskJet printer that can be used to print draft documents quickly while using less ink than normal.

Ellipsis   Three closely spaced dots used to indicate deleted or missing text. Use the ellipsis character in the ANSI character set rather than three separate periods.

Em-Dash   A dash having a length equal to the size of the font. In a 12-point font, an em-dash has a length of 12 points.

Em-Space   A space having a length equal to the size of the font. In a 12-point font, an em-space has a length of 12 points.

Embedded Commands   Commands that can be inserted into an application and subsequently sent to a printer.

Emulation   The capability of a printer to act like a printer of a different type.

En-Dash   A dash having a length half the size of an em-dash. In a 12-point font, an en-dash has a length of 6 points.

En-Space   A space having a length half the size of an em-space. In a 12-point font, an en-space has a length of 6 points.

Encapsulated PostScript   See *PostScript*.

Energy Star   A U.S. Government program that encourages the design of equipment that has a low power consumption or that automatically switches to a low-energy mode when it is not being used.

Envelope   In graphics, the overall shape that encloses an object. Ordinary text, for example has a rectangular envelope. You can use graphics applications to change text so that it fits into a different-shaped envelope.

EtherTalk   A cabling system used to interconnect Macintosh computers and other devices that communicate by the AppleTalk protocol. See also *LocalTalk*.

Factory Default   A device's default settings at the time it leaves the factory where it was manufactured.

File   A set of related data stored on disk.

Fill   To cover an enclosed area with a color, texture, or pattern.

Filter   The capability of a graphics application to change an image. Filters are used to correct defects, to enhance images, and to add special effects to images.

Fixed Space Font   See *Monospace Font*.

Folio   The printed page number.

Font   A set of characters of a specific design and style. A font usually consists of uppercase and lowercase alphabetic characters, punctuation characters, and numbers. Special-purpose fonts contain families of symbols. See also *Printer Font* and *Screen Font*.

Font Cartridge   A plug-in printer option that contains fonts. These fonts are used in the same way as *internal fonts*.

Font Characteristics   The design, size, style, stroke weight, and orientation of a font.

Font Scaling   The ability to change the size of a font.

Footer   Text or graphics that appears at the bottom of pages.

Full Color   An image stored, displayed, or printed in 24-bit or 32-bit form.

Gamma   (1) A measure of contrast in the midtones of an image. (2) The relationship between input and output levels of each color.

Gamma Correction   The process of changing the tonal relationships in a graphic, particularly the midtones.

Gamut   See *Color Gamut*.

Geographic Information System (GIS)   An application that relates data to geographic maps.

GIS   See *Geographic Information System*.

Graphic   A displayed or printed image other than text.

Grayscale   An image in which colors are represented by shades of gray.

GUI   Abbreviation for graphical user interface. GUIs, such as those used by IBM-compatible computers running under Windows and by Macintosh computers, allow users to interact with symbols on the screen.

Gutter   Extra space in the inside margins of duplex documents to allow for binding.

Halftone   An image in which gray is represented by black dots of various sizes (traditional printing) or by various patterns of dots (inkjet printing).

Hanging Indent   Paragraph in which the first line extends to the left of the remaining lines. Often used for bulleted and numbered lists.

Hardware   The electrical and mechanical components of a computer and the devices connected to it.

Header   Text or graphics that appears at the top of pages.

Headline   The title of an article.

Highlight   The brightest part of an image. See also *Midtone* and *Shadow*.

Histogram   A chart showing the number of occurrences of specific values within a range. In graphic applications, histograms are used to show how often each color occurs within an image.

Hot Key   A single key or key combination you can press to gain immediate access to something in an application that you would otherwise access by pressing a sequence of keys. Also known as *Shortcut Key*.

HP-GL/2   A graphics language that describes shapes in terms of vectors, as opposed to bitmaps. Often used with plotters.

HSB   Abbreviation for hue, saturation, and brightness. A color model used to specify colors. Sometimes referred to as HSV (hue, saturation, and value).

Hue   One of the three dimensions of color, the others being saturation and brightness. A specific color, such as blue, red, or violet; the position of a color in the color spectrum. See also *Brightness* and *Saturation*.

I/O   Abbreviation for input/output. An electrical connection for input and output of data, such as the port that connects a computer to a printer.

Image   Any shape or combination of shapes displayed on a monitor, printed on paper, or stored in a file. The process of creating on paper or film the content of an image file.

Imagesetter   A printer capable of very high-definition output such as 1270 or 2540 dots per inch. Used in the preparation of plates for printing on commercial presses.

Indent   Distance between text and the margin on a page. Indents are measured from the margin toward the center of the page.

Inkjet Printer   A printer that operates by firing jets or spots of ink onto media.

Intensity   The darkness or lightness of displayed or printed images.

Interface   The connection and interaction between a person and a computer and between a computer and other devices.

Internal Font   A font permanently stored within a printer.

Italic   The tilted version of a font. See also *Roman*.

Jaggies   The jagged effect seen in a bitmapped image caused by using square pixels to represent diagonal lines and curves.

JPEG   Abbreviation for Joint Photographic Experts Group. JPEG defines standards for compression of electronic image color files. See also *Compression*.

Jump Line   Reference to the page on which an article is continued.

Justify   To change the space between words and between characters so that the left and right ends of lines of text in paragraphs are vertically aligned.

Kern   To adjust the space between characters to improve their visual balance. Kerning is most often used with large characters.

Key   The black component in process color printing. See also *Process Color* and *CMYK*.

LAN   See *Local Area Network*.

Landscape   The orientation of a printed image across the length of a page. See also *Portrait*.

Laser   A device that produces a very uniform light that can be accurately focused. Laser is an acronym for Light Amplification from Stimulated Emission of Radiation.

Laser Printer   A printer that uses laser technology to place an image on paper or other media. The term is loosely used to refer to printers that operate in a similar manner to true laser printers, but use light from a source other than a laser.

Leader   See *Callout*.

Leading   The space between lines of type, measured from baseline to baseline (pronounced "ledding").

Legend   An area in a chart where the meaning of colors or patterns used to represent specific values is defined.

Line Art   Illustrations that consist only of solid black, with no shades of gray.

Line Screen   The lines-per-inch resolution used to screen an image in preparation for printing on an offset printing press. Also known as the *Screen Frequency*.

Local Area Network (LAN)   Several or many computers within a building (or other locality) interconnected so that they can exchange data and services.

LocalTalk   A cabling system used to interconnect Macintosh computers and other devices that communicate by the AppleTalk protocol. See also *EtherTalk*.

Lowercase   Characters in their small form, as opposed to capital letters. The traditional term for lowercase is minuscule. See also *Uppercase*.

Luminosity   The brightness of a color.

Marquee   A line, usually dotted or dashed, that indicates a selected region of an image.

Masthead   Section of a magazine or newsletter which states the publication's name, ownership, and the names of the key contributors.

Media   The material on which images are printed. The most common medium is paper. Media is the plural form of *medium*.

Midtone   Parts of an image that have a brightness halfway between that of highlights and shadows. See also *Highlight* and *Shadow*.

MIO Interface   See *Modular Input/Output Interface*.

Modular Input/Output (MIO) Interface   A Hewlett-Packard proprietary interface for printers. Printers equipped with this interface can accept plug-in cards so that they can be connected to various types of computers and networks.

Moiré Pattern   An undesired pattern in a image that results from incorrectly scanning halftone images or changing the size of bitmapped images.

Monospace Font   A font in which every character occupies the same horizontal space when it is displayed or printed. Also known as *Fixed Space Font*. See also *Proportional Font*.

Network   See *Local Area Network*.

Non-Solid Color   A color that is displayed by mixing other colors on the screen. See also *Solid Color*.

Nonbreaking Space   A space between words that cannot occur at the end of a line.

Object   An entity that can be manipulated as a whole, rather than by its component parts. See also *Object Linking and Embedding*.

Object Linking and Embedding (OLE)   The capability in Windows to link an object created in one application with another application, or to embed (place) an object created in one application in another application.

Object-Type   A graphics application that works with vector graphics images, or a vector-based image. Compare with *Paint-Type*.

OCR   See *Optical Character Recognition*.

Off-Line   Not in communication with a computer. In some cases, a printer must be off-line before the front-panel controls can be used to change its settings.

OLE   See *Object Linking and Embedding*.

On-Demand Thermal Inkjet Printing   The technology used in HP 560C and 1200C printers. Ink is forced by heat through an array of nozzles onto paper.

On-Line   In communication with a computer. A printer must be on-line in order to receive information from a computer.

Optical Character Recognition (OCR)   The process of converting an electronic image of text into a format that can be read by text-based applications such as word processors.

Orientation   The placement of an image on paper. The orientation is portrait (or tall) if the printed object is viewed correctly when the long edge of the paper is vertical; the orientation is landscape (or wide) if the printed object is viewed correctly when the short edge of the paper is vertical.

Orphan   The first line of a paragraph at the bottom of a page. See also *Widow*.

Outline Font   See *Scalable Font*.

Page Description Language   A programming language used to instruct a printer how to create the image to be printed. PCL and PostScript are page description languages.

Page Layout Application   See *Desktop Publishing*.

Page Orientation   The direction in which an image is printed on a page. See also *Landscape* and *Portrait*.

Page Protection Technology   A method of allowing a printer to print images that would normally require a larger internal memory than the printer actually has.

Paint-Type   A graphics application that works with bitmapped graphics images, or a bitmapped image. Compare with *Object-Type*.

PANTONE   A proprietary color matching system used to specify colors.

Parallel Interface   A connection between a computer and a printer or other device in which data is transmitted one byte at a time. See also *Serial Interface*.

Path   See *Print Path*.

Pattern   The method by which pixels are arranged in clusters to represent colors and gray.

PCL   Abbreviation for Printer Control Language. PCL is the page description language designed for use with Hewlett-Packard printers and other products.

PEL   See *Pixel*.

Phosphor   A substance that emits light when it is stimulated by a stream of electrons. Colors on a monitor screen are produced by phosphors.

Photo CD   A compact disk containing digitally recorded photographic images.

Photograph   An image containing black or color (or both) in shades that vary continuously, rather than in discrete increments.

Pica   A traditional unit of measurement used in typography and page layout. One pica is equivalent to 12 points. See also *Point*.

Picture Element   See *Pixel*.

Pitch   See *Characters per Inch*.

Pixel   The smallest element on a monitor screen or dot in a printed image. Pixel is derived from Picture Element and is sometimes abbreviated to PEL.

Point   A traditional unit of measurement used in typography and page layout in the United States and England. One inch is equivalent to 72 points in most personal computer applications. In traditional printing, 1 inch is 72.25 points. See also *Didot*. Point is also used as a measurement of paper thickness, in which case 1 point is one thousandth of an inch.

Port   A connector at the back of a computer into which a device cable is plugged.

Portrait   The orientation of a printed image across the width of a page. See also *Landscape*.

PostScript   A device-independent page description language used to transmit text and graphics information to a printer. An interpreter within the printer translates PostScript statements into the printer's native language. Encapsulated PostScript files contain PostScript data. These files have a file name extension .EPS.

PostScript Printer Description File   A file containing information that customizes the user interface and the PostScript output to a printer.

Primary Color   There are additive and subtractive primary colors. The additive primary colors are red, green, and blue. The subtractive primary colors are cyan, magenta, and yellow.

Print Cartridge   The housing that contains ink used for printing.

Print Path   The stages through which an image passes, starting with an original image and ending as a printed image. Typical stages are scanning in RGB, modifying with a graphics application, converting to CMYK, and printing.

Print Queue   One or more documents waiting to be printed.

Printer Driver   A file that controls a printer and allows your applications to access that printer.

Printer Font   A font that is designed to be used by a printer. See also *Screen Font*.

Printing Engine   The mechanical and electrical components of a printer that put ink on paper.

Process Color   A printed color composed of cyan (C), magenta (M), yellow (Y), and black (K) inks. The abbreviation CMYK is often used to refer to process colors. Process color inks are transparent. A wide range of colors can be printed by printing process colors on top of each other.

Proportional Font   A font in which characters do not all have the same width. A *w* in a proportional font occupies more space than an *i*. See also *Monospace Font*.

Proportional Leading   Positioning text so that character baselines are at a vertical position one-third the distance from the bottom to the top of the slug. See also *Slug*.

Protocol   Rules that govern the transmission of information between devices.

Pull Quote　A quotation extracted from the text of an article and printed in large type on a page. Often used in magazines and newsletters to attract readers' attention and to improve page layout. Also known as a blurb or breakout.

Rasterize　To convert an image to a bitmap form. Outline fonts are rasterized so that each character can be displayed as pixels on the screen or printed as dots. Vector images generated by graphics programs are, similarly, rasterized so that they can be displayed and printed.

Ream　500 sheets of paper.

Recto　The right page of an open book. By tradition, rectos have odd page numbers. See also *Verso*.

Related Color　Adjacent colors on the color wheel.

Resample　To change the size of a bitmapped image by adding or removing dots.

Resolution　Image sharpness. The perception of image sharpness can be affected by several factors, including: dots per inch, the size and shape of dots, dot placement, the type of paper on which the image is printed, and the printer driver settings.

Resolution Enhancement Technology (REt)　A technique that smoothes printed curves. REt, incorporated into the 1200C printer, enhances the appearance of text and graphics when the printer is used in High Quality mode.

Reverse　A light image displayed or printed on a dark background.

RGB　Abbreviation for the names of the additive primary colors red, green, and blue. A model used for specifying colors.

Roman　The normal, upright style of a font, as opposed to the slanted, italic style. Windows applications use *Regular* to refer to the roman style.

Rule　A horizontal or vertical line on a page that separates sections of text or separates text from graphics.

Sans Serif Font　A font in which characters do not have serifs. See also *Serif*.

Saturation　One of the three dimensions of color, the others being brightness and hue. The amount of white in a color. A highly saturated color contains no (or almost no) white. Pastel shades have low saturation. See also *Brightness* and *Hue*.

Scalable Font　A font in which each character is defined mathematically. A scalable font can be used to display or print characters in many sizes. *Outline font* means the same as *scalable font*.

Scaling　Reducing or increasing the size of an image without changing its aspect ratio. See also *Aspect Ratio*.

Scanner A device that converts a printed image or solid object into a bitmapped image.

Scatter One of the color blending methods by which clusters of pixels represent colors or gray.

Screen A gray or colored background used to emphasize certain text such as a sidebar. See also *Sidebar*.

Screen Capture Converting the image displayed on a screen to a graphics file. The graphics file can subsequently be imported into a word-processing, desktop publishing, or other applications so that the on-screen image appears as an illustration in a document.

Screen Font A font that is designed to be used for displaying characters on a monitor. See also *Printer Font*.

Screen Frequency See *Line Screen*.

Secondary Color A color produced by adding equal components of two additive primary colors. Green, orange, and violet are secondary colors.

Self-Mailer A publication, such as a newsletter, that is designed for mailing without being inserted in an envelope.

Serial Interface A connection between a computer and a printer or other device in which data is transmitted 1 bit at a time. See also *Parallel Interface*.

Serif The decorative line or other design that terminates a stroke in a traditional alphabetic character.

Serif Font A font in which characters have serifs.

Server A computer that provides information or other services to other computers on a LAN. The computers that receice data or other services are known as clients. See also *Client*.

Set Solid Type set with no added space between lines. The leading is the same as the font size.

Shade A color that varies slightly in saturation or brightness from the color on which it is based.

Shadow The darkest part of an image. See also *Highlight* and *Midtone*.

Shortcut Key See *Hot Key*.

Sidebar Text on a page that provides supporting information about the main topic, but is shown separately. Sidebars are usually enclosed within a box or emphasized with a screen. See also *Screen*.

SIMM   Abbreviation for Single In-line Memory Module. Computer and printer memory is usually supplied as SIMMs.

Size   For a font, the vertical height of characters, measured in points. The height is slightly more than the distance from the top of uppercase characters to the bottom of descenders.

Slug   The horizontal bar that contains a line of text. The height of the bar corresponds to the leading. See also *Leading* and *Proportional Leading*.

Soft Font   A font that is stored as a file on a disk. See also *Internal Font* and *Font Cartridge*.

Software   The programs that control computer operation.

Solid Color   A color that can be produced by a video adapter and color monitor. VGA adapters can display 16 solid colors. More sophisticated adapters can display more than 16 solid colors. Compare with *Non-Solid Color*.

Spooler   Derived from the acronym for Simultaneous Peripheral Operation On-line. The capability of sending data to be printed to memory or disk, and then from memory or disk to the printer. A spooler reduces the time during which a computer cannot be used because it is sending data to a printer.

Spot Color   A color printed by ink of that color, rather than by blending process colors. Spot color inks are usually opaque. Unpredictable results occur when one spot color is printed on another.

Stroke Weight   The thickness of the lines of which characters are formed.

Style   (1) A variation of a font. Roman, bold, and italic are typical styles. (2) The overall appearance of text. Word-processing and desktop publishing applications allow you to define such attributes as font, font size, font style, line spacing, indentation, and color as a style.

Subtractive Color   A color produced by mixing the subtractive primary colors (cyan, magenta, and yellow). Printed colors are created by mixing these colors. See also *Primary Color*.

Tabloid   A size of paper or publication; 11×17 inches.

Tag Image File Format (TIFF)   A standard file format for graphics files. Most graphics applications can read and write TIFF files.

Tagging   Identifying objects on a page according to their type. After objects have been tagged, each type of object can be printed optimally.

Target Printer   The printer on which a publication is intended to be printed. Not necessarily the printer connected to the computer on which the publication is created.

Text Wrap   In word processors, the ability to move a word that extends beyond the right margin to the beginning of the next line. In desktop publishing, the ability to wrap text around graphics.

TIFF   See *Tag Image File Format.*

Tint   A percentage of a process or custom color.

Tonal Range   See *Dynamic Range.*

Tracing   The process of creating a vector graphic file from a bitmap graphic image.

Track   The space between characters in text. Text with loose tracking has greater-than-normal space between characters. Text with tight tracking has less-than-normal space between characters. Desktop publishing applications allow you to change the tracking of selected text.

Transparency   An image printed on transparent material with transparent inks. Used to project images with an overhead projector. Sometimes referred to as a slide.

TrueType Font   A scalable font that can be used to generate printer and screen fonts.

TWAIN   A standard method of communicating between applications and devices (particularly scanners). No one seems to know what TWAIN stands for, although Tool Without An Important Name has been suggested.

Typeface   The general design of a character set.

Unsharp Masking   A filtering process used to make edges clearer in a bitmapped image. Contrary to its name, the process makes images look sharper.

Upload   To transfer a file from a computer to a higher level computer. The opposite of *download.*

Uppercase   Capital letters. The traditional term for uppercase is majuscule. See also *Lowercase.*

Value   The relative lightness or darkness of a color.

Vector   A mathematical description of a line in space.

Vector Graphic   A graphic image in which objects are defined mathematically. A vector graphic file contains just these mathematical definitions and is usually much smaller than a bitmapped graphic file for the same image. See also *Bit-mapped Graphic*.

Verso   The left page of an open book. By tradition, versos have even page numbers. See also *Recto*.

Virtual Memory   Hard disk space used as if it were RAM. Many applications use the hard disk in this way to allow working on projects that require more RAM than actually exists in a computer.

Weight   See *Stroke Weight*.

White Space   The areas of a page that contain no image or text.

Wicking   The result of ink being absorbed unevenly into paper, resulting in small threads of ink extending from an image.

Widow   The last line of a paragraph at the top of a page. Also, a single word or a few short words forming the last line of a paragraph. See also *Orphan*.

Windows   A visual environment for PCs in which all applications have a similar on-screen appearance and share screen, printer, and other drivers.

Workstation   A high-performance personal computer, often used for engineering design or scientific calculations. Most workstations are installed on a LAN.

Wraparound Text   Text that fits around the shape of a graphic.

WYSIWYG   An abbreviation for What You See Is What You Get. WYSIWYG refers to a screen image that closely resembles the same image when it is printed.

x-Height   Height of the main body of lowercase characters, excluding ascenders and descenders. The x-height determines the visual impact of text.

Zoom   To increase or decrease the magnification of a displayed image. You zoom in to increase the magnification and zoom out to decrease it.

Index